MODERN SCHOOL EDUCATION

MODERN
SCHOOL EDUCATION

[Strictly According to the UGC Syllabus for B.Ed. Course]

By
HASNAIN QURESHI

ANMOL PUBLICATIONS PVT. LTD.
NEW DELHI - 110 002 (INDIA)

ANMOL PUBLICATIONS PVT. LTD.
H.O.: 4374/4B, Ansari Road, Darya Ganj,
New Delhi-110 002 (India)
Ph.: 23278000, 23261597

B.O.: No. 1015, Ist Main Road, BSK IIIrd Stage
IIIrd Phase, IIIrd Block
Bangalore - 560 085 (India)
Visit us at: www.anmolpublications.com

Modern School Education

PRINTED IN INDIA

Printed at Mehra Offset Press, Delhi.

Contents

Preface ix

1. **Ideal Schools** 1
New Trend Schools • Vital Importance • Two Sides of the Coin

2. **Fundamental Issues** 7
Role of Education • Education for All • Different Stages • Teacher's Responsibilities • Educational Management • Funds and Finances • Unlevelled Field • Organisational Setup • National Integration • Non-attachment

3. **Basic Education** 35
The Structure • Beginning Level • Recommendations of the Committee • Initial Difficulties • Saturation Point • Official Commission

4. **Secondary Education** 91
Growth and Development • Historical Backdrop • The Infrastructure • Official Commission • Post-High School • Many a Committee • Hindrances in Growth • Middle Stage • Ways of Assessment • Junior High School Level • High School Level • Professional Education • Past Happenings • Model Schools • Goals and Aims • Various Difficulties • The Courses • Languages in Course

• Mathematics and Science • Social Studies • Physical Education • Education for Girls • Career Planning • Books for Course • Teaching Devices

5. **Policy on Education** 171
The Evolution • The Outcomes • The Setup • Education for Girls • Caste Categories • Special Education • Caring for Kids • Primary Education • Concerns for Kids

6. **The Facilities** 185
Education in Schools • Professional Education • Education for Health • Young Generation • Teacher Education • Educational Management • Funds for Schools • Generating Sources • New Trends • New Schemes

7. **Preparation of Courses** 199
The Perceptions • Elementary Education • The Problems • Various Types • Character and Intellect • Progressive Movements • Social Background • The Implications • The Fundamentals • Serious Deficiencies • Professional Culture • The Syllabus • Descriptions and Explanations • Dominance of Developmentalism • New Perspectives • Aims and Practices • Impact of Resource Expenditure

8. **School Administration** 257
The Administration • Focal Point • Government's Role • Role of Municipal Bodies • Major Hindrances • Various Schemes • Steps for Betterment

9. **Technical Aspects** 287
Growth and Development • Fundamental Difficulties • Role of Commission • Role of Planning

10. **Environmental Science** 303
The History • Elements in Action • Major Hindrances • Role of Education

11. Awareness on Population 321
The Perceptions • Objectives and Purposes • Due to Rise in Number • State of Affairs • Various Schemes • New Plans • Future Hopes

12. Social Goals 327
Growth and Development • Rapid Rise • Objectives and Aims • Various Streams • Execution of Schemes • The Important Aspects

13. Role of Planning 335
Fundamental Schemes • Different Approaches • Area of Operation • Role of Commission • Movement for Education • Typical Approach • At the Doorstep • Managing Institutions

Bibliography 365

Index 371

Preface

Education is a vast discipline and Teachers' Training is a vital part of it. The responsibilities of the educationists and educators are focused on the task of providing better training to the future teachers for their better learning and proper development. Needless to say that this responsibility can only be exercised, if the trainers are equipped with the required knowledge of the subject concerned. That's why it becomes essential for making adequate provisions for each course to the student-teachers or teacher trainees. The present series is designed for providing a solid workable base for all course-papers. It has been prepared strictly according to the syllabus of the B.Ed class, prescribed by the UGC for different universities.

No doubt, there are so many other books on the subject, available in the market, written by worthy authors. However, every writer has his or her own style and way of presentation. The present work also has its own features and characteristics.

In preparation of this series of texts, the editor had to refer to the works of other authors and information sources. The editor feels a deep sense of gratitude for incorporating their ideas in the text. Hopefully, this series would serve as a 'ready to refer' tool for all teachers, teacher-students and others.

—Editor

Preface

1

Ideal Schools

National Education Policy determines to provide education to each person who is interested to have it for his and his nation's welfare. In our country, there is a vast difference of living standards between haves and have nots. Psychological studies proved that brilliant and intelligent students are also found in the villages. To locate the gifted, intelligent and brilliant students from rural areas and provide an education with a difference, separate residential schools should be established. To meet this demand, Government has established Navodaya Schools in the country to fulfil the objectives of National Education Policy.

New Trend Schools

Navodaya Schools are basically pace-setting schools. There is provision for good education in these schools. In the policy, it is said, "it is universally accepted that children with special talent or aptitude should be provided opportunities to proceed at a faster pace, by making good quality education available to them, irrespective of their capacity to pay for it:' Therefore the role of Navodaya Schools is very vital. These are pace-setting schools intended to serve the purpose, and will be established in various parts of the country on a given pattern but with full scope for innovation and experimentation.

Rajiv Gandhi has rightly said, "to get together the knowledge and education, whether it is in the village or city, in tribal area or hill-track or forest area, it is the main policy of education. New policy will be of equalisation. Every person can reach to it and how one should reach to it, it should also be clear. We can not say that we can provide the common education according to the intelligence level or living standard of the peoples' class, but we can assure that we will try to provide good quality education to every child who is intelligent without considering the class, caste, area and other socio-economic factors.

"The aim of education is not limited to only reading and writing. Its objective should be character formation, personality development, sports, to foster the values and skills of art and culture and to pay attention to those areas which are important for the personality development of the individual. We have to locate best and gifted children and the areas where they can properly be developed. We will provide them the best opportunities for their all round development. We have suggested to establish Navodaya Schools to fulfil these objectives. This programme is different to those traditional schools which are run in each district. We understand that this is a noble step taken by us to provide best education to the children of weaker sections, whatsoever their family, economic, cultural and social background is."

There is a general discussion in the field of education regarding the equal opportunities of education. Kothari Commission has suggested the neighbourhood school system for this equality. In New Policy, the idea to provide the educational opportunities to the children of weaker sections was promoted and the result is that now in each State there are ample Navodaya Schools. The basic concept of Navodaya School is, that these will be run on the lines of residential public schools and these schools will develop the talents of the children coming from the rural, tribal, hill areas and from the weaker community.

Vital Importance

Objectives. The broad aims of Navodaya Schools are as under :

(i) To serve the objectives of excellence, coupled with equality and social justice (with reservation for SCs and STs).

(ii) To promote national integration by providing opportunities to talented children, largely rural from different parts of the country to live and learn together.

(iii) To develop their full potential

(iv) To become catalysts of a nation-wide programme by school improvement.

(v) The schools will be residential and free of charge.

A Progressive Step. Navodaya Schools are progressive and this system is a new and important step to locate and develop th talents hidden in remote society and culture. These schools will a boon for those who have no opportunities for their all ro development. These schools will act as pace setters in which will be complete freedom for educational innovatio experiments.

Residential Structure. Navodaya Schools will be r State will bear all the expenses for boarding, lodging educational material. There will be an entrance admission in these schools.

Students Number. There will be only 560 s Navodaya School. There will be 80 students i each class will have two sections of 40 each. 4 opened in the country.

Organisation. These schools will be ru Society registered under the Societies Regis schools will be affiliated with the Centr for academic purposes. Classes from 6 these schools.

Talent Search. These schools will environment to those who are la competitive test, there will be a prog hidden in remote areas. Educatio regarding these schools-

1. These schools will cre and equality and als reservation for SCs
2. These schools w studying in thes

areas and they will come in contact with other talented students of the other parts of the country.

3. There will be all round development of the students, i.e., mind, body and the spirit.

hese schools will provide motivation to improve the ards of school education.

The students who want to appear in the entrance admission in these schools must have completed ay and should not cross the age of 13 years. He the class V examination. These tests will be of hese will test the ability in intelligence, language

ar (Haryana) and Amravati one Navodaya n 1986-87, 81 schools were opened and in ex bols were opened. In each district of the wha least one Navodaya School.

up a n ian Express the following views have been among bjectives is not test quality education in institutiome pace-setting institutions but to build particularlyent from all strata of society especially currently enjoy limited access to

Two Sides of t any kind of standard of facility,

Following ar

1. Educationis

is maximum vour of these schools:

are well-off, en y are of the opinion that there

spend about 20 t ation. Only those persons who

ward in public sch f best education. The parents

by Navodaya Schoo ees per annum for their each

2. These schools will pro nequality will be removed

curriculum and regional onal unity through core

3. There will be better stand es.

means of instructions will education and modern

process. d in teaching-learning

4. These schools are residential and all the expenses of inmates will be borne by the State.
5. There will be no corruption as regards the admission in these schools is concerned, because entrance test will be held for such admissions.
6. Three language formula will be adopted in these schools.
7. There will be 400 Navodaya Schools in the country in which 2,24,000 students will receive their education.
8. These schools will give leadership to raise and maintain the standards of education in the country.
9. These schools will be opened in rural areas where the environment will be healthy.

Though Navodaya Schools scheme is highly ambitious, it. has created some doubts. The following are the points disfavouring these schools-

1. These schools will provide education only to 2,24,000 students, i.e., less than one per cent student population will be benefited. There are about 3.5 crores children of school-going age and among them most of the talented students will not be benefited. These schools have very limited scope.
2. These schools will admit those students who will qualify an entrance test. There is a doubt that the wards of elites will be selected through these tests. The wards of really weaker sections will not qualify these tests, because then are not acquainted with the skills of these tests.
3. There is unequal distribution of population in our country. The scheme is to open one school in each district. Therefore, there is no proper proportion for the representation. For example District Maya bandar has only 14,000 population, District Greater Bombay 25 lakhs, Mednipur in West Bengal has the population of 68 lacs. How, this injustice will be removed.
4. These schools will prove the successful experiment of Downward Filtration Theory propounded by the Britishers in this country. Apart from this, 12 Arab rupees will be spent per year for the education of only 2,24,000 students.

Only one student can get admission through this out of 1,000 families. It would be better that the existing Government primary and secondary schools raise the standard so that all round development of every student be made.

5. These schools will create the feelings of hierarchy. The students studying in these schools will create a separate class of the society.
6. Other field of education such as free and compulsory primary education, adult education, women education, vocational education, etc., will be ignored.
7. These schools will motivate the brain drain. From our country, thousands of talented students take flight for foreign countries in search of jobs. Our country does not provide them proper jobs, therefore, the talents, trained in those schools will also fly over to other countries and the problem of brain drain will remain as it is.

2

Fundamental Issues

Today, we are independent. But, despite political independence, have we become really independent? And, if we have not, then why? The reason for this is that our educational system has not broken from tradition, its basis is the system employed in the time of our slavery. Besides, we have also had to face numerous problems in the educational sphere. In this period of crumbling belief and faith, not only our country but the entire world has lost all sense of direction. As a result, the older generation wants to tie down the rising generation, breaking completely from tradition, has become filled with anger, and is now bent upon revolution. We are finding it difficult to discover the path of synthesis and harmony. at least apparently, there is no possibility of arriving at a compromise.

If our education from 1947 till the present is categorised as the aimless education of the aimless, it would be no exaggeration. The reason for this is quite explicit - we do not have before us a proper plan or sketch for building our nation. A nation does not undergo development by the building of dams and construction of factories and mills, but through the process and medium of education. There is a famous Chinese proverb, which says, "If you plan for a year, plant grain; if you plan for ten years, plant trees, if you plan for a hundred years, plant men:" And in our case, the kind of nation that will be built or created is not evident even from the declaration on the national plan for education.

Role of Education

At present, the many problems that are afflicting education have one sole cause at their root which is aimlessness. According to Dr. Radhakrishnan, the objective of education is the discovery, and the development through proper training, of an individual's inborn qualities. Universities should fulfill these two prime duties towards their students.

The significant fact before our country today is that is needs of self-reliance in foodgrains, economic development and more employment, social and national unification, and political development can be fulfilled only through the training of students in character, in profession and practice, and development of literacy, artistic and cultural interests. And these, in reality, are the objectives of education.

Education for All

The major problem confronting Indian education is the problem of compulsory primary education because the level of literacy has been very low. This shows that primary education has not expanded to the desired extent. Besides, many political, social, religious, economic and geographical factors are creating obstacles in the path of expanding primary education. This problem has been made even more complex by such contributory factors as the curriculum of primary education, problem of school, wastage and stagnation, and. many administrative difficulties.

The important aspect of the problem in primary education is the failure to fulfil the promise of the Constitution, according to which it is the duty of the state to provide for the education of all children upto the age of 14; this is stated in Article 45 of the Constitution. States have remained indifferent towards the fulfilment of this promise. In the third Five Year Plan, efforts in this direction were made, but in the fourth, this ideal was assumed to be the cause of educated unemployment. In the fifth plan, it was clearly assumed that the objective of compulsory and universal education could not be fulfilled. It was assumed that only 75 per cent of the children could be provided education.

Different Stages

Secondary education is the backbone of the country's development, and it is unfortunate that there is no uniformity at this level in our country. The curriculum is spread over 12 years in some states, over 11 years in others and over 10 in yet others. Besides, problems relating to curricula, administration, training of teachers, financial aid, etc., have combined to create obstacles. Among its numerous problems are those of the objectives of secondary education, its limits, form, curriculum, guidance, administration, substitution, finance, evaluation and examination, and the problem of a proper life for students.

Despite this, there has been considerable progress in secondary education. Between 1951 and 1974, the enrolment went up six times in the case of boys and 13 times for that of girls, though this is an average for the different rates of growth achieved in various states. With reference to the total population, admission of girls at the primary stages has decreased. Besides, secondary schools have also been afflicted with problems relating to resources, teachers and facilities. The central problem at this level is that of qualitative growth, though there is also the problem of education lacking a vocational bias.

Higher education, too, has been facing numerous problems in our country. In the main, it has failed to help students to earn their livelihood, and it has continued to expand despite the absence of employment. Its failure in this regard is the result of many factors. University education is lacking in direction because of political pressures, the sovereignty of universities themselves, the quality of student life, lack of finance and absence of clearly defined objectives. The country lacks any concrete plan for taking advantage of higher eduation, and because of this many contradications have crept in. Higher education is suffering from the problems inevitably linked with expansion. The enrolment in arts, commerce and science has risen from 3.2 million in 1968-69 to 3.5 million in 1974. Besides, since most institutions of higher education are located in cities, its benefit goes mainly to students living in urban areas: In addition, there is need for intellectual development, new curricula for the universities, etc.

India undoubtf.dly needs technical education for its rapid. development, because, a variety of highly skilled technicians are required for exploring the country's considerable natural resources. But, education in this sphere has suffered mainly from a lack of proper planning. As a consequence, while many individuals received training in one branch of technology, there was a complete absence of trained personnel in other branches. This has led to unemployment. Even today, our technical education is handicapped by lack of proper planning, absence of text-books, absence of teachers, lack of laboratories and other facilities. Its problems can be rooted out in only one way- linking it with employ-ment. It is necessary to plan, for technical education in the light of manpower needs.

The need for social education and adult education is indicative of the illiteracy prevailing in our country, because in proportion to the population, the percentage of literate individuals is very small. Besides, the very concept of social education has always lacked clarity. In this sphere, the main problem lies in not finding suitably devoted workers. Besides the administrative structure has also succeeded in covering this education with a veil of intellectuality, with the result that, instead of being something intimately concerned with the masses, it has become only a subject for intellectual discussion. This is despite the fact that, in the fifth plan, social education has been linked with continuous education. Because of this, social education is being expanded through such schemes as private candidature in examinations and correspondence education institutions. However, the problem of literacy is at the same level as in 1974. In the Sixth Plan, it has been given national importance.

Teacher's Responsibilities

The problem of teachers also afflicts Indian education. It is the teacher who is the link between education and the student. Teachers have become even more dissatisfied, since the new scales of pay favoured by the Kothari Commission were not implemented. The responsibility for this dissatisfaction rests securely with our popular government which has continued to neglect the builders of the nation in its own selfish interests. Recognising the importance of teachers, the Kothari Commission has said that a concrete programme for the professional training of teacher is essential for bringing about qualitative progress. The money spent upon teacher training can bring forth the maximum dividends, since the money spent is less but its return in the form of a qualitative improvement in the education of lakhs of individuals is enormous. The factors which influence the improvement of education and its contribution to national development are- the qualities, ability and character of the teachers. These are undoubtedly of the greatest importance. Nothing is more important than inducting good teachers into this profession. There should be professional training and the availability of satisfactory working conditions, which can influence them profoundly. The investment in the education of teachers can bring manifold advantages because the financial investment is less, but the advantages gained in the context of general education are comparatively much more.

The new problem that has arisen because of lack of foresight in education is given the name of student dissatisfaction or student unrest. The violence and destruction indulged in by our students in the entire country over the last 15 years has proved beyond doubt that there is some serious fault in our educational structure. Though the phenomenon emerged somewhat late after independence, the entire world has seen with open eyes the anger of the younger generation and the repressive attitude of the older generation. The students who were used before independence to wave the national flag and make clamorous demands for the country's freedom came to raise the flag against the same leaders who had once inspired them. This came about because of lack of direction. This has come to be called student indiscipline. When its causes were analysed, it was discovered that the students trained by crushed and dissatisfied teachers can never turn to constructive activity. Consequently, the discontentment of teachers also came to the fore in the form of the teacher's movement. This led to the opening of a new chapter, the arrest of teachers by their own students. Now, the teacher has been compelled to give up the selflessness of Dronacharya and to engage in a struggle for survival. This struggle still continues. From this, it is evident that the dissatisfaction of the students can be eradicated only when the structure of education is completely reshaped.

Educational Management

The educational system today is suffering from the problems inherent in a dual administration. The administration imposed by the Centre and the States is obstructing education at the local and individual levels. This system of providing grants is also defective. Besides, officials concerned with administration and inspection are ignorant of th real problems of schools, teachers and students. Hence, their decisions fail to benefit the educational system. If education is to be utilized for national development, there is great need for able and efficient administration and suitable educational planning. Hence, there is an urgent need for a suitable administrative and planning mechanism.

Education aims at the complete development of the individual. Today, education is based on psychology, and efforts are made to adjust students at a mass level with society, despite their individual differences. In India, the advantages of guidance and counselling services is available only to the privileged and so those lacking in opportunities remain in the condition of deprivation.

Funds and Finances

Indian education has been singularly unfortunate in that, whenever a crisis occurred, the budget of every other department remained unchanged while that of education suffered major reductions. Besides, only 2.3 per cent of the national income is usually spent on it. Other countries spend as much as 7 per cent of the national income on education. In the fifth plan, 2.3 per cent of the national income was kept apart for education, although it was planned to be increased to 4.7 per cent by 1981. The present situation is such that even if more resources are allocated for education but remain linked to traditional techniques, which have been the cause of collosal wastages, even the basic needs of educational reform will not be fulfilled for this, the present stagnation must be brought to an end.

It is becoming increasingly clear that the main cause of the decline in national character is the absence of growth and development in moral and spiritual values. The Education Commission has paid particular attention to this problem.

Unlevelled Field

The glaring fact before us today is that educational opportunities are being exploited mainly by the privileged, and that is why many brilliant individuals in society fail to develop their capacities, and the nation is deprived of their potential. Almost 20 crore individuals are living far below the ideal level of existence in our country. For children belonging to this class, equality in the opportunities for education are inconceivable as long as special provisions are not made for them. This problem is being tackled to some extent through the policy of reservations, but it is also taking the nation towards a crisis. But, if such reservations are based on income, the result will be the eradication of a caste-based communalism, and also provide equal opportunities to children in the educational sphere.

Organisational Setup

The educational structure is not uniform throughout the country; it is different in different states, and, as a result, we do not find mobility in the educational system. If the educational structure is made uniform, it will be possible to achieve a growth in social unity.

The Kothari Commission reflected on the problems of education, considering every aspect and form of education, with the exception of medical sciences. The Commission has made an effort to come to terms with all kinds of problems inherent in the educational world. However, it was found that the Commission's statement of purpose was riddled by inconsistencies. What happened was that instead of solving existing problems, the Commission became the cause of numerous other problems. It gradually became clear that the crossroads at which education now found itself was the age old crossroads, with which we have been familiar since antiquity.

One important basis of qualitative improvement in education is the pay given to teachers. The pay scales considered adequate by the Commission failed to attract the teachers. This is not surprising, in view of the rising price index. In fact, the pay scales are shameful. Connected with this problem is the obstinacy of State governments, of which the government of Uttar Pradesh has provided an excellent example, Institutions are being compelled to face numerous intractable problems in implementing the new scales of pay. The red-tapism of the Education Department must be held responsible for creating many problems.

The teachers movements give an inkling of the revolution which is brewing. Glancing at this state of affairs, the erstwhile Minister of Education, Dr. V.K.R.V Rao was compelled to observe that he had often become aware of the neglect of Indian teachers, which had been going on for decades. This neglect took two forms—denial of an adequate livelihood, denial of any suitable opportunities for his own professional development. Though some steps had been taken in this direction after independence, they were woefully inadequate. On the other hand, the teacher had adopted the method of revolution. In addition, there was a gradual assimilation of external vested interests in this movement, and consequently, the bright and respected image of the teacher in society was undergoing distortion. Dr. Rao did not deny the fact that a revolution was, in fact, necessary. In certain circumstances, revolutions become inevitable, but when they are organised by teachers, they should be in consonance with dignity of teachers so that the feelings of students, guardians and society towards the teachers should not be poisoned, and the teachers' respected image should not be destroyed.

On the other hand, the government had its own limitations. But, Dr. Rao admitted that it was the duty of administrators, politicians and elected representatives not to close their eyes towards the problems of teachers. If the government could not meet the demands of teachers because of limitations of resources, it could at least listen sympathetically to the teachers and explain to the teachers the reality of the situation. For certain unavoidable needs, available resources could be improved, while for others, steps could be taken to find a solution in the near future.

Dr. Rao's ideas are very far from reality, though he is perfectly aware of reality because of his close contact with education in the past. He is also aware of the problems of education. But the atmosphere of ministership surrounding him compels him to a kind of duplicity. This is nothing new in his case. Every teacher who became a minister soon moulded himself to the atmosphere surrounding ministers. The language of administration is marked by 'should', not by 'this is so'. In brief, what this means is that the problem cannot be solved as long as the distinction between professions and deeds continues. In fact, the commission has left no stone unturned in giving birth to class differences. The pay scales applicable to teachers, from the primary to the university level, give not even a slight indication of the principle of 'equal pay for equal ability.'

The problem of language has also added to the problem of education. The Kothari Commission is also responsible for highlighting and intensifying this problem, because it raised a storm of controversy over this question. It was perhaps not aware of the truth that Hindi is the language of the nation, and that it was being prevented from taking its rightful place by political machinations and manipulations. Dr. Ramdhari Singh Dinkar has explicated the three-language formula in the following terms: We may suppose that a student of Bengal learns Bengali in (a) and English in (b). This allows him the freedom to fulfil the requirement of (c) by studying either French or Marathi. In the same way, if a student of Bihar studies Hindi in (a) and English in (b), he may learn Urdu or Russian to fulfil the requirement of (c).

This elaboration is based on the Commission's following formula.

(a) Mother tongue
(b) The state language of the Union or any parallel state language
(c) any new Indian or European language different from those under (a) and (b).

National Integration

The Commission laid stress on the generation of national and social unity, but without clarifying how this objective was to be achieved. Besides, the Commission also failed to elaborate the meaning of Indian democracy. Dr. Sampurnanand has commented that no one dares argue that the objective of education in Soviet Russia, the U.S.A., England and France is not the comprehensive development of the country's citizens but the values which are declared to be the objective of western democratic countries are different from the values enumerated by the proponents of the Soviet Russian ideology. What is called dictatorship or tyranny by one country is called democracy by another. The term 'democracy' is one which should be clearly defined because when national and social unity reaches the hands of a dictator like Hitler, it becomes a most potent vehicle of evil.

Work Experience vs. Basic Education. The Commission has sought to introduce practical work experience at every level of education and to make education dynamic and productive. Despite the passage of considerable time since the publication of the Commission's report, no State has summoned up the courage to implement its curriculum. They see it as the productive system of Basic Education. On the contrary, the truth is that the scheme of practical work experience is the death knell of basic education. Our state governments try to imitate others or to delay action-whenever it is a question of accepting any responsibility concerning education. Dr. V.K.R.V Rao is of the view that education should be brought into close relationship with life and production. Nevertheless, before initiating this programme, the pre-existing economic situation should be observed carefully. Only then can there be any hope of success. He favours emphasis upon those schemes which do not involve economic problems, for instance, students should be given holidays during the days when they can work on their farms at home, or cooperate with their parents in other ways. By such means, education can be brought into ever closer contact with life, and it will be able to make progress as an effective instrument of society.

Curriculum and 'Teacher Training. Dr. Rao has pointed out that the view that teachers nowadays have no interest in their work was gaining currency in society. He feels this to be completely unfounded. He suggests that the same remark applies with equal truth to doctors, administrators, politicians and workers. It is a pervasive fact, a national disease. Then how can teachers remain free from its taint? For this, we need dedication, self-confidence, intimacy, and the creation of human values.

In order to increase the teacher's desire for better scholarship and greater ability, there should be some institutions whose membership should evolve great honour upon its possessor. The rules pertaining to such institutions should be based upon the objectives and activities in the educational sphere favoured by the people as a whole. Dr. Rao experesses the feeling that the honour bestowed by institutions of such a nation will be more inspiring and dignified than the awards distributed by the administrative machinery.

There is frequent mention of the decline in quality and standards in education. Qualitative, improvement presupposes the following three things- (1) Adequate material and physical resources should be available in schools, i.e., such things as libraries, buildings, laboratories, apparatus, materials, etc. (2) Capable teachers should be recruited and there should be provisions for training during employment or period of service, and (3) there should be an environment suitable to studying, and teaching in every institution. Of the three, the last factor is the most important, and it becomes possible only when teachers devote themselves dedicatedly to the task of teaching. Caution is also needed to ensure that the teachers' work is not unduly interfered with by persons not connected with education, the administration or the government. Achieving this is not as simple as it may appear. For this, it is necessary to generate the right awakening in society, it is not something which can be achieved by preparing a curriculum or providing the right text-books. Instead, it will be necessary to organise conferences and meetings at state levels for the organisers and administrators of schools in rural areas so that they are aware of their true responsibilities, and are able to manage schools in the best possible way.

From the viewpoint of education, our country is undoubtedly lagging far behind other countries. It has also faced a number of other complex problems. A solution to these problems was offered in the form of the Kothari Commission. Despite this, she path seems completely unchanged. Though government statistics give some satisfaction, the fact remains that education is in the doldrums. One must ask: why does such a state of affairs exist? The reason lies in the misunderstandings harboured by the government as well as the people as a whole, in the wrong techniques adopted, and in the fact that their basis is private self-interest. The Kothari Commission made a telling point in its observation that education must be given the form of a complete process; teachers must be given the opportunities to maintain their existence; national development should be given the greatest attention to maintain the nation's very existence. It recommended that education in agriculture, industry and other professions should be made a part of the educational structure. It advised that the principle of an education co-extensive with life should be adopted.

Need for an Educational Plan. The great educational plan for the next twenty years is unique. Its characteristic principle is that the development of the nation comprehends the development of the individual and the development of the individual contributes to the development of the nation. Because of this, the plan exhibits a touching faith in antiquity while at the same time, it gives expresssion to an attachment, faith and love for the future based on reason, not superstition.

Question of Existence. On considering the question of existence, we are faced with certain old convictions which have assumed the form of questions. The Kothari Commission has sought an answer to the problem posed by the late Jawaharlal Nehru - Can we asso-ciate scientific and technological progress with the progress of the mind and the progress of the soul? We can never be untrue to science because it puts before us the fundamental truths and facts of life. In spite of this, can we not be assured and confident about the facts which India has additionally honoured and observed? We have to take firm steps toward industrial progress, while remembering that all material thing turn to dust and ashes in the absence of charity, patience and wisdom. (Introductory page of Education Commission, para 22, 1.86).

What is to be Done? We must remember that the aim of education is to build the nation. While many factors influence nation building, in the final analysis, this objective can be achieved only through (1) self-reliance in foodgrains (2) economic development (3) political development (4) social and national unity (5) development of human resources (6) national awakening (7) growth of democratic values. This objective is possible of attainment only through a revolutionary change in education.

Suggestions by the Kothari Commission. On the subject of the complete report of the Kothari Commission and the problems it gave rise to, it can be said that it is a very significant educational plan. Society has to resort to modernisation in order to educate itself. It must make an attempt to bring into existence an educated class comprehending citizens belonging to every class, deeply imbued with the qualities characteristic of India, so that it can raise the educational standard of the average citizen. The present age with its lack of faith and sense of direction has brought aimlessness not only to our country but the whole world, and as a result the old generation wants to shackle the younger generation in its own dogmas, customs and traditions. On the other hand, the new generation is filled with the furious desire for a revolutionary change. It is becoming difficult to find the path of accommodation and adaptation.

1. Generation unrest and gap was observed obviously after independence. Students unrest now become a common regular phenomena having its roots in politics. Political leaders gave wrong direction to the youths under the names of political youth organisations.
2. Teachers were exploited by society of haves. They have followed the path of confrontation against the Government for their jobs, social, economic and cultural security and for the survival of their own-selves.
3. The problem of national language still remains unsolved. Though Hindi is declared as a link language of nation, yet it could not get its right place due to the reasons known to all.
4. There is nothing obvious between the masses and the administration. Multi-tier system of education is found in the country which is ultimately responsible for creating drama on the stage of nation.

Therefore the following points should be kept in mind while planning for the education

1. Development of national consciousness should be the important aim of education. For this we should be aware of : (i) our cultural heritage (ii) its revaluation and (iii) firm faith in future.
2. For the qualitative improvement of education due emphasis be given to teacher education. For this (i) right type of persons should be attracted towards teaching profession (ii) they must possess high character, spiritual and moral values (iii) and must have professional wealth.

Ours is a country known by the name of India; ours is the nationality-Indian; ours is the Constitution which has a common goal of achieving justice- social, economic and political; freedom of expression of thought, of development and availing opportunities, achievement of integration national, social and emotional; attaining the common bonds of fraternity and unity.

Needless to say that all these ideals and goals cannot be achieved until and unless we do not overhaul the entire curriculum, method of teaching, rather the entire system of education with our national objectives in view. It is a bare truth that uniformity at all standards of education to bring out a coordination in the prevailing system which is eventually a state subject is the dire need of the hour.

There is population-explosion and that has left a vacuum in providing the equalization of opportunities in the realm of education. The ratio between the teacher and the taught is inadequate. Dearth of foodgrains, economic development, lack of employment opportunities, wide gap between the privileged, domination of the narrow loyalties under the guise of ideology, religion, language, state, caste, creed, etc., are some of the hurdles which require immediate consideration with a concrete follow up programme if national reconstruction is to be made with sincere efforts so that we may not only be able to solve the gigantic problems our country is facing at present but also raise the status of Bharat.

Education is a powerful tool for social change. Society goes on under a continuous process of change. Emerson was right when he asserted that it is not wealth or high pillars which make a man. Education can build a nation and can lead the entire nation on the path of progress. It is only through education that we can inculcate the feeling of self-sacrifice, patriotism, critical and analytical thinking, character building etc., which may ultimately transform an individual and society as a whole. For that we will have to evolve a national policy on education. History gives an evidence that it is only the educated elite which has brought a change in the world. Education trains the mind and leads an individual towards critical thinking and analogical outlook.

Education is not something which may be discussed in an isolated water-tight compartment; it requires aims, contents, teaching points, students, teacher, time table, vocational efficiency. Keeping in view the needs of society and the national objectives and exploitation of the manpower to raise the status of the country in the international sphere. The national development has its base in economic progress and productivity. If we want to bring out a social change we will have to see the modernization without sacrificing the gems of our rich cultural heritage

Only a handful of elite dominate all walks of life. This control is due to the ignorance of the people. The privileged always rule over unprivileged and the former have been exploiting them like any thing. This tendency has been widening the gap between haves and have-nots. The social unrest caused through this can only be removed if the following programmes are implemented.

— Science as a basic component of education and culture.
— Work experience as an integral part of general education, especially at the secondary school level to meet the needs of industry, agriculture and trade, and improvement of scientific and technological education and research at the university stage with special emphasis on agriculture and allied sciences.

As for the question of the adoption of science along with culture, India has been following the same from times immemorial. It is only ignorance which is giving impetus to the technology based on experience rather than science. Work experience is a system which provides opportunities for self-employment and prepares a man for the job in his future and present. That is why the Kothari Commission visualised for vocationalization of secondary education.

There is a lot of diversity in our country. Language, provincialism, factionalism, regionalism, religion have been disturbing the nation's peace and order. National integration can only be achieved through cultural and moral integration. This needs stability in character. For this the following programme should be implemented.

— Introducing a common school system of public education.
— Making social and national service as an integral part of education at all stages.
— Developing all modern Indian languages and taking necessary steps to enrich Hindi as quickly as possible so that it is able to function effectively as the official language of the Union, and
— Promoting national consciousness.

We can breath in a traditional society but we cannot live the life in it in the sense of the term. In the fast running world, there is always struggle for existence. We can exist only when we go ahead by maintaining the progress of science and technology. "Indian society of today is heir to a great culture. Unfortunately, however, it is not an adequately educated society and unless it becomes one, it will not be able to modernize itself and to respond appropriately to new challenges of national reconstruction or take its rightful place in the comity of nations," the National Commission says. For achievement of six major universities has been recommended.

Modernization does not mean that the social, moral and spiritual values be neglected and not given due importance. It is the age of conflict of culture, materialism and ethical values. It is the conflict between discerning and non-discerning, between values, patterns and concepts and man! He is missing his path.

Now education should be accepted as a powerful means of social revolution. There should be radical changes in education. We need quality but along with action. There should be close coordination of plan and execution. We have to go, rather rush with the world in this race. It is a challenge, but who will accept it, you, he or the legislative members, students, teachers, guardians, government, public, who,? Who will decide the fate?

Napoleon once told his soldiers to have faith in God, but also to keep their powder dry, because even God could not make we-gun-powder usable. This remark seems to apply appropriately to the social forces bringing about rapid changes in today's volatile society. Education today is equivalent to Napoleon's powder and politics to God. Our powder-that is, education- has become so wet that it cannot be modified and improved in accord with circumstances. And, though politics is God, it cannot dry this wet powder. It is because of this wetness that the student and the teacher of today are completely helpless in providing society with the necessary sense of direction. The corrupt politics and society of today have completely altered the values of life. Human values now have different, unheard of definitions. National values have been swallowed by selfishness.

The life of every nation receives its truest sustenance from its system of education. A living educational system is the foundation of a life full of vivacity and energy, and it is the educational system which gives impetus to society and the life of the nation. It creates, shapes and moulds the national character. The bases of educational policy are the purposes and aims of the nation, for the fulfilment of which the country's administrative system must be possessed of honesty, dynamism and efficiency. These factors advance a nation's interests and take it towards its objectives through the medium of the educational system, and make it prosperous and contented. The individual and the nation are complementary units. In the event of any imbalance or disharmony between the two, both are destroyed. Adjustment with passing time, adaptation to a changing environment are bitter truths of life. A nation must not loose its sense of direction as time passes and circumstances change.

The history of education in India after independence establishes clearly that changing times have brought aimlessness, loss of a sense of direction. In this period of uncertainty, the life of our country is standing at the crossroads, immobile, lifeless, bewildered. It is seeking in vain for the right direction.

Our Constitution made education a subject to be dealt with by the States, not by the nation, a cruel mistake for which the new generation is paying. The acceptance of invisible responsibilities in the sphere of general and higher education was, for the Centre, no more than an escape, a flight from circumstances. Article 45 of the Constitution is a dead letter, a mere pronouncement. Even the question of achieving its implicit objective does not arise.

The Politics of Education. In theory, the basis of the politics of education is the Constitution, which we ourselves have framed and adopted, but it has completely neglected national character, and it was on the basis of this Constitution that our politicians played cruelly and willfully with the future of the nation. These politicians turned their entire energies to the physical or material development of the country. This led to cracks in dams, silence of generators producing electricity, immobilized wheels of the railways, roads leading to nowhere, and aeroplanes sitting idly on the ground. All this happened because the basis or content of education has been hollow. Our politicians lacked the foresight needed to prepare a blueprint for creating the foundation necessary for nation building.

The educational system and educational process in each state have differed so radically from those in other States that instead of encouraging national and emotional unity, it is disunity and alienation which have been promoted. Granting pensions to those who participated in the anti-Hindi movement in Tamil Nadu is an index of this national degeneration. Today, we have arrived at a stage in which citizens of one region face difficulties in working in or doing trade with other regions. Regional imbalances prove the view that making education a state subject was like subjecting the country to slow poisoning.

Non-attachment

The educational system and the social, political and economic circumstances, and the social and psychological diversity have all helped to evolve educational politics as the politics of alienation. And, today, because of this alienation, there is strong discontent in every individual's mind. Every individual is dissatisfied and anxious. It would have been far better if a single educational current had flowed through and enveloped the entire country. Such an education would have arroused social and national awareness. But narrow political interests ignored this vital national need. The consequences of such narrow-mindness are before us. When a troubled mind whispers the word of revolution into one's ears, one is advised to maintain harmony between enthusiasm and commonsense, but this policy does not apply to these politicians.

Today, education has come to be regarded, in the political field, as a device for catching votes. This has entangled the educational class in political alienation, leading to confusion. One must wonder why no attention is being paid to this. Each one of our political parties raises its voice in favour of farreaching changes in education. But these slogan-mongering parties are devoid of any national awareness, though they include members even of the party in power. In the recent election, students were given misleading and false assurances and the result was that these assurances themselves became a halter for the politicians.

Neglect of Teacher. In this field of educational politics, the present state of the teacher is not merely pitiable, it is worse. The one link that maintains the balance and liaison between bureaucrats, polycrats and students has been eliminated. Chancellors of universities do not think it necessary to take the advice of teachers when they are faced with student problems and student movements. It is the teachers who are asked to organise examinations, but directions are issued by the university administration, which drunk in the glory of its power over teachers, overlooks every important aspect.

The alienation pervading our universities and colleges has further intensified social differences, because of which harmony and balance have become impossible to maintain. Even such basic ideals as equal pay for equal work or equal pay for equal ability have been trampled underfoot. The Kothari Commission was right when it observed that, unfortunately, on the whole, our school system lacks any concrete traditions for the development of national unity and national consciousness. What is needed for developing national consciousness and cultural awareness and evaluation is an inspired devotion. This is completely lacking.

Impact of Active Politics. Now, the sole task of the teacher has degenerated into pointing out some important question and dictating the simplest possible answers to them, thus completing the courses of study. The teacher, today, is no better than an insignificant servant, who, on the one hand, must bow low before superiors, officials or suffer their anger, and on the other hand, suffer the indignities heaped upon him by his students. The general degeneration of social character is evident from numerous incidents every day. Our political parties have organised students unions into destructive forces. This is as true of one as of another student union, irrespective of whether they bear the name of Youth Congress, Vidyarthi Parishad, Yuvjan Sabha, Yuva Janta or any other name. All that students do is to wear the appropriate badge and organise political mass fights. A clear symbol of the crisis in education is the fact that central ministers and members of parliament take the deepest possible interests and give vent to their fiercest political loyalties in the elections to the students union of Delhi University.

Political statements also aggravate the crisis among students. In 1974, one newly elected minister of Uttar Pradesh went so far as to declare that students would be promoted without examinations. As a result, the entire order and timing of examinations has gone haywire. Examinations in most universities are postponed from March to May, and then again to August, when they are actually held. With the result, students suffer the loss of one full academic year.

The express demand of our time and our environment is that students should not be dragged into politics, that their creative energies should be employed to generate 'a national spirit. But, nothing concrete has been done in this direction. Our political leaders have yet to find the key to this problem.

It is a strange anomaly that, at the national political level, the education minister is not a minister of cabinet rank. One wonders why the chief executive authority in the educational sphere, though education is regarded as the foundation for nation building, is not provided with a suitable rank. This fact clearly suggests that our legislators are perpetrating a huge fraud upon the nation. State ministers of education are in an even worse position, since their voice echoes hollowly and ineffectively in the schools owned and managed by industralists and self-styled social workers. Managers of educational institutions reap rich harvests in a period in which the politics of education is riddled with corruption.

If we are to think of education in the context of a national awakening, it is necessary to change our present Constitution. As long as the articles of the present Constitution, relating to education,, stand unchanged, we cannot ever dream of a healthy educational system. Hence our objective should be-one nation, one Constitution and one educational system. In the last analysis, there should be no provision for private enterprise. Otherwise, we will continue to wander and roam, as we have been doing till the present.

The crises in education actually arose as soon as we got independence. In our ignorance, we thanked our fortune for the social structure we had inherited from our period of slavery to a foreign power. We were so deeply obliged for that we accepted it as an invariable part of our life. Before independence, we were staunch opponents of Macaulay's educational system. After independence, ironically enough, the makers of our nation and a few vested interests began regarding Macaulay as a messiah. They recklessly adhered to Macaulay's ideas, with the result that his educational system sowed the seeds of casteism and class conflict in our society and in our educational world. Education of a particular group led to the emergence of a class of bureaucrats and politicians, while on the other hand, a governing class was created in the name of education of the people. It was this class conflict that has led to the crisis in education.

The crisis in education has overwhelmed the whole world, because the rise in population brought forth increasing numbers of students. The opportunities of education did not keep pace with the rise in population. Despite this, the expenditure on education increased at a rapid pace. At the same time, education began to grow in, the form of a local industry or enterprise, and hence the crisis in education is the product of many factors.

The population has risen rapidly all over the world, while at the same time, the death-rate has registered a dramatic fall. It was only natural that the problem of providing the means of living for this increased number of people should confront the world. Educational opportunities did not increase in the same proportion, and consequently, an educational emergency arose all over the world. It is also true that a nation's educational system is closely linked with the struggle for life. There is inadequacy of money, teachers and classrooms, but there is no paucity of students. The gravity of the educational crisis confronting the world can hardly be delineated through maps.

Differences due to Local Factors. Though the educational crisis is universal, local differences have created much variety in its form and context at different places. However, the model of this crisis is the same in every country, a model which was variously called Change, Adaptation and Disparity. Since 1945, the world has witnessed a remarkable scientific and technological revolution. And, the consequent unregulated changes in educational policies led to educational crisis and conflict.

The major reasons responsible for the universal educational crisis are the following- (1) Increasing desire for education, (2) Lack or inadequacy of the means to education. (3) the internal permanent agency of education, (4) the structure of society. With the development and extension of the field of knowledge and science, the desire for education in the common people has increased, and as a result, the need for expanding education was felt. The change in the prevailing educational values in the traditional system gave rise to the view that national development was possible only through the maximum utilization of the nation's educated manpower.

Education and society must undergo adaptation in order to overcome this crisis, without which the structure of both must necessarily undergo degeneration. In order to face this challenge, the resources of domestic life, as distinct from the resources of national life, have to be adopted. Money is needed, but the allocations made for education in the national budget are not sufficient to provide all the means of education. Consequently, the optimum utilisation of the nation's manpower, should take place with a view to quality, efficiency and productivity. Transformation is possible only through ideas, courage and determination. It is here that the responsibility of the planners of education increases manifold. Each nation needs an educational system suited to its circumstances and resources.

Education is not the panacea for all the ills of society. Education-does not have adequate time to seek and provide a cure for all of society's varied ills. For the same reason, education cannot satisfy and fulfil all of society's ambitions. Education is, in fact, a faith, on the basis of which the individual undergoes development for his own benefit and the benefit of society. In providing the means for human development, the wastage that results is not due to education, but due to the circumstances of society. An important question must be asked here: Can a dogmatic faith provide assistance to any specific system in the process of rational analysis? The answer to this dogmatism gradually erodes reason in education and undermines foresight. The system of education seems to combine the teaching of folk songs with that of science and technology, it is a cruel satire on education. At the same time, from the social viewpoint, such means also suffer misuse because these means fail to satisfy the real needs of society.

On the other, it is no less a fact that, even in the absence of means, an educational system for society can be evolved by putting faith in the philosophy of 'Know Thyself.'

Attitude towards the Teaching Profession. With changing circumstances has come a change in the attitude towards teachers and the profession of teaching. With the invention of new methods of teaching and modern teaching aids, the teacher can increase his efficiency. But, the explosion in knowledge, which is also responsible for the educational crisis, has not been able to give the requisite impetus to the teaching profession. Classes are still devoid of new knowledge. Consequently; there has come about an imbalance between the expectations from education and its achievements.

Dogmatism. One cause of the educational crisis is the dogmatism of teachers. There was a time when the dogmatic farmer hesitated in introducing the new methods of farming in his field, but today, the same situation is found with regard to teachers. The position of small schools is similar to that of small and scattered fields. They are lacking in the means for research. One cause of the fragmentation of education is the transference of traditional knowledge from one generation to another, because of the traditions practised in society. Today, education is bearing a heavy load of responsibility, but, in the existing circumstances, the fulfilment of this responsibility is a complex and difficult task. The task of educating the nation is no easier than the task of putting man on the moon. Hence, in the sphere of educational conflict, it is essential to get victory over the dogmatism inherent in this sphere.

In his work *'World Educational Crisis'*, Philip H. Coomb has delineated the educational crisis in many countries, of which India is one. This crisis in India has been viewed and analysed from various points of views, such as-policy on admission, inefficient administration, students at the primary level, dropouts, economic growth, economic expenditure, college population, problems of teachers, etc.

The Kothari Commission has reflected on the educational crisis in terms of Input and Out put. the three spheres examined by it are—

1. Transformation of the internal form of the educational method, so that it can be brought into intimate relationship with the life, needs and ambitions of the nation.
2. Qualitative improvement in education so as to make the standards achieved by it adequate, and to ensure that such standards keep on improving with the aim of making them comparable to standards in the international sphere.
3. Expansion of educational facilities according to the needs of the population and stress upon equality of educational opportunities.

The three problems point towards the educational crisis. Hence education has been considered in the context of the problem of national development. Our nation's problems are-self-sufficiency in foodgrains, economic development, universal employment, social and national unification, and political development. Consequently, education must be made to conform to the lives, needs and ambitions of the people. The crisis in education can be rooted out only when education becomes flexible enough to change along with social dynamism and mobility.

Once, during a seminar, an informal discussion on educational objectives brought to light the fact that in India, the determination of educational priorities did not exist. After the analysis of the curricula of many states, it was found that they were incapable of fulfiling any educational purpose. It was felt that educational curricular are formulated merely to bestow priority on the choices indulged in by some Commissions.

Whenever I go to schools, I am overwhelmed by the feeling that we are indulging in a gigantic game in the name of education. After a glance at the results of examinations and marks obtained by my own children, I am compelled to view with alarm the yawning gap between profession and practice. On talking to lady and gentlemen principals of schools, I feel that the whole blame rests squarely on the shoulders of teachers. In talks with teachers themselves or the office bearers of teachers unions, the entire blame shifts to the government, but when I glance helplessly at the predicament of my own children, I feel that the entire fault lies with the parents themselves. The present day analysis of the educational process turns into mutual recrimination and shifting of the responsibility and blame to others. The unfortunate victim of this game of passing the buck is the helpless student.

Books on education have always provided impressive lists of the objectives of education, because they include such things as social, individual, professional, and cultural development, proper utilization of leisure and entertainment, integral development, spiritual development, and external or physical development. Students appearing for examinations learn such lists by rote, though they cannot imbibe them. They win freedom after learning of such objectives in the way best suited to them. I often see and meet many old teachers who never obtained any training anywhere, never studied the elaborate explanation of educational foundations in the context of the philosophy of education, never possessed any practical knowledge of educational psychology, and yet their students are performing their duties devotedly and faithfully in many walks of life. The success with which these untrained teachers have achieved the objectives of education is worthy of imitation.

The teacher of today receives training. In the context of its philosophical, sociological and psychological foundations, the curriculum of training is completed in one or two years. During training, he takes a variety of oaths-that he will be a devoted teacher, adopt the scientific and psychological methods of teaching, etc. But, when he enters the sphere of action his entire training goes overboard. His acquired skill becomes worthless, and like his predecessors, he anxiously waits for the 'pay-day' after making motions of having done his duty. An artificial dissatisfaction enters his life. Possibly, it may be difficult to find a better instance of the projection of reproach.

The questions staring us in the face are- why do such things happen? Have we strayed from our objectives? We are feigning ignorance, and hence, we cannot find an answer to these questions. And so, we come to feel that both our vision and our sense of direction have suffered distortion and mutilation.

Soon after independence, Dr, Radhakrishnan pointed out, on the basis of the suggestions of the Commission, that the objective of education is to discover the innate qualities of the individual and to develop them by training. Universities should fulfil these obligations towards their students. In fact, these obligations should be fulfilled not only by universities but by each and every educational institution. It is obvious that these objectives imply the development of a healthy mind. Personalities themselves lacking in harmony and balance; of which there is no dearth in any sphere of education, have failed to make students balanced and harmonious.

The crucial and challenging question before our country immediately after independence was the question of survival, or of existence. Man's existence is founded on material goods and the nation's existence on thought, awareness and consciousness. These latter elements bear a direct relation to education. Education has its beginnings at the primary level, but the suggestions of the Radhakrishnan Commission were adopted, and once again the Secondary Education Commission was granted the responsibility for determining and achieving the objectives of education. This Commission made its first attack on educational objectives. It profoundly observed that the political, social and economic circumstance had changed and new problems had emerged. It had become necessary to make a careful examination and re-determine the objectives of education at every level. This statement applies not only to the present situation, but also to the future evolution of education, the future of nature and social system, in which education has to modify itself, and to which education must adapt itself. Consequently, the foundation for the development of democratic citizenship, professional efficiency, personality and leadership was given the following shape- (1) students should be given training in character so that they may be able to take part in the democratic process, (2) students should be given practical and professional training so that they may contribute to making the country economically prosperous, (3) students should be prepared for literary, artistic and cultural interests, which are essential for man's integral development and expression of self;. in the absence of this, the country's culture will be underminded.

It is clear that the country's educationists had determined the objectives of education in conformity with the potential needs of the new democratic nation. But by the time the year 1964 came, it was felt that the implementation of the objectives of the 1953 Commission had been faulty. Students were taught mob behaviour in the name of democracy, anarchistic behaviour in the name of organisation, ignorance in the name of knowledge, irresponsibility in the guise of devotion and dedication, disbelief in the name of faith, and rights in the name of duties. The outcome was that the three points of the educational wheel-the teacher, the student and the curriculum-continued to sink steadily into a quagmire from which there was, for them, no emerging.

The declared purposes of the Commission of 1964 caused an explosion whose echoes can be heard even today. The truth of the matter is that society does, in reality, want to build the nation, but the management of society is in the hands of profiteers and black marketeers who are short-sighted and conscious only of their immediate interests. So, they regard the expenditure on education as no better than the money spent on a charity. The results of such negligence are before us. The student movements and the teacher movements are the result of this exploitation and torture. This has made it painfully evident once again that we have failed to achieve the objectives we ourselves created.

In restructuring educational objectives, we have kept before us the vision of national development. We have reflected on the possible modifications in the prevailing educational system. We have laid stress on determination and patience. Hence, the objectives of education have been determined in the new context, which comprehends such things as self-reliance in foodgrains, economic development and employment, social and national unification, development, etc.

Objectives of education have remained more or less the same in all ages. The main aim has always been-giving direction to society and the individual. But in this context, the dominating pattern has been that of the individual. Individuals have proved lethargic and negligent in honouring educational objectives, irrespective of whether these individuals are managers or legislators, teachers or parents, students or any others. Each one has given priority only to his own convenience. The teacher does not bother about fulfilling the objectives of education but about completing the course, as though that were the sole objective of his effort. The principal's sole objective is a satisfactory result. The management aims solely at grabbing money, by means fair or foul. Parents feel satisfied when they have sent their children to the prison of the school. What all this means is that there is so much variation and instability in the patterns and models of individuals that the aid which a liberal attitude has given them itself prevents them from regaining their balance.

Today, the contexts have altered. The negligence of the last twenty five years may have cheated no one else, but it has certainly cheated theyounger generation. The founders of education, who have indulged in the worst possible exploitation of and injustice towards students, should now beware. For the present, student unrest is only a foreshadow of its real self, but it has indicated that the objectives of education, modes of teaching, behaviour, all must be changed; if they are not changed, students will replace those who was responsible for education.

These questions keep flashing through my mind. I see that the form of education lies entangled in the legislative assembles of states, the chairs of ministers, the files of secretaries and the helpless shortsightedness of our legislators. There is a need for dedication to the nation, for development of the nation, for its cultural development, for religion, morality and character. All its needs are lost sight of in the futile exercises in manpower planning and determination of the objectives of education, and devising suitable plans and schemes for achieving them. It is impossible to forecast when our nation will arise from its long slumber, when it will look at itself and the people with new eyes. What I wonder is whether our people have the necessary courage, dedication and ability?

The following steps will have to be taken to resolve the educational crisis in the country—

1. Educational values must be remoulded and reshaped from the social, moral and spiritual viewpoints.
2. Education must be linked with production. Science, practical experience and professionalisation will be elements in this education.
3. A uniform system of school education must be implemented for social and national unification. A programme for national and social service will have to be implemented. The language policy will have to be geared to achieve national unity. A national awareness will have to be generated.
4. Education must be linked with modernization.
5. Teachers must be given a position of respect and honour, a high social position.
6. Administration of education must be improved.
7. Stress must be laid on job oriented education.

3

Basic Education

The Structure

In our country, there are two forms of primary education - (1) Primary education, (2) Basic Education. The first is called the general form. In it, there is provision for an education which achieves only the objective of intellectual skill. In John Ruskin's opinion, its objective can be described in the following terms. 'The meaning of education is not to educate people in the things of which they are ignorant. The real meaning of education is to teach people to conduct themselves in ways in which they do not behave.'

It has also been said in our Constitution- "The state shall endeavour to provide within a period of ten years from the commencement of this Constitution for the free and compulsory education for all the children until they complete the age of 14 years." (Article 5 of the Indian Constitution) Because of this, states and local bodies were entrusted with the responsibility of making all efforts to implement the seven-year plan of compulsory education.

In our country, general primary education is found to have different forms and names in different parts. The Kothari Commission suggested that this diversity should be ended and uniformity introduced but this uniform concept of education has yet to gain wide currency. For achieving this purpose, the Kothari Commission has put forward the following suggestions

The objective of primary education is to build up a responsible personality capable of functioning as a useful citizen. The Constitution provides for compulsory education of children upto the age of 14 years. The following programmes should be implemented for achieving this target :

1. By 1975-76, there should be adequate ar arrangements for providing effective education for every child for a period of 5 years. Providing effective education for every children for a Period of 5 years.

Existing Form	*Form Suggested by the Kothari Commission*
1. Pre-primary 2. Pre-Basic 3. Kindergarten 4. Montessary, etc.	1. Pre-primary
1. Primary (in some states) 2. Lower Primary 3. Junior Basic 4. Lower Elementary	2. Primary Classes 1 to 7 or 8 1. Lower Primary Classes 1 to 4 or Classes 2 to 5
1. Middle (in some states eg., Punjab) 2. Junior High School (U.P.) 3. Upper Primary School (Gujarat) 4. Senior Primary School 5. High Elementary School (T.N.)	2. Upper Primar Class 5 to 7 or Class 6 to 8

2. By 1986, every child should be given 12 years of education.
3. There must be very little wastage or failure in classes 1 to 7. The rate of success should be 80%
4. Children who reach the 7th class before the age of 14 and do not wish to study further should be kept in the same class. They should also be given a condensed vocational course.

5. Every state should prepare schemes for the growth of primary education.
6. A primary school should be available to every child within one mile of his residence.
7. Children between the ages of 5 and 7 should be admitted to class I.
8. The system of registering names in schools before actual admission should be introduced.
9. The rate of progress should be from 80% to 100%. A child should not be failed without sufficient cause.
10. The recommendations of the National Committee of Education be implemented.

Beginning Level

In his book *To students*, Mahatma Gandhi has written that every individual who wants to do something for the students, and every educationist, has felt that our educational system is defective. It does not satisfy the needs of poor India. It fails to establish harmony between home life, village life and education. In his analysis of contemporary education at that time, Gandhiji has said that the prevailing system was defective in three major ways-(1) it was based on a foreign culture and had no relationship whatsoever with Indian culture; (2) it neglected the culture of the heart and the hand, and limited itself solely to the culture of the mind; (3) it was impossible to have real education through the medium of a foreign language.

Gandhiji expressed his views on education on-22nd and 23rd October 1937 at the Wardha Education Conference. For him, education meant the comprehensive and integral development of the individual and the child, in other words, the development of the brain, body and the spirit. Literacy in itself does not constitute education. For this reason, he wanted education to begin with handicrafts, and he wanted such an education to be productive from the very beginning. In this way, every school would become self reliant.'

Zakir Hussain Committee. A committee was setup under the chairmanship of Dr. Zakir Hussain for reflecting upon the concept of Basic Education. Its main suggestions were :

1. Provisions should be made at the national level for providing free and compulsory education for every child.
2. The medium of education should be the mother tongue.
3. The medium of education should be productive handicraft industry.
4. The educational system, should be self sufficient itself to pay the salary of the teacher.
5. Great stress should be put upon labour, and dignity of labour should be inculcated among students.
6. Education should conform to the child's natural environment.
7. The child should be transformed into a good citizen.
8. Curriculum. (1) One of the handicrafts- such as weaving and spinning, carpentry, gardening, agriculture, leather work, or other productive industry. (2) Mother tongue. (3) Mathematics. (4) Social studies (history, geography, civics). (5) General science, practical botany, biology, hygiene, etc,) (6) Drawing and painting. (7) Music. (8) Hindustani (in the Devanagari or Urdu script).

This scheme began to be implemented in 1937. In 1939, a committee was organised under the chairmanship of Shri S.G. Kher to evaluate the system of Basic Education.

The Kher Committee. The then Chief Minister of Bombay (1939) was made the chairman of committee to evaluate Basic Education. The Committee stressed the implementation of the scheme in rural areas. Its main suggestions are:

1. In the absence of adequate finances, it is not possible to arrange for basic education. Despite this, provincial governments should establish creches and also encourage voluntary organisations in doing the same.
2. The period of Basic Education should be increased from seven to eight years, of which the first five years should be for junior basic, and the last three for senior basic.
3. At the conclusion of this education, the child should be possessed of full potential for further development.
4. The advisory board for central education should establish a permanent committee for the supervision of basic education.

Sargent Plan. In the Sargent Plan of 1944, the importance of basic education was accepted. The recommendations of the Kher Committee also found a place in this plan. It was accepted by the Central and Provincial governments.

Kher Committee 1948. Accepting the recommendations of Sargent Plan the Kher Committee recommended that basic education should be introduced throughout the country in 16 years. It was also said that non-basic schools should be converted into basic schools, and the central government should bear 30% of this expenditure on education.

National Basic Education Board. This board came to be established in view of the suggestion for establishing a permanent commission for basic education. Although the government accepted Basic Education as national education the system failed to make encouraging progress. The responsibilities of this board include research concerning basic education, training of examiners and officials, advising governments and institutions, organising seminars, and organising laboratories.

The characteristics of basic education can be stated thus :

Psychological Basis. In basic education, attention is paid to the interests of the child. Stress is laid on the natural development of the children's personality.

Social Basis. It is on Indian culture and its needs, which it successfully satisfies.

Economic Basis. Basic education makes an effort to ensure that child should be able to meet the expenses of his own education. The real truth of the matter is that the system is a great scheme for putting an end to unemployment.

Importance of Labour. Basic education has always been alive to the importance of physical or bodily labour.

Social Synthesis. It also achieves a harmonious relationship between the home, the school and the society as a whole because it is based on the foundation of reality.

Centred in Industry. The entire process of education is based on industry. Thus, the child receives a practical education because he learns by doing and thus gains experience.

Comprehensive. Being a comprehensive collection of numerous subjects, basic education makes lessons interesting, and the child obtains a knowledge of numerous subjects simultaneously and without effort.

Centered on the Child. The basis of this system is the child itself. According to H.R. Bhatia, in the basic system, the child is regarded as the customer of education, and hence it becomes necessary to study his requirements and understand them, make provisions for them and satisfy them.

Independence. Both students and teachers have a very large degree of freedom in their activities.

Many tests and experiments have been conducted to evaluate the success of Basic Education. In every state, basic schools, training centres, teacher training programmes, etc., were initiated. Many such experiments have been conducted at Assam, the Kumar Mandir, Ahmedabad, Gujarat, Navyug School, Bombay, Graduates Training Centre, Dhaarwara, Basic Training Centre, Kalmore, Poona, Basic School, Sevagam, and at other places.

Many charges have also been levelled against Basic Education. The allegations are as follows :

Craft Centered. Some people are of the view that the defects of basic education lies in the very fact of its being centered in craft and industry. The child begins to take more interest in the industry than in education.

Impracticable. Some people consider it to be impracticable. The reason for this is that it is not easy to impart this kind of education.

Lack of Self-reliance. One major charm of basic education is self reliance, but in reality children waste the materials given to them, and thus the objective of self-reliance is not achieved.

Lack of Religious Education. Gandhiji did not include religious education in basic education because the prevailing view of religion is an extremely narrow one, and it is more likely to cause harm than good.

Lack of Interest. Although basic education conceives of many industries in a single, school, it is not possible to make arrangements for every industry in every school, and hence students often lack interest in the industry available in a particular school.

Lack of Textbooks. Since the basis of this system is activity, there is a lack of text-books.

Lack of Enthusiastic Teachers. The most serious shortcoming of basic education is the lack of enthusiastic teachers, and it is because of this that Basic education has proved a failure.

Recommendations of the Committee

In 1965, the Central Education Advisory Council accepted the following recommendations of the National Basic Education Council—

1. Basic education should be given recognition at the primary level throughout the country.
2. Existing basic schools should be strengthened.
3. Primary schools should be converted into basic schools.
4. Crafts should be necessarily available in all new schools.
5. At the secondary level, post basic schools should be an inseparable part of education.
6. Post-basic schools, in particular, should be strengthened.
7. Training institutions should have facilities for providing training in basic education.
8. The knowledge and experience of administrators of education should be imbued with service and sacrifice.

Mahatma Gandhi's concept of basic education is a milestone in the history of education. It was, in fact, a revolt against the prevailing passive, book-centered education, an education dominated by examinations, and also against a tendency to blind limitation of the British government's traditional educational pattern. At the primary level, it gave birth to a national stream of thought, and it has become an important current in the stream of our national educational system. Mahatma Gandhi has clarified that our objective is not to create skilled workers or even skilled artisans and artists. What we want is the harmonious and comprehensive development of human beings.

The Education Commission (1964-66) has stated that it is our firm belief that its basic principles are sound, and that with due modification it should be closely associated with the national educational system, not only at the primary level, but at every level. Its important elements are-(1) productive activities in education, (2) correlation of the productive activity with the material and social environment, (3) close relations between the school and the community. In view of these ideas, the Commission has laid stress on work experience at every level of education. In it, education is closely related to handicraft. The Commission, too, has accepted its comprehensive form.

The Commission has caused harm to Basic Education by accepting the programme of work experience, since it is only on this basis that the National Basic Education Institute has been shut down. Having put an end to the very life of national education and its original and natural sources of inspiration, we have tried to fulfil our goal of national development through an imported and borrowed educational process.

Criticising the Kothari Commission's concept of work experience, Jugatram Dave has brought out the following points : According to him, the Commission claims to have accepted the basic principles of Basic Education in the total educational programme. These basic principles are identified as : (1) Productive tendency in education, (2) correlation, and (3) contact between school and society. These elements have been accepted at the top, and this is desirable. One additional element, a very important one, should also be included-and that is, love of country, love of indigenous things, self-reliance, courage, sacrifice, etc. The tendency towards social service has also been accepted. But these qualities will be absorbed by the children only when there is a concrete objective before them. Of course, there can be social service tendencies which can operate without giving too much importance to love of country. During Gandhiji's days, all tendencies were focussed upon the national movement for independence. Now, this movement is 20 years old. For the younger generation, it is a part of history, and it has not left its impress upon their minds. In our present day society, instead of love or worship of nation, the ideas that are present before almost every individual are those of wealth, honour, self seeking, etc. Consequently, there must be special efforts in our curriculum to introduce national ideas and patterns of conduct into our education. If this is not done, the most significant aspect of basic education- formation of character- will remain indistinct.

Shri G.N. Acharya holds the view that the Basic Education which was developed by Zakir Hussain and others was an attempt at the implementation of Gandhiji's ideas. In the preceding session of the Rajya Sabha, the President had sorrowfully declared that Gandhiji was the father of a new-born infant — basic education: The declaration of the Commission could be regarded as the death certificate of that infant basic education.

Every point in the criticism of Basic Education applies with equal validity to the concept of work experience also. The question is whether teachers want to make the child a human being or a skilled mechanic. If the child becomes a human being, he can become everything, but if the child is to be developed into a machine, then the social system will be dominated by a few who will never allow the majority to prosper. Hence, government should have no hesitation in accepting basic education as a system of mass education.

What is needed today is that the system of national education propagated by Gandhiji should be accepted as an instrument of social change. Its aim is to instill such experiences in the child as will persuade him to remain honest. Indian villages are a formidable instrument for a national social system, since they fulfil a social need. Through it, dignity of labour, social responsibility and a liberal attitude is developed.

Initial Difficulties

Like the numerous other problems facing our country after independence, our schools also faced the problem of education. The freedom from slavery made it necessary to evaluate education afresh. Hence, in this evaluation, the problems which had made this country illiterate once again ,came to the fore. Despite the introduction of a new educational policy, the progress was not satisfactory. Many factors lay at the root of this situation. In the process of evaluation, the following problems of primary education came to be identified distinctly, and these problems continue to exist even today, in one form or the other.

Problems of Administration. In India the responsibility for primary education falls fully upon the local administration and partially upon the State government. Both these administrative units manage primary education in their respective spheres in their own ways. There is lack of coordination between them, and the result is that the officials appointed by the State either fail to manage the schools established by the local administration or consider this unnecessary.

The responsibility for the conduct of education lies with the director of education in municipalities, the deputy inspector in the district councils, Communities in panchayats, and S.D.I. and Education Development Officers. All of them exhibit the tendency of passing on the responsibility to others. In America, the responsibility for primary education has been put upon the local administration, and it conducts education through the cooperation of the community. In the same way, in England; the Local Education Authority is responsible for primary education, and in both of these countries, state control is limited to providing funds for education. The local administration conducts education efficiently in its own way. Unfortunately, in India, there is a complete lack of efficiency. In this context, the Balwantrao Mehta Committee has recommended the complete decentralisaton of education at the primary level. Some of the suggestions given for bringing improvement at this level are the following-

1. The State's educational policy should be in conformity with the needs of the country.
2. The State should form a council consisting of governmental and non-governmental representatives for the development of primary education. Its prime function should be to ensure the uniform growth of primary education.
3. The State should lay down the minimum limits and standards which can easily be achieved by each school.
4. A strong administration should be formed in every State to provide compulsory education, and its aim should be to take advantage of every possible agency.
5. States should provide the necessary funds for the growth of primary education because proper management is inconceivable in the absence of funds.

6. The success of primary education depends upon administrators and inspectors. Hence, only capable and vigilant individuals should be chosen for this task.
7. On primary education, there should be uniformity in the policies of local administration, states and the Union government because, in its absence, the direction of primary education becomes lax.

Management of Schools. The 45th Article of our Constitution directs that education should be compulsory for all children, till they attain the age of 14. But this objective could not be achieved due to inadequacy of schools. Our schools are confronted with the following problems-

(*i*) *Problems of Primary schools in towns.* In towns, the number of schools is not in proportion to the population. for political reasons, many schools are set up at one place, with the result that areas requiring one school have two or three, and others which need two or three have only one.

Attendance is also a major problem in urban schools. In some schools, the number of students is so large that the teacher, after taking the attendance, has little time left for actual teaching. Such schools not only create an imbalance in the educational system, they also misuse and waste investment on education. In towns, there are very few schools near industrial establishments, though in fact more are required. In Mexico, there is at least one school with one industrial establishment. If such a policy were adopted in India too, at least one major problem would be overcome.

(*ii*) *Rural Schools.* In rural areas, the main problem of schools is the fact that they are scattered, they have dirty and kucha buildings, and inefficient teachers. The problems of housing for teachers and the indifference of parents complicates the situation.

Rural primary schools are in a much worse condition than urban schools. Since it is assumed that the reconstruction of the village is possible only through education. Education should be so organised that a child should find a school within one mile of his house. On the subject of rural schools, the editorial of American Education' opines that it cannot be said where the rural school ends and the villages began; neither can it be said where the life of the village begins and where it ends, because the school has created for itself a place as the basic or original office of the society and the community.

(*iii*) *Social Schools*. The third category of primary schools is of the schools found in tribal areas, backward mountainous regions and areas occupied by the erstwhile criminal tribes. These schools do not amount to even 5%, with reference to the population to which they cater, and consequently, instead of taking children out of the darkness of ignorance to the light of knowledge, they allow them to remain immersed in their darkness.

Provision of Finance. In India, money is spent extravagantly on every activity except education, and thus India's educational budget is much less than that of other countries. While Japan spends 6% of its national income on education, Russia 7%, England 4.5% and America 4.7%, India spends only 2.3% of its national income on education. This makes clear the financial condition of Indian education. Other countries spend 50% of the total educational budget on primary education; for India this figure is only 35%. It is obvious that unless this investment is raised, the growth of primary education will be below expectation. Without it neither the teachers will take an interest in their work, nor will the necessary means for it be provided.

Problem of Teachers. Some of the main problems being faced by primary teachers are(1) those concerning efficiency, (2) the problems of schools, (3) problem of equality, (4) problem of salary. As far as the question of efficiency and qualifications is concerned, for a primary teacher the certificate of the State Board is proof of the teacher being a matriculate and also of his being trained, but many teachers do not possess even this minimum qualification. This inevitably brings down the standard of education. Teachers in primary schools do not get an attractive salary. Consequently, they treat teaching as a kind of pension, and spend their time in other activities to supplement their income. Secondly, the salaries paid by the state differ considerably from those paid by institutions, with the result that there is widespread dissatisfaction. At places, a peon gets a better salary than a primary teacher.

The Kothari Commission has given numerous suggestions for the improvement of teachers at the primary level. Of these, the major ones, are :

1. Teachers in primary schools should be trained, as far as possible, and they should also have studied in a school for 10 years, i.e., they should be matriculates.
2. The Teacher should have gone through a training course for at least two years.
3. Untrained teachers should get an opportunity to improve their qualifications through in-service training programmes or correspondence courses.

Teachers should be aware of both urban and rural conditions, and their work should conform to it. In rural schools, it is best if the teacher belongs to the same region. Every school should have an adequate number of teachers because it has been found that single teacher schools are merely places where children collect together, but not places where they receive education. Teachers should be guided by the following motto-when you have more time, study more, but when time is short, do not study, but do. work industriously. China has organised its primary education on the basis of this principle. The immediate problem of shortage of teachers can be solved by following Denmark's plan. In this, a teacher takes one class on the first day, but a different class on the next day. Our schools at present need a minimum of 1,06,000 and a maximum of 2,64,000 teachers. Every effort should be made to fulfil this need.

Problem of Curriculum. Our schools lack a systematised curriculum. At some places, the load of work is so light that both teachers and students idle away time, but at others, children are burdened with books. In order to make the curriculum attractive, we should keep in view the needs of our country. The present curriculum does impart literacy to the child, but it cannot develop in him the qualities needed for achieving national goals. It fulfils the needs of neither the villages nor the towns.

The Kothari Commission has pointed out explicitly that students at the primary level should not be burdened with many subjects. They should be taught subjects imparting knowledge of language, arithmetic and the environment. At this level, the sole language taught should be either the mother tongue or the regional language. In arithmetic, knowledge of Roman numerals, the use of charts and maps, etc., should be imparted. Work experience should have a suitable place from the very beginning so that the child learns to work and develops the right sentiments.

The Commission says that all over the world, the curriculum is in a state of indecision. To improve the school curriculum, many steps, such as (1) research into the curriculum, (2) preparation of text books and teaching aids, (3) in-service training of teachers, etc., will have to be taken.

At the primary level, the Commission has divided the curriculum into two parts- (1) Lower primary stage (from class 1 to 4) - one language, arithmetic, study of the environment, creative activities, art, programmes, social service and health, (2) Higher primary stage (from class 5 to 8, -two languages, mother tongue or original language, arithmetic, science, social studies, art, work experience and social service, physical education, morality and spiritual values.

Problem of Space. Primary education invariably faces the problem of space. Most such schools operate in rented buildings, which usually lack adequate lighting. They are also not suitable from the environmental angle. They cast a deleterious influence upon the child's mental and physical health. At some places, such schools function even in huts and tents. During the rainy season, their difficulties increase manifold. According to Maulana Abul Kalam Azad, our attention should turn towards school buildings, the teacher and the method of education. He requests particularly the rural people to obtain construction materials from the government, and through local cooperation, construct school buildings for the community.

The Kothari Commission has recommended that state governments should provide some proportional aid for the construction of well-planned school buildings.

Problem of Resources. In primary. schools, there is generally a need for seats, blackboards, furniture and other useful materials. In addition, drinking water and urinals are also required.

Experience shows that there are very few schools which have all these facilities and materials. In some places, students do not have even jute mats to sit on. At others, one finds the blackboards lying in the store. At yet others, there is a complete absence of maps and charts, and even if available they are not used by the teachers. This problem has two aspects, first, the lack of necessary materials, and second, the failure to use them when available. Regarding the first, the Kothari Commission has recommended that the government should arrange for the cheap production of good quality teaching materials. Whenever there is a lack of teaching material, it should treat the high school as an extension service centre and provide the necessary things. The second obviously depends upon the teachers.

Problem of Ancillary Services. The ancillary services concerned with education usually include- (1) arrangement for lunch, (2) free text-books, (3) free materials, (4) hostel accommodation, (5) medical facilities.

Regarding the first, it can be said with certainty that there are very few schools in India which provide lunch to children. Children who travel two or three miles to reach the schools generally have difficulty in carrying their lunch. They take lunch only when they return home after school hours. In winters, the period in school becomes even longer. Consequently, the health of children is adversely affected. Hence, the community should make such an arrangement that it should collect foodgrains and give it to schools, so that this problem may be overcome. In some schools, a substitute for lunch is provided in the form of snacks. The Central Social Welfare Board has prepared a budget of Rs. 3 crores for providing lunch to 119 lakh children.

It is the duty of the state to provide text-books and uniforms to poor children and to fulfil the requirements of Article 45 of the Constitution. If the government is able to provide housing for primary teachers, the cause of primary education will receive great strength.

Special Problem. The special problems of education include the problem of education of girls, training of teachers, attaining proper standards among teachers and preparation of suitable literature both for students and teachers. For the solution of these problems, the Kothari Commission has suggested that special schools for girls should be opened, but it feels that the majority of schools should be co-educational. Teachers should be trained through in-service training programmes or correspondence courses and literature suitable for them should be created. The materials necessary for the teaching of science should be available in every school, so that science rooms and science corners can be set up.

Problem of Research. Education is a dynamic process and therefore, at intervals research into it is essential. The sphere of primary education is riddled with problems, and they can be overcome only through adequate research. According to Shridharnath Mukerjee, this research should concern itself with the following spheres- (1) conversion of primary schools into basic schools; (2) implementation of compulsory education; (3) the attitude of uneducated guardians; (4) teaching of multiple classes; (5) proper adjustment of the school time table; (6) wastage and stagnation; (7) school buildings; (8) study of compulsory education as implemented in foreign countries; (9) construction of school buildings; (10) inexpensive tools of teaching or teaching aids.

Research can be conducted into many areas in addition to those outlined above. For this purpose, surveys into the educational conditions should be carried out periodically. The problem is that our legislators are concerned only with their own selfish interests. In the opinion of Shri K.G. Saiyadain, although the demand of the political conditions is the immediate implementation of plans, our politicians are in no position to achieve this. Hence, educationists, the government and administrators should seek solutions to these problems so that illiteracy may be wiped out from the country by 1985-86, the date set by the Education Commission.

Dominance of Politics. A survey of primary education in many states has revealed the fact the primary education has been profoundly influenced by panchayats. As a result, the teachers have become stuck in the quagmire of local politics. One Principal pointed out that his school was often visited by some local politicians who had managed to get many of the teaching staff involved in their own activities. He subsequently found it almost impossible to get any cooperation in teaching work from those members of his staff. Teachers took advantage of this situation to neglect the school and teaching work. this has not only led to wastage and stagnation, it has also become the cause of misuse of national funds and manpower.

Lack of Lady Teachers. Even today, many schools in India have closed their doors because of the lack of lady teachers. The main reason for this is an absence of mobility among lady teachers. The question of social security is intimately connected with the status of ladies, and the fact that ladies teaching in rural schools have no security worth the name hardly needs to be proved. Local politics creates further insecurity for a lady teacher.

Non-implementation of Plans. According to a survey in Rai Bareilly, there are 867 rural schools of which 15 are for girls. In urban areas, there are 10 schools for boys and 5 for girls. In these, the average number of teachers is five. Many of the state educational plans are not implemented in such schools at all.

Slackness of Law for Compulsory Education. For the success of primary education, it is essential that a compulsory education act be passed and implemented, but the entire administrative structure in the country has shown little inclination towards any concrete work in this direction. Hence, it is essential that the entire energy of the country should be directed towards this.

Pay Scales and Service Conditions. In primary schools, the service conditions for teachers and the arrangements for disbursement of salary are inadequate. At some places dearness allowance and village allowance is not paid at all, while the salary is disbursed at intervals of six months at a time. In such a situation, many District Boards constantly face hunger strikes by teachers.

Problem of Universal Compulsory Education. The 45th Article of the Constitution provides for compulsory and universal education for children upto the age of 14 years. Although this Article is mentioned frequently enough, it has not been possible to provide compulsory education till now. There are many reasons for this :

(*i*) *Economic Causes.* The first point is that the country as well as the population are steadily moving below the poverty line.

Neither the government nor the people have the resources or the finances. Our economic structure has led to the steady enrichment of the rich and the deprivation of those already poor. In schools, students lack buildings and teaching materials. Only 30 per cent of our schools function in suitable buildings. According to governmental policy, there should be one primary school in every village with a population of 500. At present there are 3.5 lakh villages with a population of less than 500, and hence primary schools cannot be established there. Children thus have to trudge many miles to reach school. In hilly areas, the problem becomes an even more intractable one. Besides, guardians often keep the children away from school at harvest time, and consequently, their education is further curtailed.

(ii) Political Causes. Soon after independence, our country was forced to face foreign aggression on three occasions. In addition, it had to cope with the problem of refugees, and at the same time, frequent communal problems have further hindered the process of development.

A defective educational policy, defective administration and inadequate laws have created obstacles in the spread of compulsory education. The administration has failed to put pressure upon guardians to send their children to schools. And, as education is a state subject, state governments are not obliged to follow the dictates of the Central government.

(iii) Social Causes. Most guardians, being illiterate themselves, do not understand the importance of education. They regard the child as an economic unit, and hence they consider it better to engage the child in labour than to send him to school. The spread of compulsory education is further hindered by the caste system, untouchability, child marriage, dogmatism and many other social factors.

(iv) Educational Causes. The existing primary school does not conform to the child's natural environment. It does not conform either to life or to our land. It has neither utility nor creativity. There is also a lack of teachers. In remote areas, teachers do not even bother to go to school. Single teacher schools have proved almost a complete failure. The trained teachers do not teach on the

basis of the teaching principles they have acquired, while the untrained teachers have no knowledge at all of such principles.

The absence of separate schools for girls is an obstacle in the path of their universal education. Lady teachers do not emerge from the rural areas.

(v) Geographical Factors. The geographical features of our country are such that a uniform system of education is not suitable for every region. Mountains, rivers, streams, forests, the weather and other geographical features influence the life of the school. At many places, it is impossible to send young children to schools.

The 45th Article of the Constitution assures that the State will assume the responsibility of providing free education to all children between the ages of 6 and 14, within a period of ten years of the adoption of the Constitution. From this it is evident that India must aim at universal and compulsory education, but universality in this field is faced with three problems :

1. *Absence of universality in facilities.* There are very few children in India who can find a school within a mile of their houses. Many children have to walk many miles to reach their school.
2. *Absence of universality in registration.* There are many children in India who are admitted to a school at the age of 6. In many cases, children join the first class at the age of 10 or 11.
3. *Universality in drop-outs.* This problem is related to the first two problems. The child joins a school, spends a few years in it, but then, for a variety of reasons, leaves. This practice leads to extravagance and a waste of resources. The draft plan for primary education states that education cannot be effective as long as every child does not obtain primary education. The removal of immature children from school leads to a waste of resources in education. Two problems can be seen in the process of leaving school- (i) Wastage, (ii) Stagnation.

After 1921, the problem of wastage in education is becoming steadily more and more intense. Even the Hertog report made it clear that primary education would remain ineffective as long as each child did not remain in school for a minimum of four years and achieved literacy. The term 'wastage', in this context, means the dropping out of the child from the educational process, i.e., his leaving school at an unsuitable time. This wastage involves a waste of national labour and wealth and its long term consequences must necessarily be disastrous.

Single Teacher Schools. Schools with single teachers make a special contribution to wastage. According to the report of the Indian Education Survey, these schools have played a significant role in this matter. It is difficult for a single teacher to handle five classes simultaneously. If he goes on leave, the school closes down. This makes the students reluctant in going to school, and soon they drop out altogether.

Social and Economic Structure. India's economic and social structure is of a kind which encourages parents to send their children for general education. Even today, our rural population holds on to the belief that a child should only be educated to the extent of being able to read and write.

The Child as a Labourer. Children living in villages are the property of their parents who can compel their children to labour and earn on the fields. For such parents, the money earned by the child is more important than his education.

Schools without Resources. Many schools are almost completely lacking in the resource necessary for teaching, and in the absence of these means, the teacher cannot teach. Consequently, the children engage themselves in playing here and there, and in the absence of satisfactory results, soon leave the school.

Lack of space in Schools. Wastage also occurs in schools which have only make shift arrangements for housing the children.

Another factor contributing to wastage is the fact that children are admitted to schools throughout the year. Besides, lack of attention towards attendance is another factor. It has been observed that wastage reaches the figure of 36% by the time we reach class 3. About 50 per cent of the wastage occurs at the primary stage, but there is considerable difference between the wastages in the education of girls and boys. This is illustrated in Table.

Ratio of Wastage

Stage	*Rate*	
	Boys	*Girls*
Elementary	71.09	84.74
Primary	60.30	71.36
Secondary	20.43	25.95

Saturation Point

It was stated in the Hertog Report that the term stagnation was taken to mean keeping a child in one class for more than one year. R.V Parulkar has explained that schools are established to provide education to children, and not to fail them. In other words, stagnation means the continuance of a child in a single class for two or three years due to failure. This too, involved a wastage of man's ability and the nation's energy, resources and manpower.

Besides, failure encourages a sense of inferiority in the child, and when children younger than him become his classmates, his abnormality tends to increase. Every year, the level of stagnation in primary classes is between 30 per cent and 50 per cent.

Defective Policy of States. The policy of filtration which Lord Macaulay had planned in terms of providing education to a special class, and tacitly, even today, our education caters only to a particular class. In terms of proclamations on public education, our country has made spectacular progress, and in the present context, it wants to implement an idealistic policy, but it has made no attempt to keep reality in mind. There is much talk of financial restraints, but no one is ready to consider educational expenditure in the light of an investment, whereas it was the famous economist Adam Smith who pointed out that the money invested in education is returned with interest by the future generation. Besides, educational departments have not even taken the trouble of formulating a policy for combating stagnation.

Inefficient Administration. Having thrust the entire burden of primary education on local bodies, the state governments sleep the sleep of the just. But local bodies lack both finances and adequate means of raising resources, and hence they also lack any enthusiasm for the spread of education. If the local bodies serve notices on the local population for the compulsory registration of children in schools, they cannot hope to obtain popular approval in elections. Besides, the presence of inefficient and negligent officials in the local administration further encourage stagnation. Besides, schools are set up in an unplanned, haphazard manner, and this also adds to stagnation. In some areas, there are so many schools that the average attendance in them is only 100. Besides the inspecting staff is also over-burdened as it is expected to make a survey of 100 schools every year.

Lack of Money. The main stumbling block is the lack of finance. Local administration cannot spend adequate sums on education. In order to obtain grants from the state governments, it has to live at the mercy of the government. Because of this, there are difficulties in arranging not only the salaries of teachers, but even the materials needed for teaching.

Social and Religious Problems. Social and religious problems also contribute to stagnation. In schools which have a dominance of children belonging to a particular caste, tribe or group-such as tribals, scheduled castes, minority language groups, etc., other groups are neglected, and this itself becomes the cause of stagnation.

Physical Facilities. The high percentage of stagnation is also accounted for by the fact that, from the educational view point, rural areas, hilly regions and forest regions are neglected.

Educational and Economic Factors. Low standards of teaching, inadequate and unsuitable curriculum, the poverty of the people, etc., are also factors in stagnation. The two latter factors help, to a very great extent, in lowering the standard of education.

The problems of stagnation and wastage at the primary level can exist only as long as we are unable to develop the facilities for education, and fail to implement the educational policy in the right manner. Hence, this problem can be overcome if suitable efforts are made in every sphere of education.

The conclusions of a study conducted by C.M. Mehta are very revealing-

1. The annual wastage is 28%, 14.5% students do not participate in examinations, ana hence, their comparative

percentage is 39%. Of these 81% pass and 19% fail. Stagnation amounts to 19%.

2. Both wastage and stagnation are of the order of 57%. No distinction has been made between boys and girls.
3. Those failing twice had completely different causes.

Mehta has put forward the following suggestions for overcoming these difficulties, appointment of attendance officers, efficiency, regular attendance, appointment of excellent teachers, abolition of admission at a delayed time, in-service teacher training.

Official Commission

The history of education establishes incontrovertibly that wastage and stagnation have always existed in one or the other form. The general education imparted for individual development does create or rear the common man, but it has failed to develop the individual in accord with his qualities, interests, bent of mind and innate tendencies. And, how could it do so, since how can possibilities for individual training exist in a system designed for mass education? As a consequence, under the conditions of a general education policy, the failure of certain children to develop due to some specific factors, gives rise to the phenomena of stagnation and waste. In general, the term 'wastage': is understood to mean the dropping out of the child from the educational stream without completing his education, while stagnation refers to his failing in any class.

The Hertog Commission was the first to consider this problem. Since then a number of studies have been conducted. J. Paul Leonards has expressed his view on the subject by saying that stagnation and wastage imply the absence of the child from the school at some times, his becoming an obstacle in the fulfilment of society's needs (6 to 14 years), and the individual's failure to develop his powers in his preparation for a profession.

After independence, we breathed the pure air of a free atmosphere, we got freedom of action and thought, but education could not mould itself to this environment. Education continued to face the same problems. The country's legislators adopted ideals which led to the decline of educational standards. Various curricula based on English and Hindi were alternately formulated, some small, others large, sometimes the accent shifted to social studies, at others it was general education which underwent cruel surgery. But we miserably failed to adapt the means to our ends.

Today, we are neck deep in problems. The increasing population has brought with it the problem of food, the administration's lax policies have brought corruption, and our ideal of a socialistic pattern of society has left us in a dream-world. When our sovereignty was endangered, we opened our eyes and realised that every pore of our body was stuffed with debt. Mahatma Gandhi had once said that if God were forced to come to India, he would have to be reincarnated in the form of a piece of bread. In a democratic country, every individual enjoys his own separate existence, and our educational system aims primarily at the development of his individuality. The Education Commission, too has observed that in democracy, the individual himself is the end or goal, and the purpose of education is to give the individual extensive opportunities to develop in accord with his abilities. India's future is being shaped and moulded in class rooms. This statement is undoubtedly true. Education alone can safeguard the individual's prosperity, welfare and success in this constantly developing world of science and technology. It is the prime tool or instrument of social change. It is always in the forefront in providing various means for the development of material as well as human resources.

The Education Commission has opined, in one context, that the child's leaving the school is wastage. So far, educationists have continued treating wastage and stagnation as problems but we prefer to call it a process, an activity that continues to happen during the life time of a society. Wastages and stagnation have remained processes. A problem can be solved, but a process cannot be brought to an end. It continues as a stream of water continues to flow. The Education Commission itself has not been able to recognise the two firmly as problems, and the available studies lead to the conclusion that there can be no solution to a process which never ends.

The Education Commission has identified the following causes of wastage and stagnation-

1. The existence of discrimination between children of different ages in a class.
2. The admission of children to classes throughout the year, while this should occur at a fixed time only.
3. The irregularity in attending school.
4. Absence of adequate teaching aids and materials both with the schools and the students themselves.
5. Excessive number of students in classes.
6. The curriculum not being in conformity with needs.
7. The absence of ability and capacity in the teacher to teach through play, thus depriving school life of joy.

Though simple and ordinary enough, these causes compel us to think. These facts have become a part of the life of all those concerned with education, and often enough, it is felt unnecessary to devote thought to them. One often feels that if the problem had one or two causes, one might have exercised one's mind to solve it, but where the entire structure is vitiated, the exercise is entirely futile.

The following is a brief summary of a survey conducted by Leonard-

1. During 1950-1960, at the primary level, stagnation and wastage were of the order of 65.5%.
2. The rate of wastage and stagnation was highest at the primary level, it steadily declined towards class 8.
3. Both were found to be greater in the case of girls than among boys.
4. At the middle level, wastage and stagnation is 22%.
5. According to teachers and parents, the causes of this wastage and stagnation are - the involvement of children in other activities, low socio-economic level, lack of ability among students, low levels of health, lack of communication between schools and the community, indifference towards education in the family, corrupt administration and organisation of the school, defective curriculum,

absence of a suitable environment for the students, absence of emotional maturity among students, lack of motivation, etc.

6. In the rural areas, the percentage of wastage and stagnation at the primary level is 73% and at the middle level 50% among low income families, while an additional wastage of 15% occurs because of residence in towns.

This study also establishes the point that wastage and stagnation have progressed constantly, and that they themselves are not problems, but indicators or symptoms of a problem.

There is a crying need for giving a new direction to the process of stagnation and wastage. This is possible only when we decide upon the proper planning for manpower. In society, every individual is not meant for every kind of work. Each individual should be so educated that he should be able to fulfil some specific need of society. In the statement of the Education Commission, R.A. Gopalaswami has laid great emphasis upon the correlation of education with manpower planning. In this view-

1. There should be projection of the available manpower possessing higher education so that it can be utilised effectively.
2. Highly educated manpower should not be allowed to remain unemployed or be wasted.
3. Curriculum of education should be moulded in accord with social change.
4. Extension services should be organised for progress.
5. One tremendous advantage of manpower planning will be that, irrespective of the education received by an individual, his abilities and powers will be utilised efficiently in the national interest.

Stress has been laid upon work-experience by the Education Commission for reducing the incidence of wastage and stagnation: According to it, work-experience can be defined as cooperation in some productive work, in school, at home, in a place of work, in a field, in a factory or in any other productive environment.

1. No other reform or suggestion is as important as the linking of education with the individual's life, needs and ambitions so as to make him a powerful instrument of social, economic

and cultural transformation, and to fulfil national objectives through him. This is possible only when education is linked with productivity, social and national unity and strength, the state cooperates in the development of a truly indigenous life- style, the process of modernization is speeded up and importance is given to the formation of character through stress on social, moral and spiritual values.

2. The various sources of human development should be developed.
3. Efforts should be made to discover how the best form of educational development can become possible.
4. There should be planning to ensure that the right kind and quantity of education is made available to every person.
5. Suitable Traits should be generated for the development of ability.
6. The power to provide facilities should be generated.
7. Manpower should be utilised suitably.
8. Vocational and professional education should be developed.
9. The Education Commission's concept of life-long education should be followed.
10. A clearly defined national educational policy should be framed.
11. There should be rigorous control over schools.
12. The curriculum should be reformed and made useful for life.
13. Arrangements should be made for the training of teachers.
14. Laws should provide punishment for those who do not send their children to school.
15. Adult education should be extended. Education for girls should be expanded.
16. 50% of the total educational budget should be spent on primary education.
17. Classes 1 to 4 should be regarded as a unit.
18. Local cess should be imposed for financing education.
19. There should be uniformity in education throughout the country.

The Education Commission has clarified that there should be overlooking the fact that wastage and stagnation a·e not illnesses like headache and fever, but the symptoms of other diseases concealed in the educational method. Of these the main are lack of proper harmony between education and life, and the defective management of schools which fails to attract the students towards the school. Wastage and stagnation are not, in themselves problems. In fact, it is a process, the sources of which are defective system of education, absence of objectives, and narrow mindedness of our law-makers whose selfish interests have blinded them to reality. There is no need to solve the problem of wastage and stagnation. What is actually needed is a change in the nature of its source so that these symptoms of a deep malaise may disappear and every child may be able to make his own contribution to the development of the nation.

Till today, the two noticeable levels of India's educational systems are - (1) the school level, and (2) the higher level. The former is divisible into the pre-primary, the primary and the secondary levels. All these three levels lack any relation, although the three levels provide education for the periods of infancy, childhood and early youth. So far the assumption was that the primary level was the education of the masses with the secondary level provided education to a class. Primary education was imparted through the mother tongue and the regional language while the secondary level was dominated by English.

These various dividing lines and boundaries ruined the social context and many problems emerged. Of these the main was the problem of alienation, which increased to such an extent that it made the problem irremediable. For this reason, the Kothari Commission has treated primary education as a single, composite unit, consisting of the entire educational process comprehending the pre-primary, the primary and the secondary levels.

The integrated approach can be defined as the process by which various elements are collected together, or brought near to each other.

The integrated approach can be seen as an attempt to link education to life. This concept has been evolved by the Kothari

Commission, and according to it, education should be transformed in such a manner that it should come into close relationship with the needs and ambitions of individuals, and also become a powerful medium of social, economic and cultural transformations.

In the context of education, the concept can be elaborated in the following manner. The boundaries between pre-primary and primary or between primary and secondary are purely arbitrary, and so they can be changed or even eradicated. In the same manner, people no longer cling to the traditional view that a general undifferentiated education should be imparted under primary education, while variety should be introduced at the secondary level with the interests, inclinations and abilities of the children. In Russia, a curriculum was introduced to encompass pre-primary, primary and secondary education on the basis of this concept.

With the change in time, the assumptions regarding primary and secondary education have also undergone transformation. In accordance with the new light, the entire education before university education is now regarded as belonging to the same level. This, in effect, is the integrated approach.

The Basis of the Integrated Approach. In India, many false notions have arisen about the boundaries of primary education. Till the present, it was generally accepted that there should be pre-primary, primary and secondary education corresponding to the infant, childhood and early youth periods of life. for each separate level there were distinct concepts. Primary education has been regarded as that education which was to be imparted through Indian languages.

Another assumption current till the present is that primary education fulfils the needs of the masses while secondary education fulfils those of a specific class. But these false notions of classification acted as obstacles in the child's integral development. Hence, it has now become clear that it is wrong to consider each level of education as a separate and independent entity. It is, in reality, a continuous flow which flows uninterruptedly as does a stream. Consequently we regard integrated approach as that form of education in which the entire education from infancy to early youth is regarded as a composite of various streams of the same continuum. Under this, the curriculum is so designed that it is similar in every class for every age group. Thus, it does not give rise to alienation.

The foundations of the Integrated Approach are :

Achievement of National Objectives. If we want to achieve national objectives and ideals, we will have to transform the structure and approach of primary education. What it should be, depends to a large extent upon our national educational system. The Education Commission has started its entire argument by stating that, at present, the future of India is being shaped and moulded in its class rooms. The prosperity, wealth and level of security of individuals, in the modern world based on science and technology, depends upon education. Our success in the supreme work of national reconstruction depends upon the quantity and quality of our students emerging from our schools and colleges.

Educational Reform. The formation of the new generation depends upon our goals and ideals. Pointing to the basic objectives of education, the Kothari Commission has declared that the most important reform in education is concerned with its transformation into something which can be related to the life, needs and ambitions of our people, so that it can thus be used as a powerful instrument of social, economic and cultural transformation, which is essential for the achievement of national objectives.

View of Knowledge of a Unit. The main plank of the integrated approach is the view that knowledge is a unit. The famous educationist Jecktot also regards knowledge as an integral or composite unit. All the subjects that are taught are the various branches of knowledge, but each one aims at human development. Since we have been holding different views on the concept of primary and secondary education, we have been facing difficulties in adopting the integrating view.

Programme. Not only at the primary level, but at every level of education, what we need is a comprehensive viewpoint. The programme of the integrated approach should be the following:

1. Linking education with production.
2. Laying emphasis upon national and social unity through the educational programme.

3. Uniting and organising the population through education.
4. Developing social, moral and spiritual values.
5. Modernizing society through the development of skills on the basis of curiosity, inclination and values.

The Integrated Approach and the Curriculum. During the last ten years, considerable thought has been given to the curricula of the primary and secondary levels from the integrated viewpoint. In this context, the Kothari Commission has pointed out that a single, undivided curriculum for providing general education to everyone for the first seven years should be formulated. With regard to those students who continue their education beyond the seventh class, it is hoped that full-time or part-time professional education will be provided to 20% students. The other students should be given another three years of education under a single, general and undivided curriculum. In simpler words, what this means is that there will be a single indivisible curriculum from class 1 to 10, and this will come to an end at the time of the first external examination. In this general continuity, there will be no streaming of any kind.

Integrated Approach: Comprehensive, Varied Programme. The development of integrated approach depends upon the curriculum and a comprehensive programme. In the opinion of the Kothari Commission, the education of the first ten years includes four years of the lower primary level, three years of the upper primary level, and three years of the secondary level. But, there should be no break in the continuity of education at any stage. At the same time, however, at the conclusion of each partial stage, the level of knowledge obtained by the student should be clearly specified. Keeping in mind the comprehensive objective of school education, the levels of attainment should be made clear from the viewpoint of knowledge, skill, ability and attitude or tendency. The National Education Commission has suggested the following programme for giving concrete shape to this educational programme:

(*i*) *Science Education* . Education in science should be an inseparable part of school education.

(*ii*) *Work Experience* . Work experience should be brought into close contact with the curriculum, that is, there should be greater stress on activity than on theory. This should necessarily include the following four things - (1) Literacy or knowledge of language, humanities and social sciences. (2) Arithmetic and natural science. (3) Practice, (4) Social service. Every effort of industrial education should be such that it should influence the process of technology, science, and agriculture, because only then can principle of production be satisfied.

Development of Human Values. The integrated approach also makes possible the growth and development of human values, national unity and national awareness. Thus, the very values of development can themselves be evolved and developed through this approach.

Social and National Unity. Education should be so structured as to bring about growth in social and national unity. For this it is essential that the integrated approach be adopted. Nation building is possible only when the system and organisation of the country is satisfactory, and for creating such an organisation, the following programme should be adopted :

Common School. Social and national unity can be achieved within a short period of only twenty years through the effective means of the common schools intended for mass education. In such schools, every child will receive education without discrimination on the basis of religion, caste or class. This education will be completely free, and this will give relief to the parents.

Social and National Service. A programme of social and national service, should, in general, be adopted in every school. This activity should be part of the curriculum at every level ,of education. Such a programme can include the following activities: (a) At the primary level, work of social service should be introduced on the basis of basic education. (2) At the secondary or lower levels, students should be organised for social service for 30 days. At the higher level, this period should be 20 days. (3) At the degree level, students should be required to pursue social service for a minimum of 60 days. (4) Every educational institution should try to ensure that activities for the service of society and community should be organised for the students in their own regions.

Language Policy. The growth of a suitable language will contribute to national unity. It has generally been accepted that the mother tongue should be made the medium of education, and it has already been the medium in schools as well as higher education. Hence, the language policy should be conducive to the development of national unity.

Growth of National Awareness. Through the medium of education faith in and awareness of literature, language, philosophy, religion, India's history, India's past glory, sculpture, art, music, dancing, drama, etc., should be engendered.

Education and Modernization. Today, society is changing at a very rapid pace because new inventions and new possibilities are bringing changes in the structure and beliefs of society. Through an integrated approach, we can keep pace with time in the process of education and modernization. In this context, the views of the Commission are that- (1) In modern society, knowledge has grown at an amazing pace. This has brought farreaching changes in the educational sphere also. Proper development in interests, mental inclination, values and skills becomes possible when curiosity is aroused. All these things should be kept in focus both in teaching and in the training of teachers. (2) Society will have to obtain education for itself in order to bring about its own modernization. Education should also be productive of an intellectual class in society, a class which should come forward from every part of India to achieve the reconstruction of our nation.

Social, Moral and Spiritual Values. The educational system can contribute to the creation of social, moral and spiritual values in the following ways. (1) The central and state governments should implement the suggestions of the University Commission in education to bring about social, moral and spiritual development. (2) Private schools and colleges should also accept and implement these suggestions. (3) Provisions should be made in the time-table of schools for various kinds of programmes introduced by various teachers for this purpose. (4) Universities should introduce comparative studies of various religions.

Religion and Education. In a multi-religious country such as India, there is pressing need for the sympathetic study of all religions so that the country's citizens should fully understand each other. Selected ideas from these religions should find a place in the teaching of civics and general education. Such an effort will be of great aid in the comprehension of the world's fundamental beliefs,. assumptions and ideals.

The achievement of the objectives of the integrated approach, as defined and clarified by the Commission, need unremitting effort, in the sphere of primary education. For this purpose it will be necessary to change the entire form of context of primary education for the comprehensive approach: And for this, it is essential that attention should be paid to the following elements

Democratic Education. Primary education should be such that it develops democratic values. In a democracy, the individual himself is the end, and therefore, the prime objective of education is to provide him with the greatest opportunities for developing his innate powers. This view contains a great deal of truth, and hence, at the primary level, democratic qualities should be evolved in the child from the very beginning.

Relationship between Education and Production. One of the charges against Indian education is that it has helped to create unemployment. In order to overcome this shortcoming, it is essential to relate it to production. This will also create a potential for an increase in national income and wealth.

Check upon Wastage and Stagnation. In order to place a check upon wastage and stagnation, it is essential that there should be a check upon the method of examination and evaluation. Evaluative methods should be developed, but classes or divisions should not be mentioned in the certificates.

Curriculum. Reflecting upon the condition of the curriculum, the Education Commission has opined that glancing at it in the light of significant reforms in curricula in other countries, it is found that the school curriculum in India is both extremely narrow and obsolete.

The curriculum of primary education is both narrow and one-sided. It fails to attract either the teachers or the students. It also fails to bridge the gulf between the home and the school. For this reason, it has been suggested that the rural community should be brought into the school through the project method. Hence, it is clear that the social system can never change as long as the curriculum and the modes of evaluation at the primary level are not drastically transformed. These suffer from the following defects at present :

(1) A narrow approach, (2) stress on learning by rote, (3) stress on achievement of high academic levels, (4) too theoretical, (5) lacking completely in any professional tendency, (6) inattention towards the interests and inclinations of the students, (7) lack of emphasis upon manual work and practical education, (8) completely lacking in any relationship with life.

The curriculum of modern primary education is restricted and biased. It is also negligent of the child's integral development. It only determines to make the child an intellectual creature but it avoids the responsibility of making the child capable of adapting to every circumstance of life. The whole curriculum is entirely bookish and theoretical. The attempts at reform in this direction include a change in the curriculum of primary education on the basis of the concept of Basic Education. This attempt was made in the third plan. As a result, handicrafts were introduced into the curriculum. The curriculum of basic education differs in some respects from the common one. Dr. S.N. Mukerjee's view is that, at the primary level, the project method will prove more fruitful. The project should be founded in local requirements. It should be concerned not only with general agriculture, but also with handicraft industry, development of the community and the home, health, hygiene and personal cleanliness. The Education Commission, too, has felt the same. It says that since the existing curriculum does not give adequate stress to the development of productive skills, proper kinds of interests, tendencies and beliefs, it is completely unrelated not only with modern knowledge but even the real lives of individuals.

Bases of the Curriculum of Primary Education. Representatives of governments in Asia determined the objectives of primary education in the following terms in their conference, held at Karachi in January 1980-

1. Providing opportunities for learning control over the fundamental tools of teaching.
2. Bringing about the comprehensive and integral development of the child's personality through opportunities for physical, mental, intellectual, emotional, aesthetic, moral and spiritual development.
3. Preparing the children for good citizenship, and arousing love, respect and sympathy for the nation's traditions and culture.
4. Evolving the ideas of world brotherhood and international understanding.
5. Creating a scientific attitude.
6. Arousing respect for and faith in labour.
7. Preparing the children for life, providing practical experience; creative work, and work experience.

When these principles are applied to our own curriculum, it does not appear suitable or adequate. It reveals the following defects- (i) It throws light on only one aspect of life. (ii) It fails to harmonize theory and practice. (iii) The curriculum does have variety and it is also not productive of either national unity or international understanding. (iv) It fails to bring about a proper development of mental and physical powers.

Education must be related to life, because only then can education undergo a qualitative development, and also fulfil the ambitions of life. The modern explosion in knowledge is causing rapid and farreaching social changes, but we have not brought about changes in our curricula which can keep pace with the changing times. Thus, the curriculum should be made to change in step with time.

In this context, we are bringing out the suggestions given at conferences organised by the NCERTs for improving the curriculum-

1. The curriculum of primary education should conform to local conditions and requirements.
2. Its level should be nation-wide. It must bring about a growth in knowledge, awareness, skills, values and attitudes.

3. Schools should be assisted in the formulation of their curricula by administrators of education, educationists, guardians and planners.
4. The educational process should take place in the context of the individual's development, universal brotherhood and the student's attitudes.
5. State educational institutions should formulate the curriculum for the desired levels in consultation with the NCERT.
6. There should be a proper place for the enrichment of Indian culture, democratic citizenship and economic development.

The Recommendations of the National Education Commission. The suggestions of the Kothari Commission for developing a suitable curriculum of primary education are as follows-

1. At the Lower Primary level, the child should acquire control over the basic tools of learning, such as reading, writing, counting, and in order to adapt himself to the environment, they should study, in elementary terms, the social and material environment.
2. At the Higher Primary level, education should be imparted in one language other than the mother tongue, arithmetic, natural and physical science, history, geography, civics, creative and constructive skills, and physical education. The Commission's outline for such a curriculum is as follows-

Lower Primary (Class 1 to 4) level. (1) One language- mother tongue or regional language (2) arithmetic (3) study of the environment (class 3 and 4) (4) creative activities (5) work experience and social service (6) health education.

Higher Primary (Class 5 to 8) Level. (1) mother tongue or regional language (Hindi or English) (2) arithmetic (3) science (4) social studies (5) art (6) work experience (7) physical education (8) education in moral and spiritual values.

According to the Kothari Commission, the first two classes of the primary school should be dovetailed into a unit, and wherever possible, the same arrangement should apply to the third and fourth classes also. For these classes, the proposed curriculum is very simple, and it reduces the burden of prescribed courses. In order to develop learning, it is necessary to include in the curriculum such activities as a study of the environment, conversation, social studies, science, self-expression, music, art, drama, handicraft, etc. It is also necessary to discover the student's eagerness for studying, as well as his ability.

As far as the higher primary level is concerned, at this level the study of the languages, arithmetic, science, social studies, art, work experience, physical education, and teaching of moral and spiritual values should be included in the curriculum. According to the Commission, students should be given education in moral and spiritual value in order to form their character and also to generate respect in their minds for other religions. for this, one or two hours in the week should be fixed, and the activities for social service should include participation in the local social life.

In this way, we can observe that if the suggestions of the Kothari Commission for the reform of the curriculum at the primary level are accepted, there is no doubt that the standard of teaching at this level will improve.

Evaluation is a necessary evil. In India, every one is aware of the shortcomings of our system of evaluation, that is, examinations. From time to time, numerous committees and commissions have expressed their views on these defects and methods for their eradication.

Secondary Education Commission: Evaluation. The Secondary Education Commission has thrown light on the defects of the system of evaluation in the following terms:

1. The student depends upon keys or help books, and he is required to demonstrate his skills only at learning by rote and writing essay-type answers.
2. Teachers, too consider it their objective to ensure the passing of the student in the examination, instead of seeking to develop his qualities.
3. A teacher's success is judged by the number of his students who pass the examination.
4. The attitude of the guardians is that their children should, by any means, pass the examination and secure a suitable job. Those giving employment also base their judgment on the candidates certificates.

These are some of the defects found in the existing system of examination and evaluation. But examinations inspire the teacher, provide a uniform standard, form a medium for the achievement of the objective, and provide social acceptance. For this reason, this Commission offered the following suggestions for eliminating the defects of examination and evaluation :

1. The number of external examinations should be reduced and objective testing should be introduced. The form of questions should be changed. Dependence on essay-type tests should be reduced.
2. The school record of each student should be kept systematically in order to find out his over-all progress and also to determine his future. The record should demonstrate the work done by the student and his achievements in various spheres.

Kothari Commission : Evaluation— Evaluation is inseparably linked with the system of education, and it is a continuous process. It is influenced by (1) studies (2) teaching (3) method teaching. In order to arrive at a realistic evaluation of the student, we will have to modify the prevailing general method of written examinations. There are many aspects of the student's growth which cannot be tested by this technique. Hence, evaluation must be made objective. Reflecting upon the problem of evaluation, the Kothari Commission stated that in India every individual is aware of the defects of the examination system, and it is generally believed that the examination is the criterion for testing both the student and the teacher. In this, the students learn by rote the questions usually asked in the examination, so that it is difficult to assess their real intellectual development. At the primary level one major objective of the evaluation, in the light of the objectives of teaching at this level, is to discover the extent to which the student has improved his achievement in basic skills and developed the right habits and attitudes. The evaluative technique should assist in this measurement.

Concerning the criterion of evaluation at the primary level, it can be said confidently that there can be no change or improvement in the mode of evaluation as long as the teaching methods remain unchanged. For this reason, the Education Commission has put forward the following suggestions :

1. The size of the class should be around 45 to 50 students. In the lower primary, the maximum number should be 50.
2. Evaluation is an inseparable part of teaching, and hence there should be improvement in the written tests. New techniques of evaluation should be evolved.
3. At the primary level, the evaluation should concern itself with basic ability, attitude, inclination and habits.
4. Classes 1 to 4 should be regarded as a single unit.
5. At the higher primary level, written tests should be accompanied by oral tests, and there should be internal assessment. Cumulative records and diagnostic testing should be devised.
6. Evaluation should be done in a uniform manner at the end of the primary level. The techniques should be applied throughout the country.
7. Education officers of the district may organise a general examination at the conclusion of the primary level. This test should be more valid and reliable than the existing examinations. After the test, the result should be accompanied by the student's school record.
8. For grant of scholarships, there should be separate tests.

If the Kothari Commission's suggestions are put into operation, there will undoubtedly be a rise in the standard of primary education and the coming generations will be able to make our nation strong.

Working Group, Planning Commission. The working group of the commission has also suggested, with reference to improvement of evaluation that the importance of the method of continuous testing is self-evident. Planning, practice or active implementation and evaluation are organically related to each other. Evaluation tells us how we can overcome our failures. Hence, three kinds of testing have been in practice

1. The simplest evaluation is carried out by the teacher, institution and administrator. The system of evaluation is of particular significance in any scheme of education.

2. The process working at the state and district level is responsible for creating the collective standard.
3. Evaluation of educational programmes at the highest level.

Thus, if we want to strengthen the concept of evaluation, it is essential that we maintain a balance between the various tools of evaluation.

Is the Primary External Examination Inevitable? For the last few years, it has been noticed that the district education officers, at the behest of some official directives, organise a general external examination at the primary level. Its outcome is that the ratio of wastage and stagnation rise. The arguments given in favour of it are that (1) it maintains a uniform standard, (2) it helps in the selection of the curriculum, (3) it improves teaching.

These arguments do not establish the inevitability of an external examination at the conclusion of the primary level. For maintaining uniform standards, other means can be adopted: Hence, such a test should not be regarded as unavoidable. The desired results at this level can be obtained through effective tests and proper surveys.

Dr. Devendradatt Tiwari express the view that decentralisation means handing over the focii of authority and responsibility to basic units or individuals, instead of allowing them to rest with one or a few individuals. In considering decentralisation, both authority and responsibility should be considered. A distinction between them is essential, because it is usual to trust responsibility upon the lower units, without providing them the necessary authority to carry out the responsibility effectively.

The decentralisation of education finds mention in the Constitution also, and as a result of this, education was made a State subject, and thus they got the responsibility for it. Each state is trying to fulfil its responsibility in its own region, in its own way.

Efforts at the decentralisation of primary education have been continuing since the last century. In 1882, the Indian Education Committee had put forward the view that local institutions should be given the maximum possible autonomy. Later on, the Hertog Committee evaluated the achievements of decentralisation, but it found the results dissatisfying.

According to the Statutory Commission, it was felt that changes were necessary for the progress of primary education. In its view, it was correct that, in local matters, the efforts should be made by the local institutions themselves, and it is not unnatural that mistakes may be made, initially, in the absence of experience. Despite this, the commission felt that education was national service.

After independence, great importance was attached to primary education. In 1951, a committee of the states and union was appointed. It recommended that local institutions should be given the power to exercise the maximum possible control and also to improve their resources in certain specific fields.

The Balwantrai Committee suggested to the Indian government in 1957 that a three-tier system should be adopted. In its report, it said that there should be local panchayat at the village level, a regional committee or panchayat committee at the block level, and a district board at the district level for controlling education. The main difference in this case was that, while the district had been the fundamental unit in decentralisation in the past, this report gave prominence to village panchayats and areas or regional committees, in view of the increasing population of the district and the large number of problems being thrown up because of the developmental process.

The Education Commission has also stressed the fact that the local community should prefer its active and direct cooperation in the question of education. Secondly, the district should be the basic unit in the work of planned development.

The following were the suggestions given by the Kher Committee with regard to decentralisation

1. The prime objective of decentralisation should be to encourage the growth and expression of leadership, initiative and a sense of responsibility, but this objective has never been adequately stressed. On the contrary, decentralisation has so far been taken to mean nothing more than freedom in the raising of funds.
2. One general conclusion which emerges is that little attention has been paid to eliciting cooperation from the local

population in matters of educational administration. Whatever little attention was given was casual, rather than determined. Almost the same situation obtains even at present.

3. History tells us that the suggestions put forward by Lord Rippon in 1882 to make this experiment a success were never put into practice by the administrators. He had made it explicit that the experiment could succeed only if- (1) local institutions were given adequate materials, (2) additional work involving additional expenditure was accompanied by additional grants of financial aid, (3) government officials engaged themselves devotedly and enthusiastically to the small efforts in the beginning of an independent political life, and they came to feel that, because of these efforts, a better sphere for utilising administrative power management had been discovered. In such a situation, the effort could be pushed further. Unfortunately, these suggestions were consigned to oblivion very quickly.
4. People have generally been convinced that the root cause of all the trouble is the handing over of primary education to local institutions. They feel that its success is possible only if its control lies in the hands of the state government's education department. But history has completely confounded such a view.

Arguments in Support of Decentralisation. Dr. Devendra Dutt Tiwari holds the view that there are many questions which can be adequately answered only at the central level- security, national unity, national development, etc. Unity and development are spheres which comprehend every aspect of human life, and consequently, the intervention of the centre in all matters pertaining to the individuals and local units becomes unavoidable. Education has been recognised as the most significant means of social change and development, and hence the direction of education should be in the hands of the centre alone. It is for this reason that the states have implemented most of their developmental programmes under central direction. Not merely this, the centre has come to control even the awareness or consciousness of knowledge, but this can prove fatal for local enterprise. One example of this is the National Institute of Education, which has innumerable futile and meaningless departments.

Basis of Decentralisation. Decentralisation is extremely important for a country with India's diversity because the differences in culture and social traditions give rise to different local needs. Hence, decentralisation should be based on the following points :

1. Decentralisation is essential for maintaining national unity and achieving social and cultural development. Those who argue that decentralisation hurts national unity are mistaken. We must focus our attention upon the fact that decentralisation is to be accepted in the form of the objectives of a democratic nation.
2. Decentralisation brings about the development of the individual at the national level, but in consonance with local requirements. In a decentralised system, power rests in the hands of the common man, whereas centralisation leads to the concentration of power in the hands of a few.
3. In the opinion of Dr. Devendra Dutt Tiwari, the first question to be decided is the nature or form of administration in primary education. Some people argue that primary education is very important for the success of democracy. And, since the Constitution stipulates the introduction of free and compulsory primary education, it is the duty of the centre to carry out this task. Such an argument implicity strengthens the case for the centralisation of primary education. On the other hand, at the state level, many people are convinced that the Centre should not interfere in educational matters, and that the entire direction, control and guidance of primary education should be in the hands of the state governments.

Some Aspects of Decentralisation. Decentralisation is one of the fundamental problems of our state. Its numerous aspects influence it. These are :

1. Our nation is a democratic one, and our Constitution has given importance to the dignity of the individual. Hence, democracy should be guided by the dignity of the individual and his dedication to duty.
2. At present, decentralisation is taken to mean the collection of money, and not the direction of education. The result of this is that political and economic rights are not divided on the basis of suitable administration.
3. Decentralisation brings about the expression and development of the individual's innate powers and abilities.
4. The curriculum should be formulated in accordance with local needs. Our nation is marked by wide diversities, and hence the curricula here should be constructed on the basis of local needs, not an imitation of the patterns of education in Britain or the United States of America. This will become possible only when decentralisation becomes a fact.
5. The preparation of text books should also be guided by local needs and contexts. Though the Kothari Commission has recommended flexibility and lack of compulsion in matters of preparing the curriculum, some of its suggestions implicitly support the centralisation of the curriculum, text-books and methods of examination.
6. Decentralisation should permeate not only the administration but also the school so that they can be freed from official domination.
7. The most distressing situation is opposed to decentralisation- that is, the centralisation of examinations. According to Whitehead, the ability to evaluate a student lies only in the teacher who educates him, and in no one else. As far as the question of uniformity of standards is concerned, that entire notion is an illusion. The standard indicated by external examinations is merely imaginary, not real and it only turns the entire teaching process into the wrong channels.

The Kothari Education Commission appointed in 1964-66 has proved to be something of epic proportions in the educational field.

It will always be remembered by the future generations. It was at this time, that our leaders became conscious of the need for farreaching changes in the sphere of education. For the first time after independence, they came to lay emphasis upon the necessity of educational planning in consonance with the stream of social transformation.

According to Dr. Sampurnanand, the commission opines that education should develop so as to bring about an increase in production, to achieve social and national unity to give impetus to the process of modernisation and to generate social, moral and spiritual values.

The Kothari Commission has offered revolutionary suggestions for bringing about wide-ranging and fundamental change in the country's educational system. These suggestions will undoubtedly prove valuable and fruitful if they are accepted without modification by the Government of India. In its reflections, the Commission has laid the greatest stress at the following four points:

1. The various angles of the pyramid of education and their mutual relationship.
2. The total time-period of education keeping in mind its various stages.
3. The qualities of teachers, curriculum, method of teaching, evaluation, buildings and resources.
4. Utilisation of the available facilities.

These four elements create the entire structure of education for which it is necessary to consider the means and the total time period of the educational process. The Kothari Commission opines that the two efforts which need immediate attention at the school level are - the adoption of a utilitarian approach and improvement in the quality and quantity of all available things, apart from time. Through these, it will be possible to increase one year in the achievements of the school curriculum. In addition, the period of the higher secondary stage is to be increased to two years, which is to be achieved, through a continuous programme, beginning in the fifth plan and achieving completion by 1985.

New Educational Structure. The new structure of education should have the following pattern -

1. Pre-school education of 1 to 3 years.
2. 10 years of general education, which includes 7 to 8 years of primary education- 4 to 5 years for the lower primary stage, and 2 to 3 years for the higher primary stage. After this, at the lower primary level, there should be general education for 2 to 3 years, or vocational education for 1 to 3 years. The total number of students in the vocational courses should be increased by 20%.

Qualitative Aspects, Curriculum, etc. An improvement in the qualitative aspect of teachers, teaching methods, school buildings, evaluation, presentation and curriculum should be brought about. These should also be utilised to the maximum possible extent.

Utilisation of Resources. According to the Kothari Commission, the greatest shortcoming of the existing educational, system is not its structure, but its powerlessness. Hence, it is essential that greater stress should be placed upon the maximum utilisation of things usable in extra-curricular activities, and especially upon the programmes for the improvement of teachers. These form a part of our schemes for educational reconstruction. It is essential to adopt these facilities and suggestions.

1. Importance should be given to the intensive exploitation of the facilities implicit in various schemes.
2. Period of study should be divided in the following manner

School	39 weeks
Primary	36 weeks
College	36 weeks

3. The ministry of education should prepare a calendar of holidays in consultation with the State government and the U.G.C. The loss of teaching days due to examinations and other causes should not be more than 21 days at the school level and 26 days at the college level..
4. Students should fully utilise their vocations. This utilisation should be in the form of participating in social service camps, obtaining of production experience, participating in literacy campaigns, etc.

Some of the important suggestions of the Education Commission regarding primary education are-

1. There should be complete freedom from fees in schools run by local bodies and private institutions by the end of the fourth five year plan.
2. At the lower level, attention should be paid to the fact that no promising student abandons education due to lack of resources. Arrangement for necessary scholarships should be made.
3. Provisions should be make for Ashram Schools at the primary level in regions where the backward classes, the Scheduled Castes and Tribes predominate. Such schools should be located in far-flung places. For the first two years, education should be conducted through the tribal language, and later on, knowledge of the regional language should be given.
4. Objectives should be determined in the following manner for the progress of primary education- (1) There should be good and effective education for five years for every child in the country. (2) The same kind of education should become available for seven years by 1985-86. (3) Stress should be laid upon the eradication of wastage and stagnation. (4) Those children, who at the end of 14 years, have, completed seven years of education, but do not want to study further, should be given a choice of various vocational courses.
5. The spread of primary education should be planned in such a manner that every child should have available a primary school within a mile of his house. A higher primary school should also be available within a maximum range of three miles.
6. By the end of the fifth plan, the transference from class I to class 4 should reach 100%.
7. In order to get rid of wastage and stagnation at the primary level (1) classes 1 and 2, and if possible, classes 1 to 4, should be regarded as a single unit. (2) there should be a one year programme of pre-school training. (3) In class I, the play-way should be adopted.

8. At the primary level, students should be taught either the mother tongue or the regional language. At the higher primary level, two languages should be taught. mother tongue or regional language, and the official or semi-official language.

It is evident from the foregoing elaboration that the Education Commission has attached the greatest significance to the growth of education at the primary level. The need is for a proper understanding of the demands of our times and of implementing programmes in agreement with it.

As soon as our country became independent, the responsibility for the introduction- of free, compulsory and universal education, fell upon the shoulders of the popular government. During the five year plans, primary education progressed in the following manner:

1. In the first five year plan, provision was made for compulsory education, according to the Constitution for children of the 6 to 14 age group. Rs. 93 crores were allocated for this purpose.
2. In the same way, Rs. 89 crores were allocated in the second plan for the spread of primary and basic education.
3. In the third plan, Rs. 209 crores were invested on education. Arrangements were made for 76% of the children in the 6 to 11 age group, and 28% in the 11 to 14 age group.
4. In the fourth plan, Rs. 322 crores were provided for primary education.

Primary education is the basis of country's development. Its growth leads to the emergence of awareness in the social environment.

Enrolment. The major objective in primary education is to fulfil the directives of the Constitution, under which provisions must be made for the free and compulsory education of all children upto the age of 14 years. By the end of the fourth plan, it was expected that 88% children in the 6-11 age group and 44% in the 11-14 age group would receive education. In the former group, one fourth of the girls could not be enrolled by 1974. By the end of the third year of the plan, half the boys and three-fourth of the girls could be enrolled. The environment for enrolment which was created in the third five year plan (particularly for the 6-11 age group) was favourable, and as a result, during this plan, the annual enrolment for classes 1 to 5 was 17 lakhs, in excess of the expectations. From 1969 to 1972, this annual increase was found to be 27 lakhs. Under the employment scheme the appointments of 75,000 teachers was approved in 1973-74.

Enrolment has varied from state to state, district, block, city and village. There is need for a special effort at enrolment for classes 5 to 8. In many states, the percentage of girls enrolled is very low. For India, the percentage is 71.9, but in Assam it is 58.6%, in Bihar 52.3%, Haryana 58.4%, in Kashmir 79.9% in Madhya Pradesh 14.6%, Orissa 18.6%, in Rajasthan 14.0%, and in Uttar Pradesh 13.8%. In the classes 6 to 8, the percentage of girls is less than 20.

Institutions. The increase in primary schools has not been in proportion to the rise in population, but the disparity has been somewhat compensated by the setting up of Single Teacher Schools. By 1972, there were 25% of such schools, though in some states they formed 60 to 70% of all schools. These schools meet only a fifth of the demand. The reasons for this are : lack of proper training, for running such schools, lack of technical facilities, lack of insight in the surveying or inspecting authorities, and lack of necessary materials.

Teachers. Although the ability of teachers has undergone suitable improvement, on the whole, most teachers do not possess the requisite skills. Till 1968, 41% of the teachers had not obtained higher secondary education. It is estimated that, by the end of the fourth plan, about one fourth teachers were still left untrained. Training facilities have increased but the state governments could not provide the required number of jobs. Besides, private institutions too give priority to appointment of untrained teachers. According to the figures published by the Directorate of Employment and Training 1.5 lakh trained teachers were hunting for jobs, and in 1968, their number registered an increase of 25%. In 1971, 31,000 trained teachers were on the rolls of the employment exchanges. In Andhra Pradesh, Haryana, Kerala; Tamil Nadu, Punjab and Uttar Pradesh there is widespread unemployment among trained teachers. It was expected that under the educated unemployment scheme, 75,000 teachers would be appointed, and the situation brought under control.

Buildings and Equipment. The state of buildings and equipment in primary schools is depressing. According to the Kothari Commission, only 30% of school buildings can be said to be in a satisfactory condition. As far as the question of basic equipment for teaching is concerned— a proper blackboard, satisfactory library, necessary maps and charts, general scientific equipment, and materials for exhibition or demonstration— the situation is truly deplorable.

Finance. The direct expenditure upon primary education has been steadily declining from one year to the next. In 1951, the total expenditure on primary education was 38.2%, but in 1966, it had declined to 32.5%. The total additional expenditure was 22%, but on primary education, it was 8.4%. The figures for the third plan are even lower. The amount allocated for primary education was 56% in the first plan, 35% in the second, and 30% in the third plan, and now in the fourth, it has declined to 29%. What is even more surprising is that even this meager amount is not fully utilised. Comparatively speaking, during the first four years of the fourth plan, the amount not spent was of the order of 82%, whereas 67% of the educational budget had been allocated for basic education. Even those states which should have made the greatest efforts to fulfil the obligations of the Constitution have proved most lax. The reasons for this failure to utilise the allocated funds are numerous.

Quality. The teaching method at the primary level is completely lacking in quality. No significant change in wastage and stagnation is evident in this education. There is no decline in the number of students who fail or drop out without completing their education. Making the child remain at home before the proper time is clearly indicative of economic handicap. Stagnation can certainly be reduced at the school level by means of attractive teaching programmes. Success depends upon such elements as work experience, the solution of local problems, making necessary changes in the curriculum, etc.

The following efforts for the spread of primary education have been planned, in view of the shortcoming and facts outlined above :

Expansion of Facilities. The fifth plan will attempt to ensure that by its end, 100% of the children in the 6-11 age group should be able to get primary education. At the primary level, the enrolment is one-fourth, while at the junior level it is 41%. This ratio should be decreased. States made certain rules concerning compulsory element and provided uniformity in the age structures. The result was that in 1974-79, the enrolment was of the level of 120 lakhs in classes 1 to 5,165 lakhs in classes 6 to 8, and 45 lakhs in part-time classes. Numerous tests were carried out to check the facility and success of part-time classes, and it was found that radio, television, etc., had played an important contributory role.

Social efforts were made to provide educational extension and facilities in states and districts which were backward from the viewpoint of education. Provisions were made for free text-books, free lunch, free uniforms, etc. It is also evident that the benefit of these facilities should go to the rural population. Even today, in villages with a population of less than 200 there are 80% of the children who are denied education. The same situation exists with regard to middle level education in villages with population of less than 5000. The needs of such regions and people will have to be met through radio and television, and the cooperation of the educated people in the community will also have to be sought.

The proportion of additional enrolment of children belonging to the Scheduled Castes, classes and regions is fairly large. Such children not only have to be enrolled, but actually kept in the schools. for this, the following schemes will have to be implemented :

1. Free distribution of text books, stationery, writing materials, etc., to the weaker sections.
2. Establishment of 500 Ashram Schools for the tribal and socially backward children.
3. Distribution of free uniforms to 25% girl students by the end of the fifth plan.
4. Provision of free lunch to 61.5% children.

In this plan, special attention has been given to providing extra facilities for girls, because, as a result of social prejudices, they are often deprived of education. For them, it is necessary to generate a suitable environment, and for this the cooperation of the panchayat and local community is unavoidable.

There are arrangements for providing free lunch to 12 million children, with the assistance of the famous institution, CARE. This institution will bear the entire burden of the programme. Provisions have been made for spending Rs. 40 per child or a total of Rs. 240 crores for 1.20 crores children. This will benefit half the children. The plan is that the burden of the free lunch should fall upon the local community, and for this schemes based on the school will have to be implemented. The basis for such schemes will be provided by agriculture, health, school agriculture, panchayat land to be used for farming for the school, collection of funds, etc. The state will provide animals, land, facilities, poultry, etc., for this purpose. Priority will be given to soyabean and other foods rich in protein.

Qualitative Improvement. For the growth and expansion of facilities, stress will be laid upon the source of equipment or means. For this, rural schools will have to play a special role for the uplift, social and economic, of the rural areas. These schools will build suitable citizens for the future, and therefore special importance will be given to their consolidation and development. Selected programmes will be introduced in these areas to ensure that the development is permanent, and that these programmes have a permanent impact.

Curriculum Reform. A major share of the problem can be solved through curriculum reform. It will have to be related closely to local needs and problems. They must be made comprehensive enough to include work experience, improvement in the teaching of science, personal and social health, information regarding control of population, the use of local resources and means, and development of civic consciousness.

Work Experience. Work experience must be recognised as the main element in the curriculum, and for this local resources and means will have to be organised and brought into use. In the rural areas, such programmes will consist of cleaning of the school and village, creation of soakpits, levelling of roads, working on the fields, etc. They will also include simple crafts not requiring expensive machines or tools.

This will help the programme of providing free lunch from the school.

In-Service Education. Apart from reforms in the curriculum, it will be necessary to provide in-service education to teachers to acquaint them with these changes. By 1974, 11.2 lakhs or 6% of the teachers will be given in-service education and training.

As a part of the same programme, there is a need for a clear policy on the selection of teachers. With the rise in the number of educated people, the basic qualifications for teachers have also been rising steadily. Some special efforts should be made to attractable; talented and well-educated people to come and teach at the primary level. They should be given the salaries they are likely to receive in any other sphere. In addition, the pay-scales, posts, etc., should be determined not by work alone but also upon qualification.

Improvement in Existing Schools. The buildings of most schools are in a truly depressing state, and they are also lacking in the necessary materials. Hence, it has been decided that 5% primary schools and 1% middle schools will be given financial aid for constructing buildings, and the aid will take the form of a matching grant. Half the expense will be borne by the state government and the other half by the local community. The success of this programme depends upon the organisation and collection of technological knowledge.

Development of Selected Schools. When a firm basis for the growth and expansion of primary education has been achieved, then efforts can be directed at their qualitative improvement, and for this, it is essential that technological guidance, inventive ideas and activities should be adopted for this purpose. For such a programme, the steering group of the Education Commission has come forth with the following suggestions

1. A relation between schools and technological institutions should be established at the district, state and national levels.
2. In the fifth plan, the management of this work should be concerned with the school, training school, state educational institutions, and National Teacher Education Council. The last mentioned should provide the technique to training schools and the benefit should then flow to neighbouring institutions. On the whole, a School Complex programme should emerge, and in this, about 200 schools should be attached with the training schools.
3. These attached schools should perform, in addition to their routine work, the following activities also- adult education, pre-school education, distribution of literature to the newly literate, management of schools, etc.
4. 10 or 15 primary schools will be attached with the experimental schools. These will initially number 3000, and gradually they will expand themselves. They will receive developmental aid.
5. The experimental schools will get assistance from training schools and inspectors, with the result that a stream of emancipation and expansion will flow.
6. The state education institutions will require developmental aid, and for this expansion services will have to be provided in training schools. For technical and administrative assistance, a link between the training schools and the District Education Officers will be maintained.

Strengthening of Administration. The need for a strong administration has been felt for the expansion of primary education. At the district level, this administration should be strong, because the entire success of the educational effort depends upon it. It is at this level that surveys had to be carried out, qualitative programmes implemented, technical aid provided, and attention diverted to the socially backward classes.

Financial Implications. In the fifth plan, Rs. 1089 crores have been allocated for primary education. Table provides the details-

Expenditure on Primary Education

Sl. No.	*Programme*	*Amount (Crores)*
1.	Expansion Facilities	696 - 30
2.	Incentive to Enrolment	154 - 00
3.	Ashram Schools	26 - 25
4.	Teachers Training	45 - 81
5.	Qualitative Improvement of Schools	151 - 40
6.	Development of SIES	2 - 00
7.	Administration	13 - 32
	Total	**1089 - 08**

In the sixth plan, much thought has been devoted to universal education at the primary level. For this purpose, the following schemes have been taken up :

1. Accepting the principle of average attendance to overcome wastage and stagnation.
2. Ensuring that a school is available to a child within 1.5 kilometres in a town and within 6 kilometres in a village.
3. Laying emphasis upon compulsory enrolment.
4. Bringing about the expansion of part-time, informal, education.
5. Eradication of the regional imbalances.

Reader may go through for details for primary education in the details of (1) in 7th plan (2) Education in 8th Plan.

4

Secondary Education

Growth and Development

The present secondary education has behind it the growth and traditions of the last one hundred years. Alongwith the East India Company and other trading companies came the missionaries for the propagation of their religion, and they made provisions for the education of the native children. In 1830, the Directors of the Company decided to impart education of English to these children. Their purpose was, as N.N. Basu puts it, "to raise a body of native qualified by their habits and acquirements to take a large share and to occupy high positions in the civil administration of their country than as hitherto been the practice under our Indian Government." On March 7,1835, Lord William Bentick affixed his signature to the educational policy evolved by Lord Macaulay, and in 1844, Lord Hardinge opened the doors of employment for educated Indians. The outcome was that western education began to grow and spread at a rapid pace in India. By 1862, 32 approved schools had come to exist in the country.

From 1854 to 1904. In the growth and development of secondary education, the Wood Despatch played a very significant role, since it provided the foundation for secondary education.

The Wood Despatch was framed and declared in the following words- "That the people of India should be made familiar with the works of European authors with the results of the thought and labour of Europeans on the subjects of every description and to extend the means of imparting this knowledge must be the object of any general system of education."

"On the basis of this approach, universities were set up at Bombay and Calcutta in 1857. These universities began to control and administer secondary schools on the basis of the matriculation examination, and thus it became the function of these schools to create a foundation for the colleges."

In 1882, the Hunter Commission suggested various syllabi for secondary schools. It suggested that the higher classes of the secondary schools should be divided into two parts - one should prepare students for the matriculation examination, and the other should prepare youth for commercial and non-literary activities. By 1904, the number of secondary schools rose from 3916 to 5124, but this unplanned expansion soon manifested a number of shortcomings. The Department of Education had no control over the schools which did not receive government aid. The universities, too, granted recognition to schools with reluctance. In 1904, rules for the matriculation examination were framed in accord with the Indian Universities Act; and as a consequence, the secondary schools passed even more firmly into the hands of the universities.

1905 to 1917. Three notable characteristics mark this period-

Emergence of Nationalistic Tendencies. A national consciousness arose as a reaction to the educational policy of Lord Curzon. A National Council of Education was established in Bengal, and national colleges, technical institutes, etc., came to be set up.

Medium of Instruction. It came to be felt in this period that the medium of education should be the mother tongue, and not English. Shri Rayaninagar placed this question before the Council, but the proposal was objected to on the following grounds- (i) The students knowledge of English will decline. (ii) There was a dearth of text books in Indian languages. (iii) There will be numerous difficulties in places where many language are spoken. (iv) English is a language of international importance.

Control Over Secondary Schools. In this period, the schools were subjected to control by the universities for granting recognition as well as by the education department for granting aid to them. Later on, it was decided that the education department alone will exercise control over the secondary schools.

1917 to 1947. During this period, secondary education was evaluated from time to time by various commissions.

Calcutta University Commission. This Commission (the Sadlar Commission) put forward the view that "No satisfactory reorganisation of the university system will be possible unless and until a radical reorganisation of the system of secondary education, upon which university work depends, is carried into effect."

This Commission put forward a suggestion for the introduction of two examinations-matriculation and intermediate. In the same way, different inter-colleges for the arts, sciences, medicine and engineering, were established.

Hertog Report. The Hertog Report, too expressed the view that the matriculation examination had influenced the whole syllabus. It also suggested that, in the middle schools, the vernacular syllabus should aim at the fulfilment of various needs. Professional or vocational curricula should also be introduced.

Sargent Report. The Sargent Committee was set up in the context of the post-war conditions which came to exist in 1944. The suggestions of this committee were that - the secondary course should extend over 6 years, the age of admission after primary education should be 11 years, only brilliant students should be selected for the high schools, and the selection should be unbiased and effective. Besides, there should be two types of courses in the high school- (1) intellectual (2) vocational.

After Independence. After independence, the path for the progress of secondary education was charted by four important committees and commissions.

Tarachand Committee (1948). This committee suggested that multipurpose secondary schools should be established. It felt the need for the appointment of a commission.

University Commission (1948). The University Commission opined that secondary education is the basis or foundation of university education, and therefore improvements in it were essential.

Secondary Education Commission (1952-53). This commission was appointed to study the organisation of secondary education. It put forward a blue-print for the reorganisation of secondary education along the following lines-

1. An eight year syllabus for the 6 to 14 years age group.
2. Various 3 year courses for children in the 15-17 age group.
3. A 3 year degree course after the higher secondary examination.

Education Commission (1964-66). This Commission, set up under the chairmanship of Dr. Daulat Singh Kothari, recommended the introduction of uniformity in secondary education throughout the country. It also suggested that provisions be made for various syllabi, subjects and correspondence courses.

On the whole, then, it is clear that from 1830 to 1953, secondary education passed through numerous ups and downs. As time passed, the objectives, organisation, the programmes of secondary schools underwent changes. It is hoped that, since the country has now accepted national development as its objective, secondary education will change in accordance with this objective.

Historical Backdrop

In India, secondary education does not have a uniform nature throughout the country. The Secondary Education Commission, in its survey, discovered the following forms of it in the country-

Higher Elementary or Middle School. In some states, the middle schools are known as Higher Elementary, Vernacular middle schools, etc. These schools provide education for classes six, seven and eight, subsequent to primary education.

Secondary Schools. At the secondary level, education is generally split into two parts(1) Junior level, (2) Higher level. In some states, the senior basic schools also come within the ambit of the secondary schools. These schools provide education for 3 to 4 years. The high schools represent the higher level of secondary education. In some regions, the working period for this stage is more than three years.

Higher Secondary Schools. The higher secondary schools are the most modern institutions. These have provisions for education for three or four years. They have been established by taking away one year from the intermediate level.

Higher Education. In some states, the pre-university level and the first year of the degree course together fall within the sphere of secondary education.

Intermediate Colleges. As a result of the Sadler Commission's recommendations, intermediate colleges and boards of secondary and intermediate education came to be established. These institutions have a two-year syllabus, which is divided into the two classes; eleventh and twelveth.

Vocational Colleges. There are many vocational colleges at the secondary level, which provide education in engineering, technology, medicine, veterinary sciences, agriculture and commerce. Admission to them is possible, at some places, after high school, while at others, after intermediate.

Technical Institutes. At this level, there are many technical institutions, including professional colleges as well as polytechnics, many of which have arrangements for the education and training of children of 12 years of age.

Polytechnics. In many states, arrangements have been made for the setting up of polytechnic institutes which provide training in various trades and professions. Admission to such institutions is available to students possessing qualifications equivalent to high school or middle school. Such institutions provide training in technology, arts and crafts, secretarial practice, domestic science, home-craft, and general knowledge.

The Infrastructure

When the issue of restructuring secondary education was being considered, the Secondary Education Commission was confronted with the following three questions-

1. To which age-group should secondary education cater?
2. What changes should be made in the existing system?

3. How should skills be developed in schools left untouched by the new changes?

It must be remembered that the Kothari Commission regards education as a life-long process, while the Secondary Education Commission regards the various levels of education as independent units. According to this Commission, "We bave to bear in mind the principle already noted that Secondary Education is a complete unit by itself and not merely a preparatory stage; to that at the end of this period the student should be in a position, if he wishes to enter on the responsibilities of life and take up some useful vocation.

The new structure of secondary education suggested by the Commission took the following shape. Keeping in mind the comprehensive blue-print, the new structure of secondary education should become functional after four or five years of education in a primary or junior basic school.

In this, there should be a three year syllabus at the middle school, junior high school or senior basic level.

There should be a 4 year syllabus at the higher secondary level. The Commission suggested changing the existing intermediate system into the higher secondary level, comprising 4 years of education, inclusive of one year of the intermediate level.

In the same way, the degree course should be of three years' duration. Thus, the entire secondary level is broken up into two parts- (1) junior secondary level, (2) from class 9 to class 11.

The Commission clearly found the intermediate system of examination defective. It argued that the intermediate examination destroyed the continuity of college education and creates difficulties in the planning of the syllabus for the degree course. This is worst defect. Adding one year to the secondary level will bring about an increase in skill and efficiency while an additional one year with the degree course will generate educational skill. In this way, uninterrupted progress continues to take place over a three year period.

At places where the higher secondary syllabus cannot be taught, and in the colleges which have a four year syllabus- i.e., a two year syllabus for the intermediate and a two-year syllabus for the degree course, provisions should be made for introducing a one-year pre-university course before granting admission to the university. This syllabus should be implemented in colleges.

The Commission suggested the abandonment of the intermediate level, in line with the suggestion put forward by the University Education Commission (1948). Its view was that, by putting an end to intermediate classes, the standard of secondary as well as higher education can be improved. It felt, on occasion, that intermediate education has failed to achieve the desired objectives.

Official Commission

Although many states had accepted the proposals of the Secondary Education Commission, various types of institutions-middle schools, junior high schools, senior basic, higher elementary, high school, higher secondary, intermediate, etc. continued to function. In some states, pre-professional, pre-university, pre-medical, pre-engineering, and other such institutions have functioned within the sphere of secondary education. The Kothari Commission laid special emphasis upon bringing uniformity into secondary education for the whole country, at the time of implementing its new form. It divided the secondary level into two parts- (1) lower secondary level, consisting of classes 8 and 9 or 9 and 10; (2) higher secondary level, for classes 11 and 12.

Welcoming this suggestion of the Kothari Commission, National Solidarity (July 7, 1966) declared that the commission had put forth a practical curriculum for continuous education by virtue of which education would become uniform and undergo progress.

However, what actually happened was, since the Secondary Commission had declared the abandonment of the intermediate method, some states replaced it with the higher secondary system, but other states, which continued with the intermediate system fared better because the very structure of the Secondary Education Commission soon collapsed. Of course, the little that was achieved was the change in nomenclature -Kothari Commission substituted the name higher secondary for the earlier terms intermediate.

In brief, the prevalent and the suggested forms of secondary education can be represented thus through the following table -

Existing Form	*Proposed Form*
1. High School	1. Secondary class 8 to 12 or 11-12
1. Class 11 or P.U.C.	(a) Lower Secondary Education Class 8-10
2. Junior College (Kerala)	or class 1-10
3. Intermediate College (U.P., Maharashtra)	(b) Higher Secondary Education class 9-11
4. Pre-professional, Pre-medical, Pre-engineering.	

The reality underlying this whole issue is that uniformity must be imparted to the whole educational organisation in the country so that national unity and social unity can be awakened. Education should include programmes for social service and national service. These should possess infinite potential for the comprehensive and positive development of the child.

Keeping in mind the growth and tradition outlined above, it is necessary to pay attention to the fact that the very concept of secondary education has suffered a profound transformation in past years. For this reason, an eleven-year national structure was developed, comprising of five years for the primary level, three years for the secondary level and three years for the higher secondary level. As education is a state subject, some states accepted this structure while others did not. It remains to be seen how the structure proposed by the Kothari Commission is accepted.

Post-High School

The fundamental fact accepted by the Education Commission (1964-66) in its comprehensive analysis of education is that -there must be a uniform system of education for the whole country. In this country of varieties, education flows as a part of the variegated stream, with the result that it is difficult, if not impossible, to say with certainty which State has a higher standard of education than any other. The general assumption is that the standard of education is higher in states in which the medium of instruction is English. This is the reason why, in every competitive examination, success goes to those who have grown up and have been nourished in the shadow of this adopted mother tongue, while those who have suckled at their own mother's breast are compelled to mingle their existence with the mainstream of communality. They remain silent, unknown and unsung.

There is widespread discussion on the new educational structure, the much talked of 10 + 2 + 3 system. Central universities accepted it as the basis and conducted some experiments. Criteria of success were determined. But it came to be observed that these central universities, which began to search for a common educational system for the whole country, are unable to discover a suitable path to their goal. Mr. Rajni Kumar who was concerned with the formulation of this new system, asked whether we could not organise or implement a syllabus of a local philosophy for understanding the dynamic forces in society, if we could successfully implement hundreds of summer schools to orient teachers in the teaching of modern mathematics and science. This alone was the basis of a transformation in the social and economic structure. It was not possible to neglect this huge base of education.

The seeds of the 10+2+3 system are to be found in the proposals of the Hunter Commission in 1882, which has said that after the determined level of secondary education, the educational process should divide into two streams—one, that which is the threshold for university education, and two, that which is more closely oriented towards more practical, vocational or non-literary education for the masses. It was our country's misfortune that neither the government nor the people could digest this valuable peace of advice.

Subsequently, in 1929, the contemporary government appointed the Hertog Committee to assess the prevailing system of examination. The committee laid stress upon the need for vocational, technical and industrial syllabi. However, the government failed to create such a programme at the secondary level, and this suggestion continued to collect dust in official files for a very long time.

In 1935, analysing the effects of economic depression, the Central Educational Advisory Committee once again proposed the introduction of vocational courses at the secondary level. The Abbot and Wood committee was asked to give its opinion of this suggestion. The Committee offered its report in two parts in 1936. In the first part, they reflected upon the complexities of vocational education in India. In the seccond, they suggested the creation of two kinds of schools for vocational education : (i) Junior, (ii) Senior. The junior vocational schools were to be of the secondary standard. The proposal envisaged that various kinds of vocational courses would be taught in these schools. The senior schools were expected to provide specialised training. In this proposal, the continuous process of general education was adopted as the basis, as a result of the proposal, polytechnic schools came into existence in the country.

The second world war started and ended. The structure of the country began to undergo profound changes. At this juncture, another Commission was appointed under the chairmanship of Sir John Sargent to propose a restructuring of education in the country. The committee suggested the setting up of two kinds of high schools : (1) Vocational and Technical; (2) Academic. Provisions were made for imparting education of practical science and industry in the first kind, and theoretical education in the latter. In consequence, the All India Council for Technical Education was set up in 1945, and the Delhi Polytechnic for Commerce Education was born. The plan was enthusiastically received but the cry of paucity of funds prevented the dream from being translated into reality.

In the same decade, India became independent, and, focussing attention on some basic questions and the need for an educational system for independent India, the Central Advisory Board of Secondary Education emphasized the setting up of a commission. The product of his suggestion was the Mudaliar Commission. For secondary education, this commission proposed two kinds of syllabi which, along with general education, provided for certain vocational courses, such as technology, agriculture, commerce and the fine arts. The outcome of this was that there was a rapid increase, in every stage, in the number of polytechnics and multi-purpose schools. In 1950, the Central Advisory Board felt the need for the establishment of four regional colleges to fulfil the demand for teachers in these schools. In 1963, these colleges also came into existence.

In this variable host of commissions and committees, the one to achieve the maximum publicity was the Kothari Commission which, completing its horrendous task in 1964-66, put fourth a massive scheme for a uniform educational structure for the whole country. The Commission planned that by 1986, 50% of all children at the higher secondary level should be studying under a vocational syllabus. The Commission said that its main proposal was that of the registrations at 20% of the lower second level and 30 per cent of all registrations after class 10 should become involved in part-time or full-time vocational courses. Students between the ages of 14 and 18, boys as well as girls, must be encouraged, as far as possible, to adopt vocational and technical courses.

Many years have passed since India became independent. This means that one generation has now grown to adulthood. And yet, the plant of imported education has continued to flourish and prosper. The education provided by it never had any links with either national character or the task of national reconstruction. From time to time, the Emotional and National Integration Committee (1962) has pointed towards this fact. It has said that, keeping in view the interests of the student community, it felt that the nature of education throughout the whole country should be the same so that disunity may be rooted out, harmony between various parts may be encouraged and standards may be maintained. The atmosphere that has existed in the country in the last decade can be improved only if a single system of education is implemented throughout the country.

The Kothari Commission has divided education into three levels. The first level comprises all schools and primary education, the second, high school and higher secondary education, and the third, graduate, post-graduate education and research.

From this viewpoint, the form of 10+2+3 system was determined thus-

1. Completely school arrangement for one to three years,
2. The primary stage for seven to eight years, which should consist of two sub-divisions-first, lower stage of four to five years, second, higher primary stage for the next three years;
3. Lower secondary or higher school stage in which there should be 2 or 3 years of general education or 1 to 3 years of vocational education.
4. Higher secondary stage in which there should be 2 years of general education or 1 to 3 years of vocational education.
5. The stage of higher education, in which there should be a first degree course of 3 years or more, after which there should be a second degree course or courses for less than one degree, with varying periods of time designated for each.

The foundation of the 10 + 2 + 3 system is vocational education. A voice often rises in our country, and it vehemently asks-why does the existing system of education not provide jobs for the students? Why does it fail to arouse love to work, labour and duty in them? Perhaps, the Kothari Commission accepted this challenge, and that is why it fixed national development as the objective of education. It has identified self-reliance in foodgrains, economic development, universal employment, social and national unity, and political development as the most significant aspects of national development.

The new structure of education and its implementation by the central schools poses a question before the other schools in the country- will they be able to adjust harmoniously to this new structure, and will they be able to achieve the desired standards? The answer to these questions is filled with doubt. The reason is also quite obvious. These schools run by the centre have ample resources; besides admissions to them are not open to the common public. Thus, they have been created for a special, privileged class. Admission to them is controlled by competition, and hence, once the cream has been extracted from milk, it can be utilised for making either butter or ghee. The separated milk thus left is handed over to the regional schools, which may churn it as much as they like.

Setting up the aims of education in the context of the new educational structure, the Education Commission has said that the most important and essential reform in education lies in the need for changing its form, for relating it to the ambitions and needs of the people, and thus making it a powerful medium for the social, economic and cultural changes necessary for the achievement of national objectives. For this purpose, the development of education should be so designed as to bring about a large-scale social and national unity, as acceleration of the process of modernization, and the development of moral and spiritual values.

For these objectives, and for the desired social change, it has been determined to relate the 10 + 2 + 3 system to production. It has been said that the education of science and technology, industrialization and vocationalization should be brought into intimate relationship with work experience. Stress has been laid upon similar schools, social and national service, a proper policy on language, encouragement to a national consciousness, etc., for bringing about social and national unity. In order to mould education according to the mainstream of modernization and also to provide education in social, moral and spiritual values, arrangements have been made for providing religious education.

The declaration of emergency has brought about a revolution in every sphere of national life, and possibly it is because of this that every state is echoing the call to adopt the 10 + 2 system, based on the syllabus prepared by the NCERT, without giving a thought to local conditions and environments. Probably they did not consider the fact that Uttar Pradesh, too, is a part of the country, and it is a state -in which the 10 + 2 system already prevails. As far as the question of class 8 adopting the new mainstream, the syllabus upto class 4, which means the syllabus for the first eight years is general, while specialisation is to be introduced from class 9. It is at this point that the syllabi oriented to work experience are also to be introduced. By adopting them, the child can move towards vocationalization. The notion that a child-can become skilled in 16 subjects by the time he reaches class 10 has been framed by educationists and psychologists, but it is a patently unpsychological concept. Thrusting this on the child only means increasing the educational load to an unbearable extent. In fact, in the 10 + 2 system, we actually need a plan or scheme which is suitable to the soil of our own country. We cannot hope to succeed if we keep on picking up the crumbs of educational research in Russia or the USA.

In the 10 + 2 scheme, the three-language formula has been adopted in a most willful manner. It has been assumed that it is impossible for us to achieve anything without English. The Secretary of NCERT stated at one place that English could be introduced at any stage between classes 3 and 9, but he did not make any provisions ensuring that the national language Hindi should be taught in every state from class 3. Neither did he ensure that the learning of at least one of the regional languages be made compulsory. There is a grave doubt whether such a language policy in education will be able to maintain our national unity.

Our national leaders are ignorant of the fact that our bureaucrats do not want that leaders from among the masses may enter the services or the administration. What they want is that their own generations only should have access to these avenues.

In the country in which higher, education was inaugurated, the period of higher education was fixed at 4 years, the 4 years that come after the child has gone through a curriculum of study stretching over 12 years. The Mudaliar Commission recommended the abolition of intermediate, and instead proposed a higher secondary syllabus of 11 years. Most of the states accepted this proposal, but now most of them are returning to the old path. This is mere extravagance and waste, from which national welfare can never be expected to flow. Even today, it is impossible for us to switch over to the new system in the whole country. We are faced with numerous managerial, administrative, organisational and educational problems. Hence, the conjunction of the + 3 syllabus to the 10 + 2 syllabus is in itself a big question mark. The problem cannot be solved merely by increasing the time period of the syllabus to three years.

After this long deliberation, the question is; how can this powerful programme for national reconstruction be implemented? This author's suggestions are the following: -

1. The study of 16 subjects in the first 10 years is unpsychological. The uniform teaching of literature, science, mathematics and other subjects, without any attention to individual differences, is only an unwarranted assault upon the child's potential for development. Hence, the secondary school syllabus prevalent in Uttar Pradesh should be accepted as the norm. Intensive teaching in five subjects should be the aim. Among them, there are many sub-classes in which the compulsory subjects (Hindi, Mathematics) should not be combined with the optional group. Upto class 8, education of a general nature should prevail everywhere.
2. The national language should be the medium of education, and the mother tongue should be taught at a certain fixed level. It is obvious that while English does link us closely with the world, it also alienates us from our own country.
3. By preparing its text-books in English NCERT has clearly published its innate tendency and inclination. It would have been much better had these books been prepared either in the national language or the mother tongue.
4. Tying work experience to the bounds of the classroom means, implicitly, putting an end to the basic intention of linking education with production. It would have been much better if work experience could have been provided in realistic situation, where the student could be in touch with society and the community.
5. In our opinion, the new system of education should be structured in the following way-

   1- 8 = General education flow.

   9-10 = General tendency towards specialization; in this field language and mathematics should be compulsory, and the student should choose three other subjects, according to his taste, from a number of alternatives.

11- 12 = Specialization, in which the various branches can be literary, technical, vocational, fine arts, education, etc.

6. The + 3 level should be obtained at the + 2 level, but there should be intensive study during this period.
7. In the + 2 level, that is, at the post-graduate level, primacy should be given to specialization.

The foregoing suggestions will not entail any excessive financial burden on any state government, and through slight modifications in the existing circumstances, the challenge of the 10 + 2 + 3 could then be faced.

Many a Committee

Secondary education gives desired direction to the nation's power, an idea of which the government has always been conscious. Consequently, from time to time, commissions and committees have been set up to study secondary education. In the following paragraphs, there is a consideration of the Mudaliar Commission, the Acharya Narendra Dev Committee (1953), and the Kothari Commission, and their impact upon secondary education.

Secondary education is the backbone of the country's entire educational programme, and the importance that the backbone has for human physiology is shared by secondary education in the country's economy. After independence, the need for a revaluation of secondary education in the country was urgently felt, and hence a commission was appointed in 1952, and it submitted its report in 1953.

Appointment and Membership. The establishment of the Secondary Education Commission took place in compliance with the government's proposal number F: 9.5\52-BI, dated September 23, 1952. The members of this commission were the following :

1. Dr. A. Lakshmanswami Mudaliar-Chairman.
2. John Christ-Member.

3. Dr. Kenneth Rost Williams -Member.
4. Mrs. Hansa Mehta-Member.
5. Mr. J.A. Taraporewala-Member.
6. Dr. K.L. Shrimali-Member.
7. Mr. M.T Vyas-Member.
8. Mr. K.G. Saiyyadain-Member.
9. Mr. K.N. Basu-Member.

Dr. M.M. Chari performed the function of assistant secretary to the commission.

Terms of Reference. The terms of reference of the Commission were :

1. Conducting a study into the existing state of secondary education in India.
2. For the reorganisation and development of secondary education- (i) clarification and statement of the objectives, organisation and syllabus of secondary education, (ii) a study of secondary education in the context of primary, basic and higher education, (iii) a study of the correlation between various secondary schools, (iv) a study of other related problems so that, according to the country's needs, the uniformity of secondary education for the whole country could be determined.

Objectives of Education. The secondary Education Commission fixed the aims of education in the following terms -

Growth of Democratic Citizenship. In this field, praising and glorifying the social and cultural achievements of our country, removing the weaknesses of our country, arousing the desire to serve the country, according to one's abilities, sacrificing personal interests and preferences for the good of the nation.

Vocational Progress. By the end of education, children should possess sound professional knowledge.

Development of Personality. Considering all possibilities for the development of personality of the child and acting thereon.

Training in Leadership. The Secondary Education Commission has placed training in leadership among the aims of education as a necessary condition for the success of democracy.

Reorganisation of Secondary Education. The following is the scheme put forth by the Mudaliar Commission for reorganising secondary education with a view to putting an end to the alienation between secondary and university education -

Period. The period of secondary education is from 11 years to 17 years of age. There should be no contradiction between the methods of teaching at the basic and secondary levels. This period is inclusive of (1) three year education at the middle, junior, secondary or senior basic levels, and (2) a four year curriculum at the higher secondary level.

Three Year Degree Course. The Commission put an end to the intermediate level and made provisions for 11 years of higher secondary and three years of a degree course.

Varieties of Syllabi. The Commission has harmonised various syllabi so that every student may be able to choose subjects according to his talents and inclination. These syllabi begin from the first year of secondary level.

Internal Evaluation. The Commission has accorded an important place to school records in the process of evaluation. Through this method students will be assessed more accurately, and there will also be an improvement in discipline in schools.

Technical Education. Although the Mudaliar Commission put forward numerous valuable suggestions for the development of technical education at the secondary level, and on the basis of these suggestions, many multipurpose institutions came to be set up, these schools failed to fulfil the needs of the country.

The following are the Commission's suggestions in this regard-

1. Technical schools should be run, in large numbers, as multipurpose schools, or as a part of such institutions.
2. In large towns, central technical schools should be established so that the needs of local schools can be met.
3. Rules should be prepared for training through apprenticeship.
4. Technical and technological schools should be set up in constitution with educationists.
5. A cess for industrial education should be imposed.

Other Kinds of Schools. The purpose behind the establishment of such schools was the fulfilment of specific objectives. In the context of such schools, it was recommended that these schools should be set up. (1) Public schools should continue. (2) The states as well as the centre should assist brilliant students. (3) Residential schools should be established. (4) There should be more for the education of children.

Co-education. On the subject of women's education and co-education, the Mudaliar Commission said that there is no difference between the education of boys and girls, despite which, there should be provisions for education to girls in domestic science. The major recommendations in this context are - (1) Despite the absence of any difference in the education of boys and girls, the study of domestic science should be given primacy in co-educational schools. (2) Where necessary, separate schools should be set up for girls. (3) Specific conditions should be imposed upon co-educational schools.

Study of Languages. The Mudaliar Commission classified languages into five groups- (1) mother tongue, (2) regional language, if it is not the mother tongue also, (3) the official language of the Centre, (4) classified language, (5) English. It made the following recommendations regarding the study of languages- (1) at the secondary level, either the regional language or the mother tongue should be the medium of education; in this, special facilities should be provided to the linguistic minorities, (2) At the middle level, our children must know two languages. Hindi and English should be introduced at the Junior Basic level. (3) At the High School or the higher secondary level, there must be at least two languages, of which at least one must be either the mother tongue or the regional language.

Syllabus. The Commission suggested a syllabus at two distinct levels-

At the Middle Level. 1. Language, 2. social studies, 3. general science, 4. arithmetic, 5. art and music, 6. industry, 7. physical education.

At the High School and Higher Secondary Level. Complete syllabus for either the mother tongue and the regional language, or the mother tongue and a classical language.

In addition, one of the following languages—

1. Hindi (for those who do not use Hindi as mother tongue)
2. Elementary English (for those who did study English at the Middle level)
3. Higher English (for those who have already studied English)
4. Modern Indian language (in addition to Hindi)
5. Modern Foreign language (in addition to English)
6. Classical language
7. 1 Social studies.
   2 General science for the first two years.
   3 One of the following handicrafts- (i) Weaving, (ii) Wood work, (iii) Metal working, (iv) Gardening, (v) Stitching, (vi) Typing, (vii) Workshop, (viii) Stitching, knitting, etc. (ix) Modelling.

Text-Books. The following are the Commission's suggestions for the improvement of text-books-

1. A high-powered text-book committee should be set up, consisting of one judge of the high court, a member of the service commission, chancellor, headmaster, two educationists and education director, and it should function independently.
2. A fund should be created from the sale of these publications, and it should be utilised for helping students through scholarships and book-aid, etc.
3. This committee should set up at various specific levels.
4. The central government should establish art schools for the technique of text-books.
5. The central and state governments should make a collection of books which can be loaned out to the publishers.
6. One single text-book should not be prescribed for any one subject.

7. Specific text-books should be prescribed for the study of languages.
8. Any text-book hurting religious or social sentiments should not be prescribed for study.
9. The tendency to change text-books frequently should be discouraged.

Dynamic Methods of Teaching. The Commission turned its attention towards the methods of teaching also. Its suggestions in this regard are the following-

1. The method of teaching should aim not only at imparting information, but should be one which helps in the formation of desirable values, attitudes and habits.
2. Activity and Projects methods should be adopted. Students should be assigned work which allows them scope for expression.
3. In every kind of teaching, the stress should be on clear thinking and expression.
4. The tendency to work in a group should be developed.
5. Progressive educational technique, should be employed in experimental and demonstration schools.

Administration. Reflecting upon the problem of administration, the Mudaliar Commission opined that development and reorganisation in education is of no utility as long as indiscipline prevails in schools. It further said that-

1. Education for character building should not be part of the school syllabus.
2. A school government should be set up for the development of discipline.
3. Collective games should be given encouragement.
4. An act should be promulgated by Parliament, forbidding the use of students in elections.

Religious and Moral Education. Moral and religious education should be imparted in schools only on a voluntary basis, and it should be given to those who profess faith in that religion. The Commission expressed its view that religious or moral education should not be given on the criterion of education in the arts; instead, it should depend upon the influence of the school and the conduct of the teachers. Thus, religious education should be given only on a voluntary basis.

Extra-curricular Activities **.** Extra-curricular activities are of the utmost importance for the development of the child's personality. Hence-

1. Extra-curricular activities should be regarded as an inseparable part of teaching.
2. The state should extend help to the child movement.
3. The central government should promote the NCC.
4. First aid, Red Cross, etc., should be encouraged in every school.

Guidance and Counselling. The Mudaliar Commission felt the need for a programme of guidance for the students. For this reason, it has included vocational as well as intellectual syllabi in the educational plan. Its views on these aspects are the following-

1. Special attention should be given to educational guidance at the secondary level.
2. Various vocational films should be exhibited in order to increase the knowledge of students.
3. There should be an increase in the number of trained officials, career, masters etc.
4. The central government should assist in the training of guides.

Student Welfare. In the sphere of student welfare, the Commission has recommended that health and physical education should be implemented. Its suggestions are that -

1. A school medical service should be initiated in every state. In every school, students should be given a medical check-up and treated, if necessary.
2. In residential schools, nutritious food should be made available.
3. Schools should keep their environment clean, and encourage respect for work in the students.
4. All teachers below the age of 40 should participate in the physical activities of students, and a record of each student should be maintained.

Evaluation. Examination or evaluation is the very foundation stone of education, and so it is essential for teachers that they should become aware of their students' progress. Hence, the Commission has recommended that :

1. The number of external examinations should be curtailed. Individuality or subjectivity in essay-type examinations should be reduced and objective tests should be taken.
2. In order to determine a child's future, a detailed record on his development in every sphere should be maintained.
3. In the final evaluation, attention should be given to internal evaluation as well as to the school record.
4. Instead of awarding marks, the system of grading should be adopted. At the conclusion of the secondary curriculum, there should be only a single public examination.
5. Subjects should be mentioned in the certificate. Supplementary examination should also be taken.

Development of Training Skill. The Mudaliar Commission was conscious of the importance of development and improvement of teachers. In the course of its survey, the Commission felt that, without any doubt, the levels of teachers and their conditions of work had to be improved in order to overcome their despair and their existing dissatisfaction, and also to generate the requisite atmosphere for education. For this, it suggested that-

1. There should be uniformity in the selection of teachers.
2. In private schools, there should be a selection committee for the appointment of headmasters as well as teachers.
3. The period of probation should be one year.
4. Teachers teaching high school classes should be trained graduates, while those teaching the higher secondary classes should have qualifications similar or equivalent to those of teachers teaching intermediate or university classes.
5. The three benefit schemes (pension, provident fund, insurance) should be implemented.
6. At the school level, children of teachers should be given free education.

7. Houses for teachers should be constructed on a co-operative basis, and they should also be given travelling allowances for attending seminars, campus, etc.
8. Posts of teachers should be made more attractive.
9. There should be two kinds of training institutions-
   (a) those which train individuals with a high school or higher secondary qualifications.
   (b) those which train graduates.

   The first programme should be for one year, while the latter should be spread over two years.
10. For training in M.Ed., admission should be available only to graduates with three years of teaching experience.

Problem of Administration. The achievement of the objectives of education depends upon an efficient administration, besides which, the cooperation of various ministries is also essential. The Commission made the following recommendations in this context regarding organisation, administration, inspection, recognition and conditions, buildings and resources, hours of work and holidays, entry into public service, etc. -

1. The education director should be responsible for advising the education minister. He should also function as the joint secretary.
2. There should be a committee, comprising the central and the state ministers of education, which should also work for the progress of education.
3. There should be a board consisting of 25 members, with the education director as its chairman. There should also be a teachers' training board.
4. The work of inspectors should be to study problems and suggest solutions. A special panel should be appointed for granting recognition in domestic science, art and music.
5. Inspectors should have high qualifications, Teachers with ten years of experience, headmasters, etc., should be appointed teachers in training colleges.
6. New schools should be granted recognition only if they fulfil all the conditions.

7. The headmaster and representatives of teachers should be part of the management committees of schools. No member of such a committee should interfere in the working of the school. Each committee must formulate specific rules. It must adopt the policy of the education department and submit reports on its working.
8. Schools should be set up in villages. Aid for constructing buildings should be extended to them. In the schools to be set up in the future, attention should be given to introducing varied syllabi.
9. The working of the school should not create problems for the community. The working year should have 200 days. There should be summer vacations for 2 months, and brief vacations lasting 10 to 15 days twice a year.
10. In the governmental sectors, individuals in the age groups of 16 to 18, 19 to 21, and 22 to 24 should be appointed. 50% of the appointments should be made directly.

Arrangement of Finances. The Secondary Commission made a strong recommendation for the provision of adequate finances for the development of education. Its recommendations are-

1. Education should be financed by the centre and the states. A board of vocational education should be set up, for the development of vocational education. Representatives of related ministries should be members of this board.
2. An industrial education cess should be levied.
3. A cess on railways, transport, and postal services should be levied. All donations to educational institutions should be free of income tax, and the wealth of religious institutions and trusts should be invested in educational institutions.
4. Wealth tax should not be applicable to the property and playing grounds belonging to educational institutions.
5. The central and state governments should grant land to schools for buildings and playing grounds.
6. The central government should accept a part of the responsibility for restructuring secondary education.

At that time, these manifold suggestions of the Secondary Education Commission were welcomed. Now, the situation has changed, and in accordance with them, a new commission has been appointed. It has produced its own recommendations. It is to be seen how useful they are.

Background. The Acharya Narendra Dev Committee (1953) was set up for the reorganisation of secondary education. But, prior to this, before the attainment of independence, in 1938, a committee was set up under the chairmanship of Acharya Narendra Dev to look into the primary and secondary education, and particularly vocational education, in Uttar Pradesh. In 1938, this committee had put forward a comprehensive blue print. Soon after, however, the Congress governments tendered their resignations, and hence the recommendations could not be implemented. No work at all was done in the sphere of secondary education, in particular. The recommendations of the first committee are as follows:-

1. Secondary education work is a complement to college education. Hence, the secondary education system should be complete 'in itself, and hence all secondary schools should be called `colleges'.
2. Less attention should be given to (*shilp kala*), and English should be made compulsory.
3. The syllabus should be made more practical.
4. Extra-curricular activities should be expanded to include debates, study centres, students unions, dance clubs, literary clubs, national history, photography, geography, scouting, guiding, school, bank, co-operative store, youth exchange, and other such institutions.
5. Technical and engineering colleges, with syllabi for four or five years should be opened; their syllabi should be practical and utilitarian.
6. Intensive efforts and useful programmes for the expansion of women's education should be set a foot.
7. Traditional institutions (sanskrit *pathshalas* and urdu *maktabs*) should be so reorganised as to ensure that their students can continue their education in a proper manner.
8. Intelligence testing should be introduced into the examination system. Schools should be subject to

administrative inspections from time to time. The Education Council should organise tests in general knowledge.

9. Training schools and colleges should be set up for providing vocational training.
10. Text-books should be improved.
11. Education should be subject to various kinds of control. A central pedagogical institute should be established.

In addition to all these suggestions, the first committee had also expressed its views on the development of existing schools, their administration, civics; control of education, etc.

As a result of the World War II, the system of education was once again destablised, and no steps, could be taken to implement the foregoing suggestions. After independence, circumstances changed to such an extent that the Uttar Pradesh administration felt the need for appointing a new committee to look into secondary education and give recommendations for its restructuring.

The second committee was set up in pursuance of the government of Uttar Pradesh order no A/550/X-30 30-52, dated May 8, 1953. This committee consisted of 29 members, its chairman was Acharya Narendra Dev, and its secretary Shri Bhagwati Sharan Singh.

The terms of reference of the committee were expressed thus:

1. To reflect upon a new scheme for secondary education.
2. To inspect the groups A, B, C and D of the board of high school and intermediate education.
3. To consider the differences in the syllabi for boys and girls.
4. To reflect upon the utility of a syllabus in a specific field.
5. To inspect the instruments of education, and the teaching staff.
6. To look into the utility of practical and industrial subjects.
7. To harmonize and blend technical education with general education.

Eight sub-committees of this committee were also set up-(1) terms of reference and jurisdiction, A, B, C, D group syllabus, (2) women's education, (complete), (3) the achievements and practicability of groups C and D, (4) vacations and holidays, (5) education of girls, (6) harmonization of general and technical education, (7) text-books, and (8) management committee. These committees conducted their meetings and established contact with the public, from time to time.

This Committee, as a whole, put forward numerous and wide-ranging suggestions on many subjects related to education. Here, these recommendations are being given in brief, so as to bring out the standard or level of thought.

Syllabus. The committee paid particular attention to the recommen-dations of the earlier committee (1939), and also to the syllabus recommended by Uttar Pradesh (1948). It also considered the increasing needs and changed circumstances. Its suggestions regarding the syllabus were the following-

1. Sanskrit should be compulsory along with Hindi, and so should passing the examination in both languages. In addition to Hindi, another modern Indian language should be studied. General knowledge should be kept outside the prescribed syllabus. In the first two years, study of arithmetic should be compulsory.
2. In higher secondary schools, domestic science or home science should be compulsory for girls.
3. For the first two years, six subjects should be compulsory, while for the last two years this number should be reduced to five.
4. Students should be permitted to take examinations in additional subjects also.
5. Schools providing teaching in commerce, agriculture, aesthetics, pre-technical or creative subjects should be selected with great care. Institutions imparting training in agriculture must have a resourceful laboratory as well as at least 10 acres of land.

Technical Education. The committee's recommendations regarding the spread and improvement of technical education are the following:

1. Technical school should provide general education along with technical education. As far as possible, the education department should itself make arrangements for such

schools, and if necessary, their management should be entrusted to other departments as well.

2. A council should be set up to establish harmony or synthesis between industries and the education department.
3. At every level, efficient services should be organised. More schools of the technical and creative type should be established. The Board of Technical Education should issue certificates. The practical syllabus should also be stimulating. In such institutions, education should be provided free.
4. Short term courses of programmes should be conducted for training in psychological services, guidance and advice.
5. A council should be set up for the construction of tests, educational and psychological research, etc.
6. Psychological laboratories should be established at the district level.
7. Change should be made in the syllabi for training colleges and colleges granting degrees in education.

Examination System. On this issue, the following recommendations have been made after considering that; suggestions of the first committee, the Radhakrishnan Commission, etc. -

1. The intermediate examination should continue as at present. In the high school examination, the private candidates should also get benefit. A survey should be conducted for research into the system of public examination. The lowest age for sitting for the intermediate examination should be 16 years.
2. Attendance of 75% classes should be necessary for sitting for the examination, and students from the examination on account of shortage of attendance should have no right to appeal against the decision of the principal of the college.
3. At the high school level, a scholarship examination should be organised. Changes regarding promotion of students should be modified from time to time. In each class (9,10,11) there should be three mid term tests, while in class 12

there should be two such tests. Promotion should be based on the result of the collective examination.

Vacations. The committee suggested a working year of 200 days. This period of work should not exceed 235 days. Schools should open every year on the eighth day of July. There should be 31 holidays. The summer and winter vacations should be about six to seven weeks long. There should be 5 hours of teaching each day. The annual examination should take place in May, and after the declaration of the result, schools should close for the summer vacations.

Moral Education. A moral and humanistic education should be an integral part of the syllabus. Students should be made aware of the basic facts and principles of every religion. Before the start of teaching work every day, a congregation should be assembled every morning for prayers for at least ten minutes. The biographies of great persons should be studied.

Discipline. Groups or unions of students, teachers and parents should be organised for maintaining discipline. The prefect system should be introduced. The headmaster should be the highest authority in matters involving suspension from school, rustication or giving of corporeal punishment. The sentiment of social service should be encouraged. Films should be given distinctive A or U certificates to clarify whether they are suitable for all viewers or only for adults. Radio programmes for schools should be well arranged.

Management Committees. The term management committee refers to the committee of local persons belonging to the community who manage schools in their own respective ways. The committee has put forth the following suggestions in this respect-

(a) Schools which are efficiently managed should be encouraged by the government.

(b) Where the management committees perform their task unsuccessfully, the local administrator should take the management of the school into his own hands, and for this purpose, even two or three persons may be appointed.

(c) The principal and a representative of the teachers should also be members of the management committee.

(d) The practice of issuing the salary of missionary managers from the maintenance fund should be adopted.

(e) If a single trust or institution has a number of schools, the management committee for each school should be a different one. The committee should have a maximum of 12 members, and its period of office should be three years.

(f) Vacancies should be filled only through advertisements in the newspapers. Teachers should be appointed on probation, and the conditions of service should be explicitly stated in the Education Act. In the absence of written agreement, teachers should not be subjected to injustice.

(g) The government should extend the desired aid and help to management committees and schools. A development fund should be charged from the students.

Text-Books. The prevailing method of recommending text-books should be modified. The principal of a school should have the right and authority to select text-books, though the department of education may, to assist him, suggest certain books. Encouragement should be given for the production of suitable text-books, and sufficient time should be granted for their preparation. Their printing should be of a high standard.

It was on the basis of the recommendations of this committee that the monolith of the examination system and system of education in Uttar Pradesh was raised. But, circumstances have once again changed, and demands are being made for a change in the educational structure.

The Education Commission of 1964-66 held secondary education to be the very backbone of education and its growth. Its main recommendations are-

For the next twenty years, secondary education should have the following form-

(i) Proper planning of the schools to be established in the future.

(ii) Determining admissions after taking note of the facilities available so that standards can be maintained.

(iii) Selection on the basis of self-evaluation at the primary level, but at the secondary level, on the basis of an external examination, coupled with the school record.

Avoid Stagnation Wastage. In setting up new teaching institutions, the national policy should be designed to avoid stagnation and wastage. Efforts should be made to prevent the setting up of small and uneconomical secondary schools. Besides, existing schools of this nature should be restructured. Industrial training institutions should be set up in the proximity of industrial centres.

Balanced Syllabus. The variation in the syllabus at the secondary level should be arranged in such a manner that, in any one group the student should be able to study three subjects intensively. For a balanced development of personality among adolescents, at this stage, half the time should be given over to the study of optional subjects, while a quarter of the time should be reserved for physical education, art, handicrafts, material as well as spiritual education.

Study of Languages. The three language formula should be implemented after suitable modification- (1) mother tongue or regional language, (2) the subsidiary or main language of the Centre, (3) a modern Indian or European language not covered under either of the first two categories. At the secondary level, only two languages should be compulsorily taught.

Science and arithmetic should be taught compulsorily. At the lower secondary level, the teaching of these subjects should aim at making them means of mental discipline.

Social studies and social sciences should be so taught as to bring about an increase in citizenship, emotional unity, national unity and human brotherhood.

Work Experience. From the lower secondary stage, student should get an opportunity to obtain work experience through laboratory or workshop training, and at the secondary level, experience of school, workshops, fields, and, training as well as industrial establishments. This work experience should, from the viewpoint of the new social structure of the country, be a progressive one.

Social Service. Programmes which contribute to community development and which encourage social service should form a part of education at every level. In every district, an organisation should be created for this purpose.

Physical Education. The programme of physical examination needs a revaluation. It should be restructured to bring about the child's proper development.

Moral Development. One or two periods should be allotted in each week for moral and spiritual development.

Creative Activities. A committee should be appointed to study the potential for the teaching of art.

Guidance and Counselling. The work of guidance and counselling should start from the primary stage. Teachers should be acquainted with the problems of individual differences as well as remedial testing. In secondary schools, there should be a guest counseller who can visit ten schools and tender advice to students. Every teacher should have a clear concept of guidance and counselling.

Evaluation. The teachers who set examination papers should adopt new methods. The state board of school education should try to give a correct impression of the student's particular ability in the certificates issued after the external examination. It should not contain any indication whether the student has passed or failed. The student should be permitted to take an examination again in subjects in which he secured unsatisfactory marks, so that he may be able to overcome his deficiency and develop his ability. The internal assessment should be separately shown.

Hindrances in Growth

Jawarharlal Nehru was of the view that the prevailing system of education may have been suitable in past circumstances, but in the modern circumstances, at a time when stratification is taking place, it could cause nothing but harm. The new generation is the country's future hope. The manner in which we developed their innate powers and the direction in which we bent their minds would determine the future of the country. Hence, the highest priority must be given to their education.

Today, the problem which is confronting us is that of growth and expansion. In our country, public education has not grown in the desired manner, though we had decided to secure this expansion through our Five-Year Plans.

In 1951, at the beginning of the plan, the number of students in government schools was 15.7%, in local institutions 12.4%, and in private schools 71.9%. By 1962, these figures stood, respectively, at 21.3%, 11.3% and 67.4%.

The directives given by the Secondary Education Commission for the reorganisation of secondary education were implemented in the last two years of the first plan and the succeeding years of the second plan. By 1960-61, the number of multipurpose schools rose from 25 to 1187. In order to bring about development in the agricultural sphere, specially designed syllabus for teaching in agriculture was introduced in 200 secondary schools in rural areas. In order to provide useful employment to students after the completion of their secondary education, 90 low technology schools were set up to absorb them as semi-skilled workers. According to the structure proposed by the commission, 1200 schools were converted into general secondary schools. the number of students rose from 23 lakhs to 31 lakhs.

As in the case of the second plan, the expansion of education in the third plan followed the following lines- (1) additional facilities were given for teaching of science. (2) The multipurpose schools established during the second plan period were improved, and their number increased. (3) New higher secondary schools were established and the maximum possible number of existing secondary schools were converted into higher secondary schools.

In this plan period, 1550 secondary schools were converted into multipurpose schools. The major problem before them was the paucity of trained teachers. Hence, it was suggested that, along with the process of conversion to multipurpose schools, the existing schools should be given adequate facilities so that they could develop suitably. Four regional training colleges were set up to overcome the shortage of trained teachers for these institutions. It was accepted as a principle that all new secondary institutions should be of the higher secondary type. In the second plan, 2250 secondary schools were converted into higher secondary institutions.

By the end of the third plan period, it. was expected that the number of secondary schools would rise to 18 thousand. In the second plan, of 14 thousand secondary schools, 11,500 had facilities for the teaching of science, though the teaching of science faced two major difficulties — lack of adequately equipped laboratories and the shortage of suitably trained and educated teachers. In accordance with the suggestion of the All India Secondary Education Council, special programmes for teachers were implemented and standardised patterns of scientific apparatus were produced. In the third plan, 2000 schools were converted to higher secondary schools, and 4000 new ones established, thus bringing their total number to 9000, i.e., exactly half the number of all secondary institutions.

Middle Stage

At the end of the second plan period, the total number of admissions to classes 6,7 and 8 (for the age group of 11 to 14 years) was 66.56 lakhs, which meant a percentage of 22.4. In the third plan, the emphasis was upon achieving the target of 11.33 lakh admissions. Among them, the number of admissions of girls rose to 28.35 lakhs.

In the third plan, stress was laid upon improving the standard of education. Admissions rose from 10.6% to 28.87%. Importance was also given to the teaching of science. At this level, the following steps were taken- (1) Post-basic schools were made a part of the secondary education structure. (2) Secondary education made production oriented. (3) Training institutions were strengthened. (4) Educational administrators were given suitable training. (5) Multipurpose schools were improved and strengthened. (6) Suitable arrangements for the training of teachers were made, and minimum standards for them were clearly formulated.

One gigantic problem before secondary education is that many students enter active life soon after completing their secondary education, though they are not properly equipped for it. The result of this is an increase in the level of educated unemployment.

The achievements of this plan are as follows —

Registration. Secondary education expanded at a satisfactory rate. The registration of boys went girls rose. The.:e was a fall in the registration of children coming from families completely without facilities and those which received partial aid. Less facilities were made available to children coming from tribes and Scheduled Castes and Tribes.

Institutions. Because of various political factors, the number of uneconomic educational institutions increased. Half of them had a total enrolment of only 140 students. 30% of such schools were situated in towns.

Reorganisation. The Kothari Commission had recommended the restructuring of secondary education, but no efforts were directed towards this. Uttar Pradesh followed the 10 + 2 + 2 pattern, but no thought was given to the introduction of a 3 year degree course.

Quality. Efforts were made to -improve the syllabi, particularly in science and mathematics. Significant work was done in this direction by the NCERT, state educational institutions, the state science educational council, etc.

Vocationalisation. Nothing commendable was done in this direction, and students were still scampering to colleges for further education. In 1972, 19 lakh high school and intermediate students registered their names with the employment exchanges.

Teachers. By the end of the fourth plan period, 85% were expected to have received training, though even at this time, the need for a qualitative programme in this sphere was being felt.

Expansion of Facilities. Keeping in the view the pace of increase in registration, provisions were made in the fifth plan for an additional 4 million registrations. It was anticipated that by 1979, 30% of all children in the 14 to 17 age group would have registered for admission to classes 9,10 and 11, while in 1974, this percentage was 23.5. There was no particular problem regarding registration in towns, and hence special attention was needed for rural areas. For this, (1) provisions were made for 250 girls' hostels and one lakh scholarships to ensure a growth in the education of girls, (2) facilities were provided for one lakh scholarships in the rural areas and setting up of hostels. (3) one lakh scholarships were reserved for children belonging to the weaker sections.

Many programmes were devised for the expansion of secondary education during the fifth plan period. The investment on these programmes was as follows -

Secondary Education in Five Year Plan (Crores)

S.N.	*Programmes*	
1.	Expansion Facilities	191.50
2.	Depressed and Girls' Education	24.65
3.	Teacher Education	4.24
4.	Reorganisation of Secondary Schools	6.25
5.	Qualitative Improvement of Education	64.56
6.	Teacher-Welfare	6.36
7.	Research	1.10
	Total	**298.86** **or 300.00**

In addition to this, Rs. 26.25 crores were allocated for improvement in school buildings and their development, improvement in design. Introduction of the shift system, the load upon the local community and creation of 2500 new school buildings. For the remaining programme 189.15 crores were also allocated.

Education of Teachers. Arrangements were made, at the secondary level, for the qualitative development of teacher education, increase in registration, of setting up a state teacher education council, strengthening training schools and development of regional educational universities. There was also a scheme at the district level in which 300 teachers were to undergo refresher courses.

A Uniform Pattern. The plan also included a scheme for bringing uniformity into the structure of school education. There has been a tendency for the public to favour the opening of a college instead of a school. Hence, an intensive school programme was envisaged. It was projected that the standard of 250 schools would be improved and for this purpose Rs. 6.25 crores were allocated.

Qualitative Development. In this plan, attention was given to the qualitative improvement of education also. Education was linked with skill, efficiency and productivity. Since secondary education makes a profound contribution to national development, the need for qualitative improvement in this sphere was felt acutely. The following programmes were suggested for this purpose-

1. Introduction of work experience at the secondary level.
2. Vocationalization of secondary education.
3. Strengthening of guidance and counselling services.
4. Development of teaching in science and mathematics.
5. Development of selected schools.
6. Opening of Teachers Centres in every tehsil for teacher's welfare and professional development, construction of houses on a cooperative basis, provision of medical and other facilities and encouragement to research.

In view of the above facts, we conclude that secondary education determines the standard of the country, and hence, it must be allowed to expand even further.

Expansion of secondary education has constantly faced various problems, and these have influenced, in particular, efficient functioning as well as educational policy. The major obstacles to expansion are the following-

1. Lack of clarity in defining objectives in the five-year plans.
2. Absence of facilities for admission.
3. Lack of proper management by management committees.
4. Absence of growth in the number of institutions.
5. Absence of proper wages and other necessary facilities for teachers.
6. Inequality in the sums allocated in the budget for secondary education.
7. Absence of loyalty among the employees.

The suggestions of the Kothari Commission for the expansion of secondary education are the following-

1. For the next 20 years secondary education should expand in the manner outlined below: -
   (a) Schools should be located at suitable places.
   (b) Admissions should be based on available facilities.
   (c) Brilliant students should be selected.
2. Programmes for the spread of secondary education should be implemented in a planned manner at the district level so that existing schools can achieve the desired standards.
3. Students should be chosen for admission to secondary schools on the basis of self-selection. In this, attention must also be paid to the school record.
4. By 1975-76, 20% of the secondary schools should become institution providing vocational training. By 1985-86, there should be a 50% increase in such institutions.
5. Provisions for part-time as well as full-time vocational education should be made from class 7 or 8. The education of girls should emphasise training in domestic activities.
6. Education of girls should spread. At the lower stage, this proportion should be 1 : 2, and at the secondary stage 1: 3. There should be separate schools, hostels and scholarships for girls.

The chief endeavour of the commission was to ensure a qualitative improvement and development in education so that education may achieve the desired standards, which may also undergo constant upward revision and thus, at least in some spheres, conform to international standards.

Ways of Assessment

The word examination implies casting a careful look all round. An academic examination can be thought of as a systematic arrangement for the testing and measurement of the students' knowledge, general ability or particular skill by some internal authority or external institution. In fact, teaching and examination are co-extensive processes. In a more comprehensive sense, one may even say that life itself is an examination. Without examination, it is not possible to determine whether teaching is progressing in the desired direction or not.

However, the prevailing system of examination has become the subject of a widespread and bitter criticism. Examinations have come to be regarded as a horror or an evil. The Radhakrishnan University Education Commission declared that till the middle of the present century, the system of examination in India was regarded as the worst form of Indian education. W H. Ryburn expressed the view that, irrespective of context, it could be said that examinations are the enemy of creative work, especially in the form in which they are administered.

The Kothari Commission said that evaluation is a continuous process, an inseparable part of the entire educational process, which is intimately connected with educational objectives. It has a profound influence upon the student's habit of study as well as the teachers mode of teaching, and thus it is of assistance, not merely in measuring the output of education, but also in its improvement and reform.

In evaluation, the maximum importance belongs to reform and improvement in cumulative record (*sanch itvrata patraka*) and external examinations. External reforms consists in improving the ability of the examiner who sets the paper, framing question papers with clearly defined objectives, improving the format of question, scientific evaluation of answers, and using calculative mechanisms, etc. These must be considered from the practical viewpoint.

Generally, people consider examination as a means of passing from one class to the next. Thus, it has become a habit, among teachers as well as students, to think that the student is required only to memorize the given syllabus in such a way that he can pass the examination. But, such habits of thought only alienate the progress of society from the educational process. They have resulted in giving education the sole aim of passing an examination and obtaining a degree, and not the aims of becoming cultured, developing good habits and conduct, improving mental and physical well-being and health or becoming an ideal citizen and working for the nation's welfare.

An examination has the purpose of discovering the individual's achievements, abilities, standard and mental power. Its objectives are-

1. Discovering whether the student has the ability necessary for studying the given text and sustaining the role entrusted to him, or not.
2. Finding out whether the student is absorbing the material taught to him or not.
3. Determining whether the student is fit for an award or a scholarship or not.
4. Evaluating the ability and skill of the teachers.
5. Evaluating the extent to which the student possesses such qualities of character as patience, determination, ability to work industriously, etc.

Upon the importance of examinations, the Mudaliar Commission pointed out that examination and evaluation have an important place in the educational sphere. The evaluation of the degree to which the student has progressed during his period of study is of value both for the teacher and the parents. Examinations have always existed in one form or the other. In the ancient past, education was imparted in ashramas, and examinations had a form different from their present one. In India, according to the Wood Plan and declaration, London University was assumed to be the ideal, and accordingly, universities came to be established here after 1850. With them, the modern system of examination came to India. Since then, examinations have remained, in one or the other forms.

Examinations are of two kinds. (1) External, and (2) Internal.

External Examination. These examinations are conducted, by the secondary board and the university.

Internal Examinations. If the teachers of the schools themselves seek to assess how much the students have learnt in various subjects, it is called an internal examination. Among this type are such tests as admission tests, monthly, quarterly, half-yearly or annual tests or examinations.

These examinations stimulate the student as well as the teacher, and also provide the following advantages-

1. The teacher is inspired to make greater efforts for achieving his goal.
2. The teacher develops awareness of the general standard.

3. It is only because of examinations that goals are clearly defined.
4. The student is realistically evaluated.
5. Having passed the examination, the student wins social recognition.

The prevailing system of examination is defective. In it, passing from one class to the next is treated as the sole objective. Some of its major defects are: -

1. The prevailing system is defective because the student considers passing the examination as his objective. Neither the student nor the teacher pays any attention to knowledge or standards.
2. Examinations have become so important that, instead of being directed towards knowledge, they are directed towards wealth. It is felt that the sole aim is passing the examination and obtaining employment.
3. The student depends upon help-books or 'keys'. He has to display his skill only in learning by rote and providing subjective, essay-type answers.
4. The teacher, too, aims only at helping the student to pass, instead of seeking to develop the requisite qualities of character in the student.
5. The teacher's worth is measured in terms of the number of his students who pass from his class.
6. The parents, too, are interested solely in their children passing the examination and obtaining a job. Even those offering employment base their judgement upon the applicant's certificates and degrees.
7. The prevailing system does not measure the child's abilities effectively. Examinations have become a 'chance', and hence they are not a complete standard of measurement.
8. Students learn the subject by rote and succeed, but this is no measure of their intellectual prowess.
9. Education, today, has come to be dominated by examinations, and thus, the means have become an end in itself. The system of examination has become a barrier

which prevents a clear perception of the purpose of education. It appears that the future of this educational system must be dark, since its sole objective is to prepare the student for an examination.

10. This system of examination has also encouraged the tendency to copy or cheat, since the students want to pass the examination, by fair means or foul. In this connection, R.C. Wren has remarked that the examination system is a suitable servant, but it is also bad. It depends upon the headmaster whether he treats the examination system as a slave or a master.
11. At present, passing the examination is an art. Those skilled in it get success with very little study while those who study in detail but lack the necessary skill of preparing for an examination are condemned to despair.
12. The examination is taken after a year, at a fixed time. If the child unfortunately falls ill, he cannot participate in the examination, though he may have worked hard throughout the year. In contrast, one who has studied even for a few days may pass the examination.
13. In a written examination of three hours, it is not possible to test the student's knowledge of the whole syllabus. Even theoretically, this kind of testing is unsatisfactory and unjustified.

Despite all these grievous defects, the system continues to prevail for the following reasons:-

1. It is because of this system of examination that students pay attention to what is taught.
2. Millions of examinees can be evaluated within a few days, and at comparatively little expense. From this viewpoint, the prevailing system is good.
3. The modern system of examination generates the feeling of competition among children.
4. In the written examinations, the student has the opportunity to express his own views.
5. It provides insight into the teacher's depth of knowledge and his efforts.

6. This prevailing system is considered suitable for a system of collective education because it provides a single criterion for all the students. In any individualized system of testing, it becomes extremely difficult to pick out the outstanding students.
7. It is true that this system allows free play to the chance factor, but it is also true that hardly one or two out of thousands of students are able to pass without studying the books.
8. Examinations teach the student to organise and utilise his knowledge effectively.

Some of the suggestions preferred by the Secondary Education Commission are-

1. The number of external examinations should be reduced.
2. The form of questions should be changed; there should be fewer essay-type questions.
3. At the time of examination, the student's work throughout the year should be considered.
4. In order to. implement suggestions for improving the examination system, teachers should participate in the meetings of the secondary Education department and the External Department of the Central Education Ministry.
5. Before embarking upon the teaching of a subject, it is necessary to determine the increase in the child's knowledge which must be aimed at, as well as the changes in his behaviour to be brought about through the teaching.
6. Examinations should include New Type Tests, among which Objective Tests, are of considerable importance.
7. In testing a student, the focus should be on what and how much the student knows, not on what he does not know.
8. The examination should be treated, not as the end, but only as the means, since the purpose of examination is to aid education in achieving its primary goals.
9. Oral testing should be given a suitable place in the system of examination.

10. The teacher's advice is also important in this system.
11. There is great need for reform and improvement in the question papers employed under the prevailing system.
12. The questions should be so designed that the child is stimulated to think for himself in seeking for the answers.
13. There is a great need to bring about a decrease in the various kinds of public examinations, because they have a detrimental effect on the child at a time when he is passing through a sensitive age and growing quickly.

There can be no denying that teaching and examination are intimately related, and that examinations have always influenced teaching. By modifying the examination system, it is possible to spread education in such a way that it may be instrumental in the comprehensive development of the child.

According to the Kothari Commission, it is universally accepted that evaluation is a continuous process, which is an inseparable part of the educational system. It influences the student's habits as well as the teachers' mode of teaching. The techniques of evaluation are means to the preparation of a record of the child's development in the desired directions.

The following are the suggestions of the Kothari Commission with regard to reform in the system of examination-

1. Written examinations should be improved.
2. New testing techniques should be devised for testing those abilities which cannot be suitably assessed through written examinations.
3. In external examinations, questions should be of the objective type.
4. Various kinds of standardised tests should be employed for internal assessment by the teacher who can create new tests, oral tests, practical tests, and thereby evaluate the child's inclination and attitude. The results of these tests should not be compared.

5. The certificate issued by the Board after a public examination should contain the marks obtained by the student in each subject, but it should carry no statement about whether the candidate has passed or failed.
6. The student should get his school record in addition to the Board's certificate.
7. The Commission has always been committed to the improvement of public examinations by removing their defects. It has even recommended that in the event of responsible evaluation, the education department should have the authority to suspend aid to such an institution.

The existing educational system aims exclusively passing the examination and thus it fails to bring about the mental and moral development of the individual. Hence it fails to aid and guide teachers as well as famous educational institutions. It is stated that the importance of modern education lies not merely in the intellectual attainment of students, but also in the emotional, social, mental and physical development. Social adjustment and other aspects of life are also important. As a whole, education should aim at the comprehensive development of personality.

Hence, the objective is to make the child a successful citizen, a fine soldier and a great leader. Hence, education in the country must make continuous progress towards improvement and reach the peak of success. In view of this, the existing system of education deserves criticism.

In the changing concepts and beliefs of the modern age, our country lags behind other countries in terms of hundreds of years in the race for progress. We want to achieve equality with the developed countries but in this process, as we move forward, the developed countries move even faster and go ahead of us. The reason for this is that our knowledge has not been related to modern science and technology. In view of this, the education commission has proposed the vocationalization of education at every level, not only at the secondary stage. The Commission has sought to base this vocationalization upon production. Hence, after considering the mutual relationship between education and production, it has proposed the basis of the scheme for the restructuring of education in the following terms :

1. Science should be the basis of education and culture.
2. Work experience should be an integral part of general education.
3. Education at the secondary level should be vocationalized in order to meet the needs of industry, agriculture and trade.
4. Laying special stress upon agriculture and related sciences, scientific and technological education at the university level should be developed.

For vocationalizing secondary education, the Commission has considered in detail the vocationalization at both its levels—the lower secondary and the higher secondary. In the Commissions' view, 20 per cent students in classes 8 to 10 should obtain vocational training. In the same way, 50 per cent of the students in classes 11 and 12 should receive vocational education. The Commission clearly accepted the principle that among the most important reforms is that of vocationalization of higher secondary education. 50% of all students should take admissions to the vocational courses. The views of the Commission regarding vocationalization at both levels are as follows-

Junior High School Level

1. Industrial training centres have courses suitable to post-primary educational levels. If the age of admission to such courses is set at 14 years, the number of students entering such institutions after completing primary education will be very large. (This age limit was 16 years, and was subsequently reduced to 15).
2. Students who stop studying after class 7 or 8 usually take up their family profession, while some of them hope to set up a small scale industry of trading organisation. For such people, arrangements should be made for short term or

part-time syllabi so that they may be able to develop their abilities and skills. The Commission purposed that a separate department should be set up within the education department to keep in touch with youth and provide them with suitable opportunities for receiving vocational training on a part-time basis, along with their general education.

3. Most students belonging to the rural areas will work on their ancestral fields. They should be given opportunities for general education, professional skills, etc.
4. A large number of girls get married soon after leaving schools. For them, arrangements should be made to provide them general education as well as education in domestic science.

High School Level

At this level, the Commission has made provisions for, a very large number of vocational courses.

1. Along with an expansion in facilities for full-time study, there should be provisions for part-time syllabi at the higher secondary level, though it may be arranged through industries, evening classes, part-time or correspondence courses.
2. The syllabi in the industrial training centres should be such that the minimum qualification for admission to them should be class 10.
3. These syllabi should provide training in health, trade, administration, small scale industries, etc., through courses lasting for six months to three years. At the completion of the course, students should be given diplomas or certificates.

In view of the importance it has attached to the vocationalisation of secondary education, the Commission has proposed that the central government should aid the state governments in implementing such a programme. Citing the example of the USA, the Commission has thrust the entire responsibility for the vocationalisation of secondary education upon the Union government.

At present, the existing system of secondary education does not make provisions for vocationalization which will satisfy the needs for skilled workers in the next twenty years.

At the secondary level, these schools satisfy only 3% of the need. In 1965-66, there was increase of 2.2%. The Commission projected that by 1985-86, there should be an increase of 20% at the lower secondary level. For the next twenty years, the Commission made provisions for the admission of 24,13,000 students to vocational schools. In the same manner, the projected figures of admission to professional universities is 6,87,300 students, which is 43% of the total number of students. The Commission set for itself the target of 50 percent.

Professional Education

Regarding the vocational education at the school level, the Commission has expressed the following ideas :

1. The Central government should introduce a variety of courses for boys and girls in 14-18 age group. The responsibility for this should fall upon the Union government, thus creating a parallel with the Smith Hughes Act of the USA.
2. As far as the question of outstanding students is concerned, instead of putting them into special courses, they can be made to do intensive work within the same syllabus thus the deficiency can be made up.
3. At present, there are 356 polytechnic institutions in which 1,13,000 students can study.
4. The Commission recommended that the name of Junior Technical Schools should be changed to Technical High Schools.

Past Happenings

The Commission has suggested that work experience is essential for arousing loyalty towards the vocation. In its view, work experience can be defined as any productive activity which contributes to productive work in the school, house, laboratory, fields, factory or at any other place.

The Commission has recommended that work experience should be introduced at every educational level. The concept of work experience is based on the principle that the process of generating knowledge and wealth should be co-extensive.

The reality is that work experience evolves an attitude of loyalty towards the profession. Because of this liberal attitude, it , is proposed that, at the higher secondary level, a variety of specialized courses should be available. The student should be allowed to make his choice from among them according to his interests and inclinations, and thus be prepared to choose a career of his liking. This will also facilitate his adjustment in life.

With reference to this attitude, as regards the higher classes, the Commission has argued that in these classes, it can take the form of teaching of art which will lead to the development of the student's creative ability and technological thought. Work experience can be imparted in the actual circumstances of real life, for instance, working in fields at the time of sowing or harvesting, or engaging in productive work in a family unit. Such situations can be exploited to the maximum possible extent.

The Commission has declared that, in the coming years, one workshop should be arranged for every school, or at-least for a group of schools. At the lower secondary level, work experience can take the form of laboratory training. At the higher secondary level, where students are more mature, and they are comparatively less in number, they can be given work experience in workshops, fields, industrial and trading enterprises.

Many kinds of materials are needed in school teaching. Work experience relating to the production of these materials should be available in schools and institutions. It has been suggested that (1) in some selected institutions (scientific and technological) students should engage in full-scale production. (2) In some institutions the apparatus used in school and college laboratories and workshops should be produced. (3) Some institutions should manufacture some things like furniture, etc.

The Commission has suggested that arrangements for scholarships on a large scale are desirable with a view to promoting vocationalization of secondary education. It has said that in vocational colleges, there are more provisions for scholarships, and that the proportion there is greater than in general education. For future progress, the following principles should be adopted (1) Liberal policy in granting admissions, (2) An increase in the amount of the scholarships.

In a country like India, the majority of parents cannot, afford a vocational education for their children because of poverty. It is because of this that the Commission has sought to make the programme of vocationalization of education successful through liberalisation of the number and amount of scholarships.

Many problems will come to an end with the vocationalization of secondary education, though at present, these problems have a gigantic and daunting size. The Commission has not encouraged employment, as was the case in Basic Education. It has opined that every individual should work to fulfil the needs of the country, and every aspect of his work should contribute to national development. The fruits flowing from vocationalisation will be the following:-

1. There will be a direct relationship between employment and education.
2. The individual will depend, for his livelihood, upon his limbs rather than upon offices.
3. The country's economic condition will improve and its manpower will be put to constructive use.
4. The Commission hopes that, in this way, every educated individual will be given a job along with his certificate.
5. Students will be convinced that education is purposeful, and that they,. too are needed for the building of their nation. The Commission views this change as the most profoundly significant.
6. The vocationalization of secondary education will make possible the best utilisation of the country's resources and circumstances. In 1882, the Hunter Commission had proposed a plan of education very similar to the present one.
7. Science and technology will be accepted as the foundation stones, and so, in modernisation, religion and work will be harmoniously blended together.

However, the important question is : when and how will these achievements take a concrete shape? Reflection upon this question turns our attention towards the following proposals of the Commission : (1) It is essential, for the vocationalization of secondary education, that vocational courses should immediately be made available to at least 20% of the students, and 50% students should be admitted to the higher secondary level. (2) At the secondary level, the opportunities for education should be available equally to everyone. A comprehensive programme of scholarships should be introduced.

The goal of vocationalization is to train and develop one stream of the educational flow in the country, in the context of the country's manpower and economic development. Through the development of vocational skills and suitable training, students are prepared for Middle Level employment in agriculture, industry, commerce, etc. The introduction of such courses in polytechnic institutions and provision of suitable training results in the student coming into direct contact with the employer. Hence, in secondary schools, educational and vocational guidance should be organised and provided so that students obtain awareness of training in various skills. Educational departments should develop vocational skills particularly in those areas in which institutional facilities are not available. These courses should be organised in cooperation with units which can provide employment. The experience obtained from multipurpose schools indicate that vocational training cannot be effectively organised until they are in close contact with those employers who will provide employment to the students trained in such schools.

Variations and modifications in vocational courses should only be made with the greatest care by highly skilled and qualified persons. However, geographical mobility among qualified people is quite limited, and so, vocational courses should be given a shape in accord with local circumstances and requirements. For this purpose, it is more convenient to carry out surveys at the district level before framing schemes for educational and vocational courses providing training in specific skills.

A powerful programme based on work experience and vocationalization can be effective in this direction. For this, contact between institutions and government agencies must be maintained. At various administrative levels, organisational facilities should always be available. At the national level, the NCERT can function as an effective clearing house and source of information for programmes of vocationalization and work experience. At the State level, independent man-power cells should be created under the management of the chief minister or the planning minister, and these cells should make, from time to time, declarations of policy on manpower. The state education institutions should take the help of employing authorities for creating research blocks, training blocks, extension blocks, etc. At the district level, project officers should be appointed for establishing harmony between work experience, teacher training and polytechnics. An employment committee should be set up under the chairmanship of the district magistrate.

In the plans work experience and vocationalization have been conceived of as mutual complements. This view finds expression in the plan in the following manners:

Work Experience. It has been presented from the perspective for development. Provisions have been made in the plan for initiating work experience in 50,000 schools, strengthening state educational institutions, employment of district project officers, training of one lakh teachers, and the setting up of 125 Common Facility Centres. For this purpose, a sum of Rs. 10.60 crores has been allocated.

Vocationalization. At the secondary level, the programme of vocationalization has been implemented in many parts and regions. It has been extended to take within its purview health, agriculture, labour and employment and polytechnic education. An additional provision of Rs. 1 crore has been made for setting up institutions for survey, collection of information, training, etc., at the district level.

Counselling. In order to strengthen vocationalization and make it effective, provisions have been made for the training of 20,000 teachers as career masters. There are arrangements for the appointment of State Bureau and District Guidance Officers. Rs. 2 - 5 crores will be spent upon this programme.

In reality, the vocationalization of secondary education is not a novel scheme but, in view of the country's present circumstances, it is essential that we provide employment to every individual according to his innate abilities. This will become feasible only when vocational education is available at every stage of the educational process. And, of all the stages of education, the secondary stage is the most important because 50% of the students have to struggle for employment and livelihood after completing their secondary education. If they are denied jobs at this stage, it will mean a wastage of valuable manpower, and this wastage represents a great loss for the country. From this point of view, the vocationalization of secondary education is of the utmost importance.

Model Schools

In India, the process of setting up multipurpose schools was set in motion by the recommendations of the Mudaliar Commission. Supporting the idea, the Kothari Commission opined that it was their purpose to introduce varied courses which would be taught in multipurpose schools. It stressed the need for establishing such institutions.

It is obvious that provisions were made for the teaching of various subjects in these schools. Even before the appointment of the latter commission, there were numerous subjects and also considerable diversification in the syllabus, but there was no school in which every course or subject was taught. The Secondary Education Commission laid stress on the creation of multipurpose schools so that all the varied objectives of education could be achieved in a single school.

The term 'multipurpose school' applies to that school which makes arrangements for the teaching of all kinds of courses which can satisfy the interests, objectives and talents of the students. It inspires the students to choose courses of study according to their interests. The Mudaliar Commission, too, said that the purpose of the multipurpose school is to provide for the education of students according to their interests and abilities. These schools should try to provide students with opportunities to develop themselves in harmony with their nature, tendency, attitude and abilities.

The Mudaliar Commission stressed the need for establishing multipurpose schools on the basis of the following arguments :

1. In the USA multipurpose schools had proved more successful than schools which had only one purpose.
2. These schools destroy the feeling of inequality in the child's mind and help to develop human equalities and values in them.
3. In such schools, the child is free to choose subjects in accord with his interests.
4. Students who fail to progress in one class can easily be transferred to a more suitable class or course, without their being any need for the student to change the school.
5. In multipurpose schools, there are arrangements for teaching every course, and so the students undergo comprehensive development.
6. Multipurpose schools can fulfil the country's need for technicians and contribute to the development of technical education.
7. In such schools, it is possible to organise courses of study which are in harmony with social, economic and psychological needs.

Goals and Aims

K.G. Saiyadain expressed the profound view that if a student; in the absence of proper counselling, takes up humanities instead of science, or vice versa, it is not only his school life which is ruined but also his entire future life, because he chose the wrong profession. It is in order to overcome this shortcoming that stress has been laid upon the setting up of multipurpose schools.

The main objectives of multipurpose schools are the following :

1. Making continuous efforts for the multi-faceted development of schools.

2. Guiding them to train the abilities and talents of students for the creation of national character and national wealth.
3. Creating skill in handicraft work.
4. Providing education in social and constructive or creative activities.

Their importance has been accepted in the Third Five-Year Plan, in which it was stated that although the concept of multipurpose schools had been accepted immediately, and the scheme had progressed rapidly, there were a few obstacles. It was argued that the attention of planner should be focussed on strengthening the institutions which had been established so that the whole scheme may rest on secure foundations.

Various Difficulties

While multipurpose schools can be credited with achieving a comprehensive development of the child's personality, it is also obvious that they suffer from certain problems. These difficulties are :

Difficulty in Converting a High School. Generally speaking, there is great difficulty in converting a high school into a multipurpose institution. And, where some high schools were given this form, there was no real need. The difficulty arises because of local conditions, lack of adequate space, buildings and facilities for travelling or materials needed for teachings.

Opposition from Parents. Parents often express their opposition to multipurpose schools if these institutions do not provide course of study related to local needs. In the absence of a definite policy on the teaching of crafts and industry, many problems are generated.

Division of Time. In multipurpose schools the problem of division of time is a very complex one, because it is a very difficult task to arrange a suitable and convenient timetable in such a vast programme.

Lack of Textbooks. Multipurpose schools have had to face great difficulties because, so far, they have lacked both in suitable text-books as well as trained teachers.

The Principal's Problem. Very often, parents do not agree with the course of study selected by the teacher for their children, and this leads to a conflict between the parents and the principal of the institution.

Economic Difficulty. These schools need buildings, laboratories, workshops, teaching material, etc. The government has faced great difficulty in making all this available, because in the absence of adequate finances, the government failed, on the one hand, to equip them with good laboratories, and on the other, to make them so attractive that students could be attracted towards the courses.

Ignorance of the Method of Working. Multipurpose schools can be successful only if a particular method of working is adopted but since the staff in many of them was not acquainted with it, they have had to face ignominious failure.

Difficulty in Changing Courses. If a student of a multipurpose school wishes to change the subjects of study, he has to face many difficulties.

Lack of Conformity with Local Needs. When the multipurpose schools were established, attention was not paid to local needs, and the result was only a wastage of money and manpower.

The government should consider the following facts in setting up new multipurpose schools

1. Multipurpose schools should be set up in prosperous regions because it is possible to get local help and cooperation in making school building and other activities.
2. Before setting up a multipurpose school in a particular place, it is essential to carry out a survey of that area. A school should be set up there only if the locale is suitable, and if such a school is really needed there.
3. Initially, multipurpose schools should be started as an experiment. They should be made permanent only if they are successful.
4. Guides should be appointed in multipurpose schools so that they can test the students and give them useful advice on the selection of courses.

5. It is not possible to meet the need for teachers for all multipurpose schools through four Regional Colleges. Hence, either the existing colleges should be expanded or new colleges established.
6. Suitable text-books should be published.

Hence, it is obvious that although multipurpose schools are necessary for our country, there is need for necessary reforms and improvements in them. They will prove useful for the country only if these reforms are carried out.

The Courses

It is ironical that, in our country, considerable thought has been devoted to the syllabi for boys and girls. The views of the Secondary Education Commission on the prevailing system were that political, social and economic circumstances had changed and new problems had emerged. It was, therefore, necessary to, make a careful study to determine the objective of education at every level. This idea was felt to be applicable not only to the existing situation but also to the direction of development, - nature and the determination of the future of our social structure, which itself had to be changed.

The Secondary Education Commission has determined the objectives of education in the following terms-

1. Students must be given training in character so that they can take a constructive part in our democratic social structure.
2. Students must be given practical and vocational training so that they can help to make the nation prosperous.
3. Students should be given training in literary artistic and cultural interests which may contribute to comprehensive human development and self expression, because without this, the culture of our country will be annihilated.

In addition, the Kothari Commission tied the objectives of education into a five point programme

1. Linking education with production.
2. Strengthening national unity and social unity through educational programmes.

3. Strengthening and vitalising democracy through education.
4. Evolving social, moral and spiritual values.
5. Modernising society through the development of skills by exploiting curiosity, inclination and values.

When we reflect upon these objectives, many questions arise to confront us. For instance: Is it necessary to differentiate between the syllabi for boys and the syllabi for girls ? Is co-education a solution to this problem ?

The Mrs. Hansa Metha Committee expressed its views on the question of differentiation between a syllabus for boys and that for girls in the following terms- (1) In the democratic and socialistic society of which we dream, education will be linked with those individual abilities, inclinations and interests which, in reality, have no relationship with difference in sex. For this reason, in such a society, there is no need to create different syllabi for the two sexes. (2) In a changing situation, it will be necessary to accept the fact of certain psychological differences between men and women. It will also be necessary to accept the fact of certain differences in their respective departments of work, and to make such differences the basis upon which the syllabi for them should be framed. However, in doing so, it should be kept in mind, that the desired and necessary values and attitudes should be evolved both in men and in women, with the passage of time, but that no step should be taken which may help to harden these differences between men and women or aggravate them.

In order to get an adequate answer to these questions, we must turn to the survey carried out by the Secondary Education Commission. During this survey, the following criticisms came to light (1) The present syllabus is narrow. (2) It is bookish and theoretical. (3) It has a long list of subjects which are not useful. (4) It leaves no scope for practical and other kinds of activities; it also lacks the necessary facilities for the proper development of personality. (5) It neither satisfies the needs of youth nor develops its abilities. (6) Excessive emphasis upon examinations is harmful. (7) It lacks technical and vocational subjects which are necessary, both for the student and for the country's economic development. The Commission's view is that the first thing, which should be clearly comprehended, is that, according to the most enlightened modern educational thought, the term syllabus does not apply to the subjects traditionally taught in schools, but rather the sum total of the various experiences gathered by students through varied activities, the experiences they gather from the school, art, liberary, laboratory, the playground, and even the mutual relations between themselves and their teachers. In this way, the entire life of the school is comprehended in the word 'syllabus', which helps the students in the development of their personality at every point.

The Secondary Education Commission has suggested a syllabus for the Middle level consisting of the following subjects- (1) Language, (2) Social Studies, (3) General Science, (4) Arithmetic, (5) Art, (6) Handicrafts, (7) Physical education.

The Commission's views on this issue are the following :

1. (a) Mother tongue, or regional language, or both, or a mixed programme.
   (b) One of the following languages should be selected
      (1) Hindi, for those whose mother tongue is not Hindi.
      (2) Elementary English, for those who did not study English upto the Middle level.
      (3) Advanced English, for those who studied English.
      (4) One modern Indian language (in addition to Hindi).
      (5) One modern foreign language (in addition to English).
      (6) One classical language.

2. (a) Social Study (for the first two years).
   (b) General science, arithmetic (for the first two years).
3. One handicraft from the following list should be chosen Carding or wea;ing, wood working, metal work, gardening, stitching, practice of typography, workshop, modelling, etc.
4. Three subjects are included in these groups :

Group. 1. (Humanities). 1. One classical language, or one language from group (a), which has not been studied in the past. 2. History. 3, Geography. 4. Economics and Civics. 5. Psychology and Logic, 6. Arithmetic. 7. Music. 8. Domestic Science.

Group. 2. (Science). 1. Physics. 2. Chemistry. 3. Biology. 4. Geography. 5. Mathematics. 6. Health science and Anatomy.

Group. 3. (Technical). 1. Practical mathematics and geometrical drawing. 2. Practical science. 3. Mechanical Engineering. 4. Electrical Engineering.

Group. 4. (Agriculture). 1. Harmonised Agriculture. 2. Veterinary. 3. Horticulture and gardening. 4. Agricultural chemistry and Botany.

Group. 5. (Commercial). 1. Commercial Practice. 2. Book-keeping; 3. Commercial geography or economics, or civics 4. Shorthand and typewriting.

Group. 6. (Arts). 1. Art and history. 2. Drawing and (aale-khan). 3. Painting. 4. Modelling. 5. Music. 6. Dance.

Group. 7. (Domestic Science). 1. Domestic economics. 2. Nutrition and cooking. 3. Maternal care and child welfare. 4. Domestic organisation and home nursing.

In addition to the above subjects, a student can also take one alternative subject from the above groups, irrespective of whether he has chosen any other subject from that group or not.

A syllabi is always the foundation of education. It is through a syllabus that we seek to fulfil the desired objectives. Educationists have, for long, been harping on the fact that the syllabus, which has been made the vehicle of education, has imparted inertia to education. The Commission has given careful thought to all the possibilities inherent in the syllabus.

The syllabus is one of the three pillars of education. It influences the entire educational process. Hence, in order to reform and improve, it is essential that the following steps be taken

1. Education departments must prepare the syllabi for schools on the basis of research.
2. Frequent revisions should be carried out in this research.
3. Text-books and reading materials should be created.
4. Teachers should be made to undergo refresher courses through in-service courses.
5. Schools should have the freedom to experiment with new syllabi. Thus work should be done particularly in schools attached to training colleges.

6. The state board of school education should prepare syllabi for every subject and implement them in schools which posses all facilities.
7. The syllabi should be prepared with the help of teacher councils, national councils and State institutions for various subjects

The syllabus should be compiled with the objectives of education in view. For this it is necessary that :

1. In non-vocational schools, a syllabus of general education should be the basis of education for 10 years.
2. At the end of this period, the level of achievement of the syllabus should be found out.
3. At the primary level, a heavy load of subjects should not be imposed upon the student. Subjects pertaining to language, arithmetic and environment should be taught.
4. The syllabus at the higher primary level should be more comprehensive and intensive. Methods of teaching should be systematically employed.
5. At the lower secondary level, the teaching should be in detail and indepth.
6. There should be diversification in subjects at the higher secondary level.
7. At the higher primary level, brilliant children should be given more facilities. They can be taught one subject in depth.
8. At the secondary level, there should be two kinds :
   (i) Ordinary. (ii) Advanced.

Languages in Course

1. In the context of education, there should be a new language policy.
2. The language formula should be structured as follows :
   (1) After the mother tongue, Hindi should be assumed to be the language of the Union.
   (2) Practical knowledge of English is useful for the students.
   (3) The development of language depends upon the teacher and his abilities.

(4) By the 10th class, the child should have knowledge of three languages.

(5) Two additional languages should be taught.

(6) Hindi and English should be applied where they are needed.

(7) At no stage should four languages ever be made compulsory.

3. The three language formula should be based on the following principles. (1) mother tongue and regional language. (2) The official and the semi-official language of the Central government. (3) One modern Indian or European language which is not covered under either (1) or (2) above, and which is used as a medium of education.
4. (1) At the lower primary level, in general, one language should be taught: it should be either the mother tongue or the regional language. (2) At the higher primary stage, two languages should be taught - mother tongue or regional language and the official language. (3) At the lower secondary language, three languages should be taught-(A) mother tongue or, regional language, (b) official or semi-official language, (c) modern Indian language,, (d) At the higher secondary level, two languages will be compulsory.
5. The study and teaching of modern literary languages (with the exception of English) should be made available in selected schools. In non-Hindi areas, arrangements should be made for the teaching of Hindi and English.
6. Hindi or English should be taught respectively for three or six years as the official and semi-official languages.
7. The study of language should not be compulsory in higher education.
8. Efforts should be made to propagate Hindi at the national level, but it should not be forced upon those not willing to adopt it.
9. Good literature should be published in the Devnagri and Roman scripts.
10. The teaching of English should not begin before class 5.

11. The classical languages (Sanskrit, Arabic, Persian, etc.). should be introduced as alternative languages from the eighth class.

Mathematics and Science

Every student should be made to study science and mathematics as part of his general education.

1. At the lower primary stage, science should be taught as environment education. In class 4, knowledge of roman numerals, charts, maps, etc., should be imparted.
2. At the higher primary level, logic should be developed. It is necessary for the child to develop his power of logical thought and deduction of conclusions.
3. In a lower primary school, it is necessary to have a science corner, while in the upper primary, there should be a laboratory and an auditorium.
4. At the lower secondary level, science should be developed as a form of mental discipline.
5. At the lower secondary level, there should be provisions for an advanced course for brilliant children.
6. The education of science should serve to relate and link agriculture and technology with each other.
7. Proper attention to the teaching of mathematics is essential for mental development.
8. At every educational level, the courses in mathematics should be modernised.
9. The methods of teaching science and mathematics should be as modern as possible.

Social Studies

1. Social study is essential for good citizenship. The course in social study must lay stress upon the strengthening of national unity and unity of man.
2. At all levels, the method of social study should be infused with a scientific spirit and temper.

Work experience implies taking full advantage of past experiences and linking education with production. Through work experience, the country can hope to achieve self-reliance in foodgrains, economic development, expansion of employment, social and national unity, political development, industrial progress, etc. For this reason, the Commission has made the following recommendations with regard to productivity :

1. At the primary level, a programme of work experience should be introduced. At the secondary level, it should function as a workshop. It should provide for work in agriculture, industry, etc.
2. Where a workshop does not exist, sets of tools and apparatus should be made available.
3. The necessary literature should be created, teachers should be trained and workshops established.

In the opinion of the Commission, work experience means being engaged in productive work at home, in school, in a shop, field or workshop, i.e., anywhere. Mahatma Gandhi introduced a revolutionary experiment in the form of Basic Education, and in fact, the concept of work experience is very similar to Gandhiji's concept. It can even be said that the kind of education which Gandhiji had envisaged for a society standing on the road to industrialization was similar to the notion of work-experience.

1. A social service programme should be introduced to achieve community development. It should be introduced at every level of education.
2. Camps should be organised for labour and social service activities.

Physical Education

Physical education should be imparted to bring about formation of character and to maintain mental awareness, physical ability and physical skill. This education, which is based on the principles governing the development of the child can be modified.

1. In an organised manner, the provision of moral education should lead to the creation of spiritual values.. For this, both direct and indirect methods of teaching should be used.
2. There should be at least one or two periods per week in the time table for the development of moral and spiritual values.

The subjects through which these are inculcated should be related to the syllabus.

Creative Activities

1. The government should set up a committee to examine the potential for the teaching of art.
2. Children's Homes should be established in every part of the country with the help to local groups, or organisations.
3. In selected universities, departments of art should be established.
4. Co-curricular activities should be encouraged for self-expression.

On the lines laid down by the report of the Hansa Mehta Committee, the Kothari Commission has stressed the principle that there should be no differentiation in the syllabus on the basis of sex. Domestic science should be available for girls, but it should not be compulsory. Encouragement should be given for receiving education in music, the fine arts, science and mathematics.

The basis of Basic Education is production, the idea that the syllabus should forge ahead through productive activities. The child should come into contact with the community. It should assume such a form that the method of education at every level should become definite. Every stage of education should be a basic one. There is no need for a separate class of education in the name of Basic Education.

The Kothari Commission devoted serious thought to the problem of preparing the most appropriate syllabus. Fresh suggestions have been invited. There is still a difference of opinion on the subject of language. Some people argue that Hindi is being throttled. In reality, however, the difficulty is that we are unable to grapple with concrete facts. The formula compounded above is similar to the Russian formula for doing away with linguistic disputes. We should take care to deal honestly and fairly with the languages of our own country.

Education for Girls

A committee was set up, under the chairmanship of Shrimati Hansa Mehta, to bring about development in the education of women and to formulate a suitable syllabus. The committee has held the view that in a democratic society, education is related to individual abilities, interests and bent of mind, and hence it emphasised the view that differentiation in the syllabus on the basis of sex should be avoided. Because of this, the Education Commission has formulated a common syllabus upto class 10. Despite this, it is desirable that the syllabus should conform to the tastes and interests of both boys and girls.

1. Home Science should be kept as an optional subject upto the Higher Secondary level. Though this subject is very popular among girls, it should not be made compulsory for them.
2. Special facilities should be provided for the study of music and fine arts.
3. Girls should be encouraged to study science and mathematics.
4. Lady teachers proficient in science and mathematics should be trained.

In addition, these suggestions should be given importance so that the education of women may gain strength and develop.

Accepting the recommendations of the National Council on Women's Education, the Commission has said that :

1. The gap between the education of men and women should be removed as soon as possible.
2. A special fund and special schemes should be generated for this purpose.
3. There should be a separate department at the Centre as well as in the States looking after the education of women.
4. Arrangements for vocational education of every kind should be made as part of women's education.
5. Vocational training courses should be initiated for adult women also.

The Commission has given great importance to the suggestions of the National Committee on Education for Women. The main suggestions are the following-

1. In the coming years, more emphasis should be laid upon the education of women so that the difference between men

and women, from the educational viewpoint, can be eliminated.

2. Special programmes should be prepared for this purpose.
3. Both at the State and Central levels, there should be special machinery to supervise the education of girls and women.

From this, it is evident that attention should be paid, in preparing the syllabus, to differences in interest and ability.

Career Planning

There is now a crying need for educational as well as vocational guidance because of the individual differences among students. Stressing the need for a programme of guidance, the Secondary Education Commission has elaborated that because of the multipurpose syllabus, the teachers and managers of schools have an additional burden of responsibility, the responsibility of providing proper guidance to students in their educational and vocational choices.

The Kothari Commission, too, has voiced similar views on the questions of guidance. According to it, at the secondary level, the main function of guidance is to recognise the abilities of youth. It will help the students to understand their abilities and limitations, to make a proper choice of academic subject in view of their qualities. Besides, it will provide them with educational as well as vocational information, make education realistic and also provide a sound basis for individual and social adjustment in the school.

The following are the purposes of setting up a guidance programme:-

1. Collecting all relevant information about the student.
2. Providing opportunities for participating in all intellectual, social and cultural programmes.
3. Providing guidance through information about educational and vocational matters.
4. Establishing a service centre.
5. Solving problems through collective and individual guidance.
6. Creating an atmosphere suitable to guidance in the school.
7. Winning the cooperation of students and parents.
8. Winning the cooperation of the entire community.

The purpose of guidance is to discover the abilities of a student which may aid him in his individual development. Three kinds of activities are important for the individual-educational, personal and vocational. Hence, guidance also takes three forms :

Educational Guidance. In such a programme, the students are given guidance regarding the syllabus. It is needed for the following reasons-

Individual Differences. Suggesting a syllabus on the basis of the child's interests and ability.

Intellectual Differences. Providing guidance on the basis of intelligence quotient or level, of the individual.

Syllabus. Guiding the students in the choice of a suitable syllabus in view of the varied courses of study available.

Polluted Atmosphere. Guiding the students to overcome the polluting effect of the unsuitable atmosphere prevailing in the school or at home.

Vocational Guidance. The purpose of this is to guide the student in his vocation while he is still at school and also acquainting him with the opportunities open to him. Its need is for the following reasons:-

1. Vocational guidance is necessary for proper choice of career.
2. Special training is necessary for specialised vocations.
3. Creates an opportunity for choosing careers on the basis of individual differences.

Individual or Personal Guidance. The purpose of such guidance is to eradicate tension, frustration or conflict.

A guidance programme can be organised in the following manners:-

Director. It is necessary to have a Director for a guidance or counselling programme. His task is to bring about harmony between the teachers and workers.

Psychologist. His task is to identify the individual qualities and abilities of the student.

Psychiatrist. His function is to diagnose, identify and carry out treat of diseases among the children.

Counsellor. The function of the counsellors is to- (i) organise psychological tests, (ii) collect data, (iii) collect information about the defects of the syllabus, (iv) provide information about various professions, (v) provide vocational guidance, (vi) organising and implementing a follow up programme.

Social Worker. He is needed to study the social and family circumstances and situation of the children in school.

Teacher Counsellor. In schools, the task of counsellors should be performed by the teachers.

The guidance cell or department should make an effort to implement its programme in each school.

The view of the Mudaliar Commission is that the secret of good education lies in the fact that it must acquaint the students with their inclinations and tendencies and also generate in them the power of social adaptation and finding suitable employment. In this regard, its recommendations are as follows:-

1. Administration in education should pay more attention to educational guidance.
2. Films should be made to create awareness in the students regarding various industries, their sphere and nature and importance. In these films, the method of working in many industries should be brought to light. The films should be based on direct observation.
3. The services of trained counsellors or career masters should gradually be made available to all educational institutions.
4. The Centre should shoulder the responsibility for setting up training centres for training counsellors and career masters in various parts of the country. Able individuals can be sent to such institutions from each state.

A guidance and counselling programme makes a very important contribution to education since it recognises the students' abilities and tendencies. The main purpose of such a programme is to recognise the talent of every student in the secondary schools. Dr. Vimleshwar De has offered the following comments upon the recommendations of the Kothari Commission on the subject of counselling.

He has argued that the Commission has not done justice to the particular nature of education, along with counselling, by regarding it as a process, (*abhikrama*). This has been done at a moment when the objectives of counselling were said to be adaptive and developmental. The preface declares that guidance or counselling should be regarded as an inseparable part of education and not as a special psychological or social service which merely assist in the fulfilment of the objectives of education. Everyone agrees that counselling should be inseparable from education, but this does not mean that counselling is not a special kind of service, or that counselling maintains its position as a matter of right. Dr. De wonders whether the Commission has implicitly given recognition to the invalid views of John and Hand (1938), which declare that guidance or counselling is the pressure that is put upon the individual through the educational process. The writers quoted above also said that they could not implement their plan of counselling because of a lack of specialists, such as counsellors, school psychologists or other professional experts at the time in question. The Commission has clearly given considerable thought to the nature of guidance and counselling at the primary and secondary levels, but it has not laid sufficient emphasis upon their services. If guidance or counselling are not regarded as special services, one may ask what was the need for special courses for training in guidance programmes, which were organised at the post-graduate level? Hence it is difficult to conceive how the commission came to make such a fundamental mistake, though it is composed of eminent educationists.

Even more significant than this is the fact that more light has been thrown upon the search for talent and its development, the education of backward children, the guidance of retarded children. Unquestionably, a theoretical consideration of counselling and its importance is important for education. What is more important, in Dr. Vimleshwar's view, is the implementation of the schemes which give concrete shape to the counselling programme. Such programmes should work as powerful media to the extent to which they allow us to make progress towards efficient and effective counselling in the peculiar circumstances prevailing in our country.

The Kothari Commission has put forth the following suggestions for the growth and development of counselling programmes.

1. Guidance and counselling services should be regarded as inseparable elements in education.
2. At the primary level, the following programme should, in general, be put into operation(1) during training itself, teachers should be made acquainted with remedial tests, (2) in-service courses should be organised for primary teachers. (3) occupational literature should be generated, (4) both students and parents should be given advice regarding the future education of children.
3. At the secondary level, such programmes should be conducted by trained individuals in the schools- (1) guidance programmes should function in every school, (2) in certain selected schools, intensive programmes should be made operative, (3) A bureau of guidance should be established and inspection staff should be appointed, (4) in training colleges, emphasis should be placed upon the importance of guidance.

Today, each one of us is aware of the fact that an organised movement is taking place for guidance and counselling. Hence in the present context, it has become necessary to provide the best possible guidance to students to ensure the suitable development of their innate capabilities. At least ten schools should take advantage of each counselling centre. There should be at least one central school in each district for organising a comprehensive programme. Inspection officers must be appointed to ensure that the programme gathers the necessary momentum. These centres should also provide vocational information and, in addition, make arrangements for part-time employment. Only then can the guidance and counselling programme achieve success.

Books for Course

Text books are symbolic of national culture. It is necessary to study the text-books of any country in order to form an estimate of its culture. The ideas, values and patterns. of a country can be known through its text-books. Though it cannot be denied that the teacher is of prime importance in the educational process, and that text books occupy the next place, the fact remains that during the early years of education, the child needs a teacher for such subjects as language, mathematics, writing, reading, etc., he still depends much more upon text-books after having learnt to read and write. Text-books perform the following functions: -

1. Even in the absence of a teacher, many more presons can take advantage of text-books.
2. The field of text-books is wide.
3. Text-books are helpful in the progress of individual as well as social life.
4. Text books hold a relationship with the parents, student, teacher, writer, the education department examiners and the publishers. Hence, they can be called the backbone of education.

The need for text-books came to light during the period of the East India Company's rule. Prior to this, one or two books were used as fundamental books or text-books in the Sanskrit *pathshalas* and the Urdu *maktabs* and *madrasas*. In the absence of printing presses, manuscript books were more commonly used, but those were more expensive because of the labour and time consumed in their production. The Company administration and Christian missionaries set up schools at many places and to teach according to a pre-planned syllabus, they published text-books. In these text-books, the major portion comprised the writings of Europeon scholars. In 1825, Mr. Elphinstone expressed the view that translations of particular books in specific languages should be prescribed for the literary development of the students. Adam had proposed that in accord with the Indian circumstances, European books should be made a part of the syllabus. He was of the view that the translation of European literature into Indian languages is compulsory so that Indians may be able to assimilate European literature through their own languages.

In 1854, in the Wood Despatch, too, emphasis was placed upon the translation of scientific terminology-into Indian languages, in addition to the establishment of oriental colleges. In 1882, the Hunter Commission commented upon the importance of text-books. It stated that scholars should be members of the text-book committees in various regions. These persons should be capable of representing the various classes of the community, as well as of reflecting upon the worth of the text-books in English and Vernacular languages put up for their consideration. In the same manner, the Secondary Education Commission, too made strong recommendation for the re-assessment and provision of text-books.

The Kothari Commission also expressed its dissatisfaction with the existing mode of preparation of text-books. Both the commissions on education have recommended that the text-books. Should be in consonance with the classroom situation and the child's mental ability should also be conducive to the achievement of the objectives of education. They also recommended that the production and publication of text-books should be nationalised so as to curb the willfulness of publishers. The secondary commission suggested that a committee should be set up for the production, selection and publication of text-books. It said that the committee should consists of the vice-chancellor of the state, one teacher, two educationists, one representative of the various classes of society, one judge. It should be presided over the director of education. The Commission also recommended the setting up of a bureau for the production of text-books as well as the syllabus. This bureau is now known as the Department of Text-book Research and Curriculum. These recommendations of the commission were considered in depth by the government, and as a result, the state and central governments have published some text-books for certain classes. The Kothari Commission has almost repeated these recommendations.

However, we can see that the manner in which text books have developed in the, country has not helped in achieving the objectives of education. There is considerable scope for improvement and growth in this field.

Text-books are important tools in the educational process. Today they are performing the role of a foundation for the development of education, but they have not succeeded in completely achieving the objectives of education. The main reason for this is that the text-books have not been prepared with the interest and inclination of the child in view. They have, therefore, failed to bring about the harmonious development of the child. In short, the following defects can be seen in most text-books:-

1. Uninteresting and unrelated lessons.
2. These are not useful for the student because they are lacking in the situation existing in the class-room.
3. In these books, the subject matter is put together unscientifically and unpsychologically, because of which the children do not understand the subject clearly.
4. These text-books are found lacking in the ideals of democracy, human rights, emotional and national unity, and international brotherhood.
5. Some text-books are written by foreign authors. These are not useful for Indian students. Besides, some of these books are written by the learned scholars of universities, who are completely ignorant of the real conditions obtaining in schools.
6. Till recently, the books were published by publishers who have been completely lacking in the necessary experience of publishing text-books.
7. They also suffer from certain technical defects such as inferior quality of paper, bad printing, weak binding, etc., which have an adverse impact upon the child.
8. Prejudice often mars the selection of text-books. Publishers get third-rate text-books selected by using unfair and unethical means.
9. Text-books of the desired standard in the regional languages have not been possible because of the absence of authors in these languages.

In view of these defects, the Secondary Education Commission had recommended the nationalisation of text-books. In its opinion, these text-books should seek to achieve the objectives of basic education, in view of the new educational policy. It suggested that they should be low priced so that cheap publications can be prevented, and also that the educational departments should not work with a view to earning profits on text-books.

The commission recommended that, in order to eradicate their shortcomings, a text-book committee should be set up. Its membership should consist of the judges of the state, one member of the public service commission, one vice-chancellor of a university of the state, one teacher (male or female), two renowned educationists and the State's Director of education. The committee should work exclusively upon the selection of text-books, and the prepared text-books should be sent to specialists without mentioning the name of the author or the publisher.

The commission also recommended that, if the education department does nationalise textbooks, it must fully implement its own policy regarding the quality of paper, the nature and quality of diagrams, printing and book-binding. The Central Government should set up a new department for the production of text-books based upon scientific research. Individuals should be given training for preparing art books to be used in Arts Colleges.

On the basis of these recommendations, a department for conducting research into text-books and curriculum was established. The department produced many text-books upto the secondary level, but it could not succeed in fulfilling the needs of the country.

The editorial comment in the *Times of India* (July 10,1964), lands support to this view. It says that children are compelled to read books which are inferior and in which hardly any sentence is grammatically correct. These books double the teachers' work, because they first have to correct them and then use them for teaching.

An almost similar comment was made in the Russian newspaper '*Pravda*' on November 30,1954. It said that in many countries the profession of text-books is not properly organised. At some places, there is a complete absence of such books while at others they lie unused in storing places.

The importance of text-books in education has been accepted by the Kothari Commission also. Text-books enlarge the mode of education, but unfortunately, the writing and publication of textbooks has not achieved the desired standard. In the opinion of the Kothari Commission, the text-book is that which is written by an able and talent specialist, properly published from the viewpoint of printing, etc., inspires the interests of the students and gives suitable help in the process of teaching. Many of the existing text-books are not only sub-standard, they are also very badly printed.

In regional languages the condition of text-books is completely pitiable. Many reasons are responsible for this situation-

1. Scholars take almost no interest in text-books. Consequently the publishers get text-books prepared by inefficient authors at very cheap prices, but this economy proves very expensive for the country.
2. Many publishers adopt extremely immoral and unethical means in order to get their text-books selected, but these adversely affect both students and parents.
3. The use of unethical means in the selection of text-books is indicative of this tendency.
4. The absence of research in the preparation and production of text-books is painfully obvious.
5. Publishers get help-books, keys and other aids to study published. The evil consequences of these practices are self-evident.

Keeping in mind these glaring shortcomings, the Kothari Commission has suggested that the NCERT's work of preparing and publishing text-books must be encouraged. This council has made considerable progress even at the central level.

Having reflected on all these points, we are faced with the following questions-

1. Will the problem of text-books be solved through nationalisation?
2. Will the government not indulge in indoctrination of its own objectives and selfish interests through nationalisation?
3. Will such a step not hinder the development of the child's personality?

When we meditate upon these questions and seek answers, due attention naturally turns towards the Red Tapism existing in all government activity. The Madras government nationalized text-books, but because of this Red Tapism, it was compelled to have its text-books published by private publishers. Even in Punjab and Delhi, the official text-books are often not available even two months after the opening of schools. As far as indoctrination is concerned, it is possible to harbour the fear that the government may, if it is so inclined, inculcate only its own version of events and facts, as the Chinese Government does. However, in a democratic system, the opposition parties function as instruments of social control, proof of which lies in the storms of controversy that often arose, from time to time, on various lessons printed in official text-books. As regards the final question, we can answer it by saying the child's development of personality will not be imperiled if the text-books are objectively prepared, and if they are in keeping with the child's interests.

The National Book Development Board was established in 1967 for the preparation, printing and publication of text-books and other kinds of help-books. The Board also lay down certain guiding principles for the book industry. In 1969, the Central Government also set up the National Board of Text-Books. This Board is functioning as a clearing house for the book producing profession. In the 4th Plan, provisions were made for spending Rs.12 crores on this work. In the same way, the National Book Trust, the Children's Book Trust are performing similar functions. In the Fifth Plan, the following provisions were made for the production of books-

Expenditure on Book Production (Crores)

Sl.	*Standard*	*Amount*
1.	University Level	15
2.	National Training Centre	1
3.	Other Programme N.B.T., Low Cost Book, M.B.D.B., etc.	14
	Total	**30**

In this way, it becomes apparent that, if we want to impart dynamism to the important functions performed by text-books in the educational process, it is necessary to nationalise both their production and their preparation. For this purpose, the government can also seek the co-operation of reputed publishers.

Teaching Devices

Both teaching and studying have become very scientific activities in the present age, and hence, teaching aids are no longer limited to a stick of chalk and a blackboard. Planning has become essential at every stage and at every level. It is only through planning that we can complete a given task according to our present time-table. In the field of teaching, the outline of the curriculum, which is to be completed in a given number of years, is reflected in the text-books.

At present, the teachers in India are almost completely lacking in proper guidance. In the view of the Kothari Commission, a good text-book, which has been written by a talented and brilliant specialist, and which is satisfactory from the view point of printing, diagramming and publication, inspires the student to read it, and also helps the teacher in performing his duty. Superior text-books and other suitable teaching aids play an incalculably important part in raising the standards of teaching.

The commission has also accepted the virtues and shortcomings of text-books in India. It has cast its eye upon the lack of interest among scholars towards the writing of text-books, corruption in the selection and prescription of text-books, corrupt methods used by publishers, absence of research, the exclusive concern with profit, etc. The Commission has expressed some ideas on the setting up an institution in the public sector for this purpose. It has felt that text-books of the desired standard are not written because authors do not get an adequate return for their labours. To overcome this, many authors should be asked to prepare text-books in manuscript form for every subject.

Emphasis has also been laid upon supplementing text-books by guide books for teachers and other material aids. It has been suggested that the All India Radio and Doordarshan should improve the quality of their programmes intended for students.

In the publication of text-books, the needs of the teacher himself are completely ignored, a fact which has not been considered important even by the Commission. In fact, guides and useful material studies should be prepared for the teachers. The Kothari Commission's suggestions in this regard are-

1. It should be the prime task of the administration to ensure that text books and other teaching materials are available at low prices.
2. Teachers should fulfil the need for guides and teaching aids.
3. In every school, at every level, a list of the necessary teaching aids should be prepared, and these aids should be available in every school.
4. The teaching department should maintain contact with the All India Radio stations and provide information regarding the lessons to be broadcast, as well as the materials or books published for teachers and students. Special radio programmes should be broadcast in the mornings and evenings so that teachers may get help in preparing the lessons to be taught in the class.
5. For teachers, the teaching materials prepared by them should be available locally and at economic prices. If certain teaching aids are expensive, they can be purchased by two or three schools together.
6. Teachers should be trained in the art of preparing teaching aids.
7. The workshops of the school should be utilised for preparing teaching aids within the school itself.

The experience of the Commission in the course of its survey can be expressed thus,- it received many suggestions pointing out that new methods of teaching should be adopted. These methods use films, film strips; radio, tape recorders, audio-visual equipment, open and closed circuit television, language laboratories, programme instructional methods and many ordinary teaching tools. Most of these things can be made use of through a School Complex.

5

Policy on Education

Education in India stands at the crossroads today. Neither normal linear expansion nor the existing pace and nature of improvement can meet the needs of the situation.

—*National Policy on Education, 1986*

1. Education has continued to evolve, diversify and extend its reach and coverage since the dawn of human history. Every country develops its system of education to express and promote its unique socio-cultural identity and also to meet the challenges of the times. There are moments in history when a new direction has to be given to an age-old process. That moment is today.
2. The country has reached a stage in its economic and technical development when a major effort must be made to derive the maximum benefit from the assets already created and to ensure that the fruits of change reach all sections. Education is the highway to that goal.
3. With this aim in view, the Government of India announced in January, 1985 that a new Education policy would be formulated for the country. A comprehensive appraisal of

the existing educational scene was made, followed by a countrywide debate. The views and suggestions received from different quarters were carefully studied.

The Evolution

4. The National Policy of 1968 marked a significant step in the history or education in post-Independence India. 'It aimed to promote national progress, a sense of common citizenship and culture, and to strengthen national integration. It laid stress on the need for a radical reconstruction of the education system, to improve its quality at all stages, and gave much greater attention to science and technology, the cultivation of moral values and a closer relation between education and the life of the people.
5. Since the adoption of the 1968 policy, there has been considerable expansion in educational facilities all over the country at all levels. More than 90 per cent of the country's rural habitations now have schooling facilities within a radius of one kilometre. There has been sizeable augmentation of facilities at other stages also.
6. Perhaps the most notable development has been the acceptance of a common structure of education throughout the country and the introduction of the 10 + 2 + 3 system by most states. In the school curricula, in addition to laying down a common scheme of studies for boys and girls, science and mathematics were incorporated as compulsory subjects and work experience assigned a place of importance.
7. A beginning was also made in restructuring of courses at the undergraduate level. Centres of Advanced studies were set up for post-graduate education and research. And we have been able to meet our requirements of educated manpower.
8. While these achievements are impressive by themselves, the general formulations incorporated in the 1968 policy

did not, however, get translated into a detailed strategy of implementation, accompanied by the assignment of specific responsibilities and financial and organisational support. As a result, problems of access, quality, quantity, utility and financial outlay, accumulated over the years, have now assumed such massive proportions that they must be tackled with the utmost urgency.

9. Education in India stands at the crossroads today. Neither normal linear expansion nor the existing pace and nature of improvement can meet the needs of the situation.
10. In the Indian way of thinking, a human being is a positive asset and a precious national resource which needs to be cherished, nurtured and developed with tenderness and care, coupled with dynamism. Each individual's growth presents a different range of problems and requirements, at every stage from the womb to the tomb. The catalytic action of education in this complex and dynamic growth process needs to be planned meticulously and executed with great sensitivity.
11. India's political and social life is passing through a phase which poses the danger of erosion to the long-accepted values. The goals of secularism, socialism, democracy and professional ethics are coming under increasing strain.
12. The rural areas, with poor infrastructure and social services, will not get the benefit of trained and educated youth, unless rural-urban disparities are reduced and determined measures are taken to promote diversification and dispersal of employment opportunities.
13. The growth of our population needs to be brought down significantly over the coming decades. The largest single factor that could help achieve this is the spread of literacy and education among women.
14. Life in the coming decades is likely to bring new tensions together with unprecedented opportunities. To enable the people to benefit in the new environment will require new

designs of human resource development. The coming generations should have the ability to internalise new ideas constantly and creatively. They have to be imbued with a strong commitment to human values and to social justice. All this implies better education.

15. Besides, a variety of new challenges and social needs make it imperative for the Government to formulate and implement a new education policy for the country. Nothing short of this will meet the situation.

The Outcomes

1. In our national perception education is essentially for all. This is fundamental to our all-round development, material and spiritual.
2. Education has an acculturating role, it refines sensitivities and perceptions that contribute to national cohesion, a scientific temper and independence of mind and spirit-thus furthering the goals of socialism, secularism and democracy enshrined in our Constitution.
3. Education develops manpower for different levels of the economy. It is also the substrate on which research and development flourish, being the ultimate guarantee of national self-reliance.
4. In sum, education is a unique investment in the present and the. future. This cardinal principle is the key to the National Policy on Education.

The Setup

1. The Constitution embodies the principles on which the national system of education is conceived of.
2. The concept of a national system of education implies that, up to a given level, all students, irrespective of caste, creed, location or sex, have access to education of a comparable quality. To achieve this, the Government will initiate appropriately funded programmes. Effective measures will be taken in the direction of the common school system recommended in the 1968 policy.

3. The National System of Education envisages a common educational structure. The 10 + 2 + 3 structure has now been accepted in all parts of the country. Regarding the further break-up of the first ten years efforts will be made to move towards an elementary system comprising five years of primary education and three years of upper primary, followed by two years of high school.
4. The National System of Education will be based on a national curricular framework which contains a common core along with other components that are flexible. The common core will include the history of India's freedom movement, the constitutional obligations and other content essential to nurture national identity. These elements will cut across subject areas and will be designed to promote values such as India's common cultural heritage, egalitarianism, democracy and secularism, equality of the sexes, protection of the environment, removal of social barriers, observance of the small family norm and inculcation of the scientific temper. All educational programmes will be carried on in strict conformity with secular values.
5. India has always worked for peace and understanding between nations, treating the whole world as one family. True to this hoary tradition, education has to strengthen this world view and motivate the younger generations for international co-operation and peaceful co-existence. This aspect cannot be neglected.
6. To promote equality, it will be necessary to provide for equal opportunity to all not only in access, but also in the conditions for success. Besides, awareness of the inherent equality of all will be created through the core curriculum. The purpose is to remove prejudices and complexes transmitted through the social environment and the accident of birth.
7. Minimum levels of learning will be laid down for each stage of education. Steps will also be taken to foster among

students an understanding of the diverse cultural and social systems of the people living in different parts of the country, besides the promotion of the link language, programmes will also be launched to increase substantially the translation of books from one language to another and to publish multilingual dictionaries and glossaries. The young will be encouraged to undertake the rediscovery of India, each in his own image and perception.

8. In higher education in general, and technical education in particular, steps will be taken to facilitate inter-regional mobility by providing equal access to every Indian of requisite merit, regardless of his origins. The universal character of universities and other institutions of higher education is to be underscored.
9. In the areas of research and development, and education in science and technology, special measures will be taken to establish network arrangements between different institutions in the country to pool their resources and participate in projects of national importance.
10. The Nation as a whole will assume the responsibility of providing resource support for implementing programmes of educational transformation, reducing disparities, universalisation of elementary education, adult literacy, scientific and technological research, etc.
11. Life-long education is a cherished goal of the educational process. This presupposes universal literacy. Opportunities will be provided to the youth, housewives, agricultural and industrial workers and professionals to continue the education of their choice, at the pace suited to them. The future thrust will be in the direction of open and distance learning.
12. The institutions which will be strengthened to play an important role in giving shape to the National System of Education are the University Grants Commission, the All India Council of Technical Education, the Indian Council of Agricultural Research and the Indian Medical Council.

Integrated planning will be instituted among all these bodies so as to establish functional linkages and reinforce programmes of research and postgraduate education. These, together with the National Council of Educational Research and Training, the National Institute of Educational Planning and Administration and the International Institute of Science and Technology Education will be involved in implementing the education policy.

13. The constitutional amendment of 1976, which includes education in the concurrent list, was a far-reaching step whose implications-substantive, financial and administrative-require a new sharing of responsibility between the union government and the state in respect of this vital area of national life. While the role and responsibility of the stages in regard to education will remain essentially unchanged, the union government would accept a larger responsibility to reinforce the national and integrative character of education, to maintain quality and standards (including those of the teaching profession at all levels), to study and monitor the educational requirements of the country as a whole in regard to manpower for development, to cater to the needs of research and advanced study, to look after the international aspects of education, culture and Human Resource Development and, in general, to promote excellence at all levels of the educational pyramid throughout the country. Concurrency signifies a partnership which is at once meaningful and challenging ; the national policy will be oriented towards giving effect to it in letter and spirit.

Education for Girls

1. The new policy will lay special emphasis on the removal of disparities and to equalise educational opportunity by attending to the specific needs of those who have been denied equality so far.

2. Education will be used as an agent of basic change in the status of women. In order to neutralise the accumulated distortions of the past, there will be a well-conceived edge in favour of women. The National Education System will play a positive, interventionist role in the empowerment of women. It will foster the development of new values through redesigned curricula, text-books, the training and orientation of teachers, decision-makers and administrators, and the active involvement of educational institutions. This will be an act of faith and social engineering. Women's studies will be promoted as a part of various courses and educational institutions encouraged to take up active programmes to further women's development.
3. The removal of women's illiteracy and obstacles inhibiting their access to, and retention in, elementary education will receive overriding priority, through provision of special support services, setting of time targets, and effective monitoring. Major emphasis will be laid on women's participation in vocational, technical and professional education at different levels. The policy of non-discrimination will be pursued vigorously to eliminate sex stereo-typing in vocational and professional courses and to promote women's participation in non-traditional occupations, as well as in existing and emergent technologies.

Caste Categories

4. The central focus in the SCs' educational development is their equalisation with the non-SC population at all stages and levels of education, in all areas and in all the four dimensions - rural male, rural female, urban male and urban female.
5. The measures contemplated for this purpose include :
   (i) Incentives to indigent families to send their children to school regularly till they reach the age of 14 ;

(ii) Pre-matric scholarship scheme for children of families engaged in occupations such as scavenging, flaying and tanning to be made applicable from class I onwards. All children of such families, regardless of incomes, will be covered by this scheme and time-bound programmes targeted on them will be undertaken;

(iii) Constant micro-planning and verification to ensure that the enrolment, retention and successful completion of courses by SC students do not fall at any stage, and provision of remedial courses to improve their prospects for further education and employment.

(iv) Recruitment of teachers from Scheduled Castes;

(v) Provision of facilities for SC students in students hostels at district headquarters, according to a phased programme;

(vi) Location of school buildings, balwadis and adult education centres in such a way as to facilitate full participation of the Scheduled Castes ;

(vii) The utilization of NREP and RLEGP resources so as to make substantial educational facilities available to the Scheduled Castes; and

(viii) Constant innovation in finding new methods to increase the participation of the Scheduled Castes in the educational process.

6. The following measures will be taken urgently to bring the Scheduled Tribes on par with others :

(i) 'Priority will be accorded to opening primary schools in tribal areas. The construction of school buildings will be undertaken in these areas on a priority basis under the normal funds for education, as well as under the NREP and RLEGP tribal welfare schemes, etc.

(ii) The socio-cultural milieu of the STs has its distinctive characteristics including, in many cases, their own spoken languages. This underlines the need to develop the curricula and devise instructional materials in tribal languages at the initial stages, with arrangements for switching over to the regional language.

(iii) Educated and promising scheduled tribe youths will be encouraged and trained to take up teaching in tribal areas.

(iv) Residential schools, including Ashram schools, will be established on a large scale.

(v) Incentive schemes will be formulated for the scheduled tribes, keeping in view their special needs and life styles. Scholarships for higher education will emphasis technical, professional and para-professional courses. Special remedial courses and other programmes to remove psycho-social impediments will be provided to improve their performance in various courses.

(vi) Angaawadis, non-formal and Adult Education Centres will be opened on a priority basis in areas predominantly inhabited by the Scheduled Tribes.

(vii) The curriculum at all stages of education will be designed to create an awareness of the rich cultural identity of the tribal people as also of their enormous creative talent.

7. Suitable incentives will be provided to all educationally backward sections of society, particularly in the rural areas. Hill and desert districts, remote and inaccessible areas and islands will be provided adequate institutional infra-structure.

8. Some minority groups are educationally deprived or backward. Greater attention will be paid to the education of these groups in the interests of equality and social justice. This will naturally include the Constitutional guarantees given to them to establish and administer their own educational institutions, and protection to their languages and culture. Simultaneously, objectivity will be reflected in

the preparation of textbooks and in all school activities, and all possible measures will be taken to promote an integration based on appreciation of common national goals and ideals, in conformity with the core curriculum.

Special Education

9. The objective should be to integrate the physically and mentally handicapped with the general community as equal partners, to prepare them for normal growth and to enable them to face life with courage and confidence. The following measures will be taken in this regard:-
   - (i) Wherever it is feasible, the education of children with motor handicaps and other mild handicaps will be common with that of others.
   - (ii) Special schools with hostels will be provided, as far as possible at district headquarters, for the severely handicapped children.
   - (iii) Adequate arrangements will be made to give vocational training to the disabled.
   - (iv) Teachers' training programmes will be reoriented, in particular for teachers of primary classes, to deal with the special difficulties of the handicapped children; and
   - (v) Voluntary effort for the education of the disabled, will be encouraged in every possible manner.

10. Our ancient scriptures define education as that which liberates-i.e., provides the instruments for liberation from ignorance and oppression. In the modern world, it would naturally include the ability to read and write, since that is the main instrument of learning. Hence the crucial importance of adult education, including adult literacy.

11. The critical development issue today is the continuous upgradation of skills so as to produce manpower resources of the kind and the number required by the society. Since participation by beneficiaries in the developmental

programmes is of crucial importance, systematic programmes of adult education linked with national goals such as alleviation of poverty, national integration, environmental conservation, energisation of the cultural creativity of the people, observance of small family norm, promotion of women's equality, etc., will be organised and the existing programmes reviewed and strengthened.

12. The whole Nation must pledge itself to the eradication of illiteracy, particularly in the 15-35 age group. The Central and State Governments, political parties and their mass organisations, the mass media and educational institutions must commit themselves to mass literacy programmes of diverse. nature. It will also have to involve on a large scale teachers, students, youth voluntary agencies, employers, etc. Concerted efforts will be made to harness various research agencies to improve the pedagogical aspects of adult literacy. The mass literacy programme would include, in addition to literacy, functional knowledge and skills, and also awareness among learners about the socio-economic reality and the possibility to change it.

13. A vast programme of adult and continuing education will be implemented through various ways and channels, including:-
    (a) establishment of centres in rural areas for continuing education;
    (b) workers' education through the employers, trade unions and concerned agencies of government;
    (c) post-secondary education institutions;
    (d) wider promotion of books, libraries and reading rooms;
    (e) use of radio, TV and films, as mass and group learning media;
    (f) creation of learners' groups and organisations;
    (g) programmes of distance learning;
    (h) organizing assistance in self-learning ; and
    (i) organizing need and interest based vocational training programmes.

Caring for Kids

1. The National Policy on Children specially emphasises investment in the development of the young child, particularly children from sections of the population in which first generation learners predominate.
2. Recognising the holistic nature of child development, viz., nutrition, health and social, mental, physical, moral and emotional development. Early Childhood Care and Education (ECCE) will receive high priority and be suitably integrated with the Integrated Child Development Services Programme, wherever possible. Day-care centres will be provided as a support service for universalisation of primary education, to enable girls engaged in taking care of siblings to attend school and as a support service for working women belonging to poorer sections.
3. Programmes of ECCE will be child-oriented, focused around play and the individuality of the child. Formal methods and introduction of the 3 R's will be discouraged at this stage. The local community will be fully involved in these programmes.
4. A full integration of child care and pre-primary education will be brought about, both as a feeder and a strengthening factor for primary education and for human resource development in general. In continuation of this stage, the School Health Programme will be strengthened.

Primary Education

5. The new thrust in elementary education will emphasise two aspects: (i) universal enrolment and universal retention of children up to 14 years of age, and (ii) a substantial improvement in the quality of education.

Concerns for Kids

6. A warm, welcoming and encouraging approach, in which all concerned share a solicitude for the needs of the child, is the best motivation for the child to attend school and

learn. A child-centred and activity-based process of learning should be adopted at the primary stage. First generation learners should be allowed to set their own pace and be given supplementary remedial instruction. As the child grows, the component of cognitive learning will be increased and skills organised through practice. The policy of non-detention at the primary stage will be retained, making evaluation as disaggregated as feasible. Corporal punishment will be firmly excluded from the educational system and school timings as well as vacations adjusted to the convenience of children.

6

The Facilities

1. Provision will be made of essential facilities in primary schools, including at least two reasonably large rooms that are usable in all weather, and the necessary toys, blackboards, maps, charts, and other learning materials. At least two teachers, one of whom a woman, should work in every school, the number increasing as early as possible to one teacher per class. A phased drive, symbolically called operation blackboard will be undertaken with immediate effect to improve Primary Schools all over the country. Government, local bodies, voluntary agencies and individuals will be fully involved. Construction of school buildings will be the first charge on NREP and RLEGP funds.
2. A large and systematic programmes of non-formal education will be launched for school drop-outs, for children from habitations without schools, working children and girls who cannot attend whole-day schools.
3. Modern technological aids will be used to improve the learning environment of NFE centres. Talented and dedicated young men and women from the local community will be chosen to serve as instructors, and particular attention paid to their training. Steps will be taken to facilitate their entry into the formal system in

deserving cases. All necessary measures will be taken to ensure that the quality of non-formal education is comparable with formal education.

4. Effective steps be taken to provide a framework for the curriculum on the lines of the national core curriculum, but based on the needs of the learners and related to the local environment. Learning material of high quality will be developed and provided free of charge to all pupils. NFE programmes will provide participatory learning environment, and activities such as games and sports, cultural programmes, excursions, etc.
5. Much of the work of running NFE centres will be done through voluntary agencies and Panchayati Raj institutions. The provision of funds to these agencies will be adequate and timely. The Government will take over-all responsibility for this vital sector.
6. The New Education Policy will give the highest priority to solving the problem of children dropping out of school and will adopt an array of meticulously formulated strategies based on micro-planning, and applied at the grass-roots level all over the country, to ensure children's retention at school. This effort will be fully coordinated with the network of non-formal education. It shall be ensured that all children who attain the age of about 11 years by 1990 will have had five years of schooling, or its equivalent through the non-formal stream. Likewise, by 1995 all children will be provided free and compulsory education upto 14 years of age.

Education in Schools

1. Secondary education begins to expose students to the differentiated roles of science, the 'humanities and social sciences. This is also an appropriate stage to provide children with a sense of history and national perspective and give them opportunities to understand their constitutional duties and rights as citizens. Conscious internalisation of a healthy work ethos and of the values of a humane and composite culture will be brought about through appropriately formulated curricula.

Vocationalisation through specialised institutions or through the refashioning of secondary education can, at this stage, provide valuable man-power for economic growth. Access to secondary education will be widened to cover areas unserved by it at present. In' other areas, the main emphasis will be on consolidation.

2. It is universally accepted that children with special talent or aptitude should be provided opportunities to proceed at a faster pace, by making good quality education available to them, irrespective of their capacity to pay for it.
3. Pace-setting schools intended to serve this purpose will be established in various parts of the country on a given pattern, but with full scope for innovation and experimentation. Their broad aims will be to serve the objective of excellence, coupled with equity and social justice (with reservation for SCs and STs), to promote national integration by providing opportunities to talented children largely rural, from different parts of the country to live and learn together, to develop their full potential, and, most importantly, to become catalysts of a nation-wide programme of school improvement. The schools will be residential and free of charge.

Professional Education

1. The introduction of systematic, well-panned and rigorously implemented programmes of vocational education is crucial in the proposed educational reorganisation. These elements are meant to enhance individual employability, to reduce the mismatch between the demand and supply of skilled manpower, and to provide an alternative for those pursuing higher education without particular interest or purpose.
2. Vocational education will be a distinct stream, intended to prepare students for identified occupations spanning several areas of activity. These courses will ordinarily be provided after the secondary stage, but keeping the scheme flexible, they may also be made available after class VIII. In the interests of integrating vocational education better with

their facilities, the Industrial Training Institutes will also conform to the larger vocational pattern.

3. Health planning and health service management should optimally interlock with the education and training of appropriate categories of health manpower through health-related vocational courses. Health education at the primary and middle levels will ensure the commitment of the individual to family and community health, and lead to health-related vocational courses at the +2 stage of higher secondary education. Efforts will be made to devise similar vocational courses based on Agriculture, Marketing, Social Services, etc. An emphasis in vocational education will also be on development of attitudes, knowledge, and skills for entrepreneurship and self-employment.
4. The establishment of vocational courses or institutions will be the responsibility of the Government as well as employers in the public and private sectors; the Government will, however, take special steps to cater to the needs of women, rural and tribal students and the deprived sections of society. Appropriate programmes will also be started for the handicapped.
5. Graduates of vocational courses will be given opportunities, under predetermined conditions, for professional growth, career improvement and lateral entry into courses of general, technical and professional education through appropriate bridge courses.
6. Non-formal, flexible and need-based vocational programmes will also be made available to neo-literates, youth who have completed primary education, school drop-outs, persons engaged in work and unemployed or partially employed persons. Special attention in this regard will be given to women.
7. Tertiary level courses will be organised for the young graduates from the higher secondary courses of the academic stream and may also require vocational courses.
8. It is proposed that vocational courses cover 10 per cent of higher secondary students by 1990 and 25 per cent by 1995. Steps will be taken to see that a substantial majority

of the products of vocational courses are employed or become self-employed. Review of the courses offered would be regularly undertaken. Government will also review its recruitment policy to encourage diversification at the secondary level.

Education for Health

1. Sports and physical education are an integral part of the learning process, and will be included in the evaluation of performance. A nation-wide infrastructure for physical education, sports and games will be built into the educational edifice.
2. The infrastructure will consist of playfields, equipment, coaches and teachers of physical education as part of the school improvement programme. Available open spaces in urban areas will be reserved for playgrounds, if necessary by legislation. Efforts will be made to establish sports institutions and hostels where specialised attention will be given to sports activities and sports-related studies, along with normal education. Appropriate encouragement will be given to those talented in sports and games. Due stress will be laid on indigenous traditional games. As a system which promotes an integrated development of body and mind, yoga will receive special attention. Efforts will be made to introduce yoga in all schools ; to this end, it will be introduced in teacher training courses.

Young Generation

1. Opportunities will be provided for the youth to involve themselves in national and social development through educational institutions and outside them. Students will be required to participate in one or the other of existing schemes, namely, the National Service Scheme, National Cadet Corps, etc. Outside the institutions, the youth will be encouraged to take up programmes of development, reform and extension. The National Service Volunteer Scheme will be strengthened.
2. Assessment of performance is an integral part of any process of learning and teaching. As part of sound

educational strategy, examinations should be employed to bring about qualitative improvement in education.

3. The objective will be to re-cast the examination system so as to ensure a method of assessment that is a valid and reliable measure of student development and a powerful instrument for improving teaching and learning. In functional terms, this would mean
   (i) The elimination of excessive element of chance and subjectivity;
   (ii) The de-emphasis of memorisation;
   (iii) Continuous and comprehensive evaluation that incorporates both scholastic and non-scholastic aspects of education, spread over the total span of instructional time;
   (iv) Effective use of the evaluation process by teachers, students and parents;
   (v) Improvement in the conduct of examinations;
   (vi) The introduction of concomitant changes in instructional materials and methodology;
   (vii) Introduction of the semester system from the secondary stage in a phased manner; and
   (viii) The use of grades in place of marks.

4. The above goals are relevant both for external examinations and evaluation within educational institutions. Evaluation at the institutional level will be streamlined and the predominance of external examinations reduced.

Teacher Education

1. The status of the teacher reflects the socio-cultural ethos of a society; it is said that no people can rise above the level of its teachers. The government and the community should endeavour to create conditions which will help motivate and inspire teachers on constructive and creative lines. Teachers should have the freedom to innovate, to devise appropriate methods of communication and activities relevant to the needs and capabilities of and the concerns of the community.
2. The methods of recruiting teachers will be reorganised to ensure merit, objectivity and conformity with spatial and

functional requirements. The pay and service conditions of teachers have to be commensurate with their social and professional responsibilities and with the need to attract talent to the profession. Efforts will be made to reach the desirable objective of uniform emoluments, service conditions and grievance-removal mechanisms for teachers throughout the country. Guidelines will be formulated to ensure objectivity in the posting and transfers of teachers. A system of teacher evaluation-open, participative and data-based-will be created and reasonable opportunities of promotion to higher grades provided. Norms of accountability will be laid down with incentives for good performance and disincentives for non-performance. Teachers will continue to play a crucial role in the formulation and implementation of educational programmes.

3. Teacher's association must play a significant role in upholding professional integrity, enhancing the dignity of the teacher and in curbing professional misconduct. National level associations of teachers, could prepare a Code of Professional Ethics for Teachers and see to its observance.
4. Teacher education is a continuous process, and its pre-service and in-service components are inseparable. As the first step, the system of teacher education will be overhauled.
5. The new programmes of teacher education will emphasise continuing education and the need for teachers to meet the thrusts envisaged in this policy.
6. District Institutes of Education and Training (DIET) will be established with the capability to organise pre-service and in-service courses for elementary school teachers and for the personnel working in non-formal and adult education. As DIET's get established, sub-standard institutions will be phased out. Selected Secondary Teacher Training Colleges will be upgraded to complement the work of State Councils of Educational Research and Training. The National Council of Teacher Education will be provided

the necessary resources and capability to accredit institutions of teacher education and provide guidance regarding curricula and methods. Networking arrangements will be created between institutions of teacher education and university departments of education.

Educational Management

1. An overhaul of the system of planning and the management of education will receive high priority. The guiding considerations will be :-
   (a) Evolving a long-term planning and management perspective of education and its integration with the country's developmental and manpower needs;
   (b) Decentralisation and the creation of a spirit of autonomy for educational institutions;
   (c) Giving pre-eminence to people's involvement, including association of non-governmental agencies and voluntary effort;
   (d) Inducting more women in the planning and management of education;
   (e) Establishing the principle of accountability in relation to given objectives and norms.
2. The Central Advisory Board of Education will play a pivotal role in reviewing educational development, determining the changes required to improve the system and monitoring implementation. It will function through appropriate committees and other mechanisms created to ensure contact with, and co-ordination among, the various areas of Human Resource Development. The Departments of Education at the Centre and in the State will be strengthened through the involvement of professionals.
3. A proper management structure in education will entail the establishment of the Indian Education Service as an All India Service. It will bring a national perspective to this vital sector. The basic principles, functions and procedures of recruitment to this service will be decided in consultation with the State Governments.
4. State Governments may establish State Advisory Boards of Education on the lines of CABE. Effective measures should

be taken to integrate mechanisms in the various State departments concerned with Human Resource Development.

5. Special attention will be paid to the training of education planners, administrators and heads of institutions. Institutional arrangements for this purpose should be set up in stages.
6. District Boards of Education will be created to manage education upto the higher secondary level. State Governments will attend to this aspect with all possible expedition. Within a multi-level framework of educational development, Central, State, District and Local level agencies will participate in planning co-ordination, monitoring and evaluation.
7. A very important role must be assigned to the head of an educational institution. Heads will be specially selected and trained. School complexes will be promoted on a flexible pattern so as to serve as networks of institutions and synergic alliances to encourage professionalism among teachers, to ensure observance of norms of conduct and to enable the sharing of experiences and facilities. It is expected that a developed system of school complexes will take over much of the inspection functions in due course.
8. Local communities, through appropriate bodies, will be assigned a major role in programmes of school improvement.

Funds for Schools

9. Non-government and voluntary effort including social activist groups will be encouraged, subject to proper management, and financial assistance provided. At the same time, steps will be taken to prevent the establishment of institutions set up to commercialise education.

Generating Sources

1. The Education Commission of 1964-65, the National Education Policy of 1968 and practically all others concerned with education have stressed that the egalitarian

goals and the practical development oriented objectives of Indian society can be realised only by making investments in education of an order commensurate with the nature and dimensions of the task.

2. Resources, to the extent possible, will be raised by mobilising donations, asking the beneficiary communities to maintain school buildings and supplies of some consumables, raising fees at the higher levels of education and effecting some savings by the efficient use of facilities. Institution involved with research and the development of technical and scientific manpower should also mobilize some funds by levying a cess or charge on the user agencies,, including Government departments, and entrepreneurs. All these measures will be taken not only to reduce the burden on State resources but also for creating a greater sense of responsibility within the educational system. However, such measures will contribute only marginally to the total funding. The Government and the community in general will find funds for such programme as: the universalisation of elementary education ; liquidating illiteracy ; equality of access to educational opportunities to all sections throughout the country ; enhancing the social relevance, quality and functional effectiveness of educational programmes ; generating knowledge and developing technologies in scientific fields crucial to self-sustaining economic development ; and creating a critical consciousness of the values and imperatives of national survival.
3. The deleterious consequences of non-investment or inadequate investment in education are indeed very serious. Similarly, the cost of neglecting vocational and technical education and of research is also unacceptable. Sub-optimal performance in these fields could cause irreparable damage to the Indian economy. The network of institutions set up from time to time since Independence to facilitate the application of science and technology would need to be substantially and expeditiously updated, since they are fast becoming obsolete.

4. In view of these imperatives, education will be treated as a crucial area of investment for national development and survival. The National Policy on Education, 1968, had laid down that the investment on education be gradually increased to reach a level of expenditure of 6% of the national income as early as possible. Since the actual level of investment has remained far short of that target, it is important that greater determination be shown now to find the funds for the programmes laid down in this Policy. While the actual requirements will be computed from time to time on the basis of monitoring and review, the outlay on education will be shaped up to the extent essential for policy implementation in the Seventh plan. It will be ensured that from the Eighth Five Year Plan onwards it will uniformly exceed to 6% of the National income.
5. The implementation of the various parameters of the New Policy must be reviewed every five years. Appraisals at short intervals will also be made to ascertain the progress of implementation and the trends emerging from time to time.

New Trends

1. The future shape of education in India is too complex to envision with precision. Yet, given our tradition which has almost always put a high premium on intellectual and spiritual attainment, we are bound to succeed in achieving our objectives.
2. The main task is to strengthen the base of the pyramid, which might come close to a billion people at the turn of the century. Equally, it is important to ensure that those at the top of the pyramid are among the best in the world. Our cultural well-springs had taken good care of both ends in the past ; the skew set in with foreign domination and influence. It should now be possible to further intensify the nation-wide effort in Human Resource Development, with Education playing its multifaceted role.

New Schemes

The need for National Education Policy was felt after 1947. Kothari Commission had recommended for National Education

Policy in 1966 and for the first time Policy for Education was declared in 1968. Due to political instability during 1971-79, Congress Jad to leave power and the then Government also declared its own National Policy on Education. Again, Congress came into power and deceased Prime-minister Shri Rajeev Gandhi took interest in Education and declared his National Education Policy in 1986 and proposed an action plan.

This document was published in 1986. Honourable Governor of Gujarat, Mr. R.K. Trievedi expressed his views on this policy- "Considering the all round development of the country, the structure of Education Policy was erected. Education is not considered within four walls of the schools. Teaching is not 'limited to the curriculum but it is a source of developing national unity, cultural preservation and indication of moral, social and ethical values."

Education Policy provides a sound basis to National Progress. Every ruler in India gave preference to Education according to its need. Present Government declared its National Policy on Education. Following are the main features of National Policy on Education 1986.

Role of Education. Education is responsible for the all round development of the individuals. It is also responsible for cultural assimilation and provide strength to democracy, secularism. Education constructs the nation at every level, creates self-sufficiency and search new areas of development.

National System of Education. Though Education is a state subject, this policy provides a National System of Education, i.e., 10 + 2 + 3 system.

Equality. This policy provides equal opportunities to all for education. Navodaya schools have been opened for socially and economically deprived but to talented children. Regional imbalances are also being removed

Women Education. New Education Policy gave special emphasis to Women Education. This statement owes that women are the keys to nation's progress. Education of illiteracy vocational curriculum, Nutrition and child care courses, Home management, etc., are given priority.

Education of Scheduled Castes. Socially and economically deprived Scheduled Castes are the back bone of our society. They need proper development and place in the society. Scholarships, hostel facilities, adult education programmes are being introduced.

Education for Tribes. This policy gave main emphasis to the education of tribes. Residential Ashram Schools have been opened for them, scholarships for higher education are given.

Education for Donor Backward Classes. A large number of backward classes, minority classes have not been given any opportunity for education. These classes have a very crucial situation. They are socially and economically deprived due to their profession, but they usually linked themselves with higher varnas. Thus upper castes do not give them social sanction. Education is the only way to give them chance to co-operation with the society.

Adult Education. Education Policy gave a programme for adult education to remove the illiteracy from the masses. For this, adult schools, libraries, distance education, T.V. programmes are being introduced.

Reorganisation of Education. National Policy on Education 1986, gave more emphasis on the reorganisation of educational pattern. First ladder is pre-primary or pre-school education. At this stage, training for child rearing and care is provided to new parents. Also, more attention is paid to the physical, mental and emotional development of the children. At primary stage, child is the centre of education. Each primary school should have at least have two such rooms to be used for in every season. Free and compulsory education be provided to the students and non-formal education will also be given to those who would have left their schools before time.

As far the secondary education is concerned, vocationalization of it is introduced. At Higher education stage, autonomy will be given to good colleges.

New Dimensions. This policy provides new dimensions to education-such as Distance Education through open universities. Indira Gandhi Open University has been established for this purpose at centre. Similarly some states have also opened, Open Universities. Declining the employment with degree, establishment of Rural universities, technical and management education, innovation, research and development, organising the new educational programmes, rationalization of educational activities and process, evaluation system, status of teachers, women education and creating means for it are some of the new dimensions.

Though, New Policy gave a new direction in the field of education in the light of national unity and development this is the preparation to welcome the 21st century. Life deal, family structure, social organisation, national consciousness are influenced by the scientific and technological advancement. Moral, social, ethical and human values need development. This is a felt need of our new policy. Common man is on the cross roads. He does not find his way to destiny. Growing population, expansion of social distances and economic disparities put some questions before the new policy. Those questions are as under-

1. Whether new policy will create class difference?
2. Is this policy competent to shape the socialistic society?
3. Will it be possible to make free and compulsory education to all the children upto the age of 14 ?
4. How will this be helpful to reconstruct the nation?
5. Will social justice be possible through it?
6. Reservation policy will not give the passage to new policy?
7. What will be the shape of future? This indication is not given by the policy.
8. Language problem is a very big problem before new policy?
9. No equality is possible through it.

Though these questions are before our policy makers, even then they are much hopeful to build new India. In the words of our deceased Prime-minister Rajeev Gandhi- "We will have to build our society, such a society where education must be honoured. Education does not end after learning school or college. It is a life long process. We cannot progress until our education be honoured and we could not face the challenges in future to save our country."

In the end past is gold, present is full of dust and future is indefinite. New Education Policy is the determination of youth. This will create a faith for future, develop our determination, thus distance will be dispersed.

7

Preparation of Courses

The Perceptions

The concept of 'primary education' as a distinct area of development was fully established five years before the next report of the Consultative Committee appeared. Certainly the Board did everything it could to keep the concept alive, and after its publication in 1928 *The New Prospect in Education, L.E.A.s* drew up schemes for the full provision of 'post primary' education for children of 11+ along with the lines indicated in the Hasow Report. There is a tendency to look upon it as little more than a historical curiosity; certainly beside the Plowden Report of 1967 it appears a very slim and modest volume, indeed, and although it took two years to produce its gross cost was minute compared with the cost of Plowden.

After a fairly lengthy introduction on general principles, the report provided a historical sketch of the development of the idea of primary education from the beginning of the nineteenth century. It went on to describe the physical and mental development of children between the ages of seven and eleven; and it is interesting to note that, just as Plowden leans quite heavily upon Piagetian thought, the 1931 report used and quoted Padget's *Le Language et la Pensee chez l'Enfant,* published in France in 1923 and translated into English in 1926.

Elementary Education

The report then went on to consider the age limits for the upper stage of elementary education, which it felt should be fixed at the age of eleven; that is, the transfer from the primary to the secondary school should take place between the ages of eleven and twelve. It went on to discuss in some detail the arguments against separate 'infant' and 'junior' schools, but finally recommended that, in those areas where it was possible, there should be separate schools for children below the age of seven, and that in all primary schools there ought to be a well-defined line of education between the younger and older children.

The report made it clear that the primary school should not be regarded merely as a 'preparatory department for the subsequent stage' : primary school. course were to be planned and conditioned by the specific needs of the child at that particular phase in his development, both physical and mental.

The internal organization of primary schools was next discussed, including such problems as the size of classes and co-education at the upper stage of primary education. The report adduced evidence from a variety of sources to establish that classes in junior schools should be kept small, preferably about thirty five, and it further made the point that it would be impossible to put into operation many of its suggestions if large classes were retained in primary schools. The size of primary classes was indeed one of the most urgent problems facing education administrators. Concerning co-education the conclusion was that there was no valid objection on general or sociological grounds, provided due regard was paid to the differing needs of girls and boys in games and physical activities generally.

The Problems

Problems of mental and educational retardation were considered in detail, and the chief causes, detection, diagnosis and treatment dealt with. Retarded children required special attention between the ages of seven and eleven, and it was recommended that special classes should be organized for this purpose and that they should be small.

The traditional curriculum of the public elementary school was next analyzed, and the general principles on which the upper stages of primary education should be based were elicited. The report considered the complexity of 'modern industrial civilization' and the bearing this has upon the work of the primary school. It emphasized the uselessness, as well as the innate danger, of seeking to inculcate what AX Whitehead has termed "inert ideas'; and it deplored and deprecated the fact that, whilst a great deal of teaching was good in the abstract, too little of it directly assisted children to enlarge and vivify their instinctive hold on the condition of life by enriching, illuminating and giving point to their growing experience.

In its further consideration of curriculum detail the report emphasized the desirability of devising new methods on approaching its various branches, and in particular dealt with the project method and 'centres of interest' as set against the traditional practice of treating the curriculum in terms of 'subjects'. It warned, however, against the dangers of such methods when used without due consideration or caution-music and drama were often merely 'dragged in' in order to fulfill what were regarded as the claims of a principle. The staffing of primary schools and the training of teachers were next considered, and it was argued that teachers with general qualification rather than specialists were best suited for work in primary schools.

A brief survey was made of school premises, equipment, school and class libraries, visual and auditory aids to teaching, school visits and playing fields. There followed a discussion of examinations in primary schools and it was recommended that, in classifying pupils leaving the infant school, of consultation between the teachers concerned. Any classification should be merely provisional, and should be subject to frequent revision.

Various Types

The council felt that as the provision of various types of secondary education was extended in the way proposed in the report on The Education of the Adolescent, the need for selecting by competition those children who would pass on to grammar and selective modern schools would diminish. It was convinced, however, that some sort of qualifying test or examination would always be required for the purpose of classifying pupils, and argued for the use of written papers in English and arithmetic as a basic test of capacity and attainment of children at the age of eleven, together with carefully devised group intelligence tests. Throughout the report of The Primary School there was a lively sense of the needs of the children themselves. It considered that what any wise and good parent might desire for his own children was precisely what the nation as a whole must desire for all children.

The primary school was on the way to becoming what it should be, namely, the common school of the whole population, so excellent and so genrally esteemed that all parents will desire their children to attend it. In 1933 the Hadow Report on the Infant and Nursery school was published and, like its predecessor, it emphasized the need to build new schools for young children more on an open-air plan. It also made it clear that the best place for very young children was in the home; but if this were not possible there was a great deal to be derived from attending nursery schools.

Character and Intellect

There is a recognition of the child as a total being who has specific and differing needs within the realms of character and intellect, and additionally the need to be initiated into the world of work and life itself in such a way as to be able to cope practically as well as intellectually. Eaglesham may be right when he comments that whilst there is to be preparation for life there is to be no vocational education.

The children are to be trained in habits of careful observation and clear reasoning so that they may gain some intelligent acquaintance with some of the facts and laws of nature and this is hardly 'followership'! The school must further arouse in its pupils a lively interest in man's ideals, achievements, literature and history; it must give them 'some power over language as an instrument of thought and expression'-surely more keeping with education for leadership! All sound education should make pupils and students aware of the limitations of their knowledge and encourage a due sense of humility within the realms of learning-whether they are leaders or followers.

The code consequently adds that, while the school should make pupils conscious of their limitations it should provide thoughtful study as it will enable them to increase that knowledge' when their school career is over, and by their own efforts. This, indeed, is still one of the prime purpose of education-to demonstrate to pupils how to acquire knowledge and learning for themselves. The influence in practice of the 'sloud' movement is to be seen in other elements of the introduction which suggests that the school should encourage the natural activities of the child's hand and eye 'by suitable forms of practical work and manual instruction'; and the general, though gradual, movement towards hygiene and health is suggested by the training of pupils in physical exercises, organized games and the simple laws of health.

It is true that the code saw the possibility of discovering 'individual children who show promise of exceptional capacity', and that such children should be qualified to pass at the appropriate age into the secondary schools and there be enabled to derive the maximum benefit from the education offered them. Whilst this was a recognition that some children rather than others were fitted for further education it is worthy of note that there was a clause in parenthesis which had the sort of contention which many educators have put forward in more recent years against the streaming of children in primary schools for the 11+ examination, and the gearing of the whole of the primary curriculum for the benefit of the academic few to develop their special gifts. The introduction was not an exhortation to industry, respect and reverence in quite the same sense as that implied in pervious codes and reports.

There was little or no suggestion of 'fellowship' subservience in the terminology of the code. It was implied that there was a great responsibility on the part of the teachers to lay the foundations of conduct; and by their influence, example and personal sense of discipline, which should pervade the school, to inculcate in the children 'habits of industry, self control, and courageous preference in the face of difficulties' training suited, surely, to the middle and upper classed as well as the working classes. Reverence was to be taught not for the nobility bur for what was noble; and children were to be ready for self-sacrifice and to strive to the uttermost for purity and truth. The respect which was to be fostered was not that for 'their betters', but for others, 'which must be the foundation of unselfishness and the basis of all good manner's. The corporate life of the school was the basis for the development of the instinct for fair play and sense of loyalty to one another-the very 'germ of a wider sense of honour in later life'.

Some of the introduction, for good or ill, reads almost like a public school code. The introduction concludes that school, parents and home should all unite in an effort to enable the children to reach their fullest development as individuals, and also to become useful and upright citizens in their community. Whether Morant was interested in forwarding elementary education or not, there was a certain liberalizing and humanizing purpose expressed in this introduction. And this was supported by the Blue Book issued by the Board of Education in 1905, which was a handbook of suggestions for teachers involved in the work of public elementary schools.

Uniformity of practice throughout such schools was not desirable, but rather that each teacher should think for himself and work out his own methods according to the school's conditions and requirements. Above all the teacher should know and sympathize with the children he was teaching. The entire process of education was viewed as a partnership for the acquisition of knowledge.

Facts were not to be dealt with in isolation but in relation to the total experience of the child 'each lesson must be a renewal and an increase of that connected store of experience which becomes knowledge' The Blue Book was in line with the introduction to the code in that it insisted that the latter should fully realize his duty to use his innate powers to the best advantage.

Life must be presented as something at once pleasant and serious, and in consequence the work being pursued in the schools was in a real sense a preparation for life. Moreover, the teacher's influence in all this was a very vital one, however short the period of influence might be. The First Education Act of 1918 enforced compulsory attendance at school up to the age of fourteen years, and it also underlined the need for a complete reorganization of what today is more specifically referred to as primary education, that is, the education of young children below the age of eleven years.

Progressive Movements

Officialdom had learned a lot from the less orthodox and more progressive movements already mentioned, but despite all this, many of the school buildings were inadequate and unhygienic. And despite the general desire expressed to make the primary school curriculum free from the pressures of selective examinations at the upper end of the school, in practice their classes were geared largely to preparation for secondary school work at the subject level and to some sort of 'scholarship' examination at 11+.
The White Paper on Education Reconstruction which appeared in 1943, suggested in particular that children of 11+ should not be classified on the basis of a competitive test, but rather upon the assessment of their aptitudes based largely upon school records and intelligence tests. It felt that competitive examinations at the age of eleven were wrong in principle, not only because of the strain to which children were subjected but also because the future schooling and careers of children were largely decided at this one point in time. An age when children's minds were nimble and receptive, when their imagination and curiosity were strong and fertile, they were subjected to a cramping and stultifying curriculum in which considerable emphasis was placed upon 'ways and means or creating the examiners. The White Paper also stated that there should be separate schools for infants and juniors; and, whilst attendance was not compulsory before the age of five, L.E.A.s must make adequate provision for either nursery schools or, where these were considered expedient, nursery classes in infant schools.

The Butler Education Act of 1944 gave the primary school statutory authority in this country, and it defined primary education in Section 8 as full time education suitable to the requirements of junior pupils'. The Act forced a clear break between primary and post-primary education between primary and secondary education. We are not here secondary education, the developing tripartite system, put ever increasing pressures upon primary schools to act as forcing grounds for grammar schools.

The aims, so clearly expressed in the Hadow Report on The Primary School, were very soon forgotten in the cut-throat competition for grammar school places, and the more enlightened development of primary school methods was somewhat delayed. There was a very real sense in which the firm, separate, statutory establishment of primary and post-primary educational institutions postponed the liberation of primary school methods and the Central Advisory Council for Education was probably not being over-pessimistic when it stated in 1947 that "the gap between a reasonable provision of primary schools and the existing provision was formidable" 'half a century's unremitting efforts will be required before we can hope to have good primary schools for all'. A lot, of course, depends on the connotation of the word 'good' in this context: the verdict of the Plowden Report, twenty years later, was quite simply expressed in these words, 'the primary schools are giving good value for the inadequate amount of money spent on them'. But it made it quite clear that the financial inadequacies has seen severe educational repercussions, as we shall presently see.

In August 1963 the Central Advisory Council for Education was asked by Sir Edward Boyle, then Minister of Education, 'to consider primary education in all its aspects, and the transition to secondary education'. Their report was concluded in October 1966 when it was presented to Anthony Crosland, Secretary of State for Education and Science, and it was published in January 1967. Volume I presented the report, and Volume II the statistics derived from a national survey of 20,00. schools. The total cost of the report was slightly over 120,000. Part one formed an introduction to the whole investigation and referred in particular to the close association between the home background and academic achievement.

Social Background

The importance to individual of his family and social background was emphasized, and among question raised in general terms was that of whether 'finding out' had really proved to be better than 'being told' and stressed the enormously wide variability in physical and intellectual maturity amongst children of the same age, particularly during adolescence, and the tendency for children to mature physically earlier than formerly.

It went on to discuss the interaction of heredity and environment, the stages of child development as outlined by Jean Piaget, and the measurement of IQ. It found a correlation between children's IQs and parental occupations-the children of professional parents have an average IQ of 115, emphasized that the child was a total personality, and that its emotional, social and intellectual aspects were closely intertwined.

The Implications

Some of the implications of this section include the fact that individual variations between children of the same age are so great that any class, however apparently homogeneous, must always be treated as a body of children needing individual and different attention. Until a child is ready to take a particular step forward, it is useless to try and teach him to take it. Since any child grows up intellectually, emotionally, and physically at different rates, his teachers need to know and take account of his 'developmental age' in all three respects.

The child's physique, personality and capacity to learn will develop as a result of continuous interaction between his genetic inheritance and his environment. Whilst the genetic factors are not as yet under our control, the environmental factors largely are. Part Two of the report, therefore, suggested the need of a very personal approach to the pupil in the primary school, with a special study of each child's 'readiness' for any particular form of learning or operation; and, at the same time, the provision of a sound, healthy, amenable sort of environment in order to present the best learning situations and conditions.

A minimum programme was suggested for the participation of parents in the education of children a welcome to the school, meetings with teachers, open days, information for parents via brochures about the organization of the school, and reports for parents. There should be a concerted effort that the primary school should be used as fully as possible, out of ordinary school hours, as a sort of community centre. Community schools should be developed in all areas, but particularly in educational priority areas, where there was need for constant communication between parents and teachers if the schools' aims were to be completely understood. The report emphasized the need for colleges of education to have stronger and more efficient links with such schools and to develop courses to meet the needs of immigrant children in particular.

There was a very strong suggestion that the training of teachers generally should take more account of those social factors which affect school performance, and also of the structure and functions of the school services. It recommended the initiation of experimental schemes in the joint training of teachers and social workers, and already there are colleges of education which are devising courses for social and youth wing work as well as general welfare work. The report made it very clear indeed that the primary school has a social role in the community, as well as an immediate and individual adductive role.

There should be three years in the infant school and children should not be transferred until the age of 8 years; this would permit both children and teachers to work steadily and without anxiety. The age for admission to a secondary school was suggested as 12+, since this would give a four-year course in the junior or middle school, with a median age range from 8 years 6 months to 12 years 6 months. It should be noted here that the definition of primary education provided by Section 8 of the 1944 Education Act was amended by Section 3 of the 1948 Education Act.

Primary education was there defined as 'full time education for children below 10 years 6 months and children above that age but below 12 years who it is expedient to educate with them'; whilst the 1964 Education Act allowed proposals to be submitted to the Secretary of State for the establishment of new schools with age limits below 10 years 6 months and above 12 years. The report emphasized the need for the fullest possible documentation of each pupil before transfer to the secondary school, and it detailed the type of contents that a folder on each child should contain.

The ill effects upon primary education of selection for secondary schools were lessening, and the council recommended that authorities still employing selection procedures should no longer rely on an externally imposed battery of attainment and intelligence tests. Part five dealt with the children in the schools, with curriculum and internal organization. Among a large variety of aims and purposes mooted, and dangers to be avoided, the following aims of primary education were accepted in somewhat general terms, with the provison that generalities have limited value and can quickly become little more than platitudes; it was agreed that a pragmatic approach to the purposes of education was more likely to be fruitful'.

(a) Adaptability-to fit children for the society into which they will grow up, and to train them to be capable of adjusting to their changing environment.
(b) The all-round development of the individual child.
(c) The acquisition of the basic skills necessary in contemporary society.
(d) The religious and moral development of the child.
(e) Physical health, intellectual development, emotional and moral health, aesthetic awareness, a valid perspective, practical and social skills, and personal fulfilment.
(f) Values and attitudes must be mediated to the children. The school is not merely a teaching shop but a living community in which pupils learn primarily to live as children and not as future adults.

The work of Piaget was emphasized as a sound developmental approach to children's learning, and the importance of children's 'cultural' play was made clear. The report went on to consider certain particular aspects of the curriculum, and throughout there was an enlightened approach to both content and method, and a balanced attitude towards heuristic principles.

The council has no doubt that 'children's questions about sex ought to be answered plainly and truthfully whenever they are asked'. It gave validity to the modern, both relaxed and friendly, approach within the primary schools as a much better preparation for life in contemporary society than the old authoritative one.

Whilst accepting "discipline", the council were clear that this connoted neither heavy punishment nor soft and flabby relationships; discipline, it felt, was impaired by such elements as disorder, untidiness and slackness. It could flourish only in an ethos of order and purposefulness, in which boredom had been eliminated. There must be, in all this, a healthy combination of individual, group, and class work and learning. Due consideration was also given to the education of both handicapped and gifted children. The role of the teacher was discussed, and it was argued that teachers must enlarge their endeavours and enlist to a greater extent parents' interest in their children's education. It was extremely important to diagnose the child's needs and potentialities and there would be increasing demands on the knowledge of the teacher, whether literary, scientific or mathematical.

Teachers said the Report 'cannot escape the knowledge that children will catch values and attitudes far more from what teachers do than what they say. Unless they are courteous, they cannot expect courtesy from children: when teachers are eager to learn and turn readily to observation and to books, their pupils are likely to do the same'. The report, in effect, asked not only for more teachers but also for better quality ones, It went on to discuss teachers' aides, or trained ancillaries, who might give substantial help to teachers inside and outside the classroom, and who would have equal status with nursery assistants and have comparable training.

The council considered that colleges of education, in general, were too remote from the problems of the school; it recommended a full inquiry into the system of training of teachers, and suggested that there should be more joint appointments to college and school staffs. Further, a network of residential teachers' courses should be developed.

(i) The Department of Education and Science should consider taking steps which would require all independent schools to state on their prospectuses whether the schools were recognized or registered and what this implies. The Department of Education and Science should reconsider the terms "recognized" and "registered" and try to devise more informative ones.

(ii) The Secretary of State's powers to serve Notices of Complaint on independent schools should be based on more stringent criteria. The construction of "objectionable" should be widened to include any conditions, physical or educational, in which children's welfare was not thought to be adequately safeguarded.

(iii) All head teachers of independent schools should be qualified teachers. After a data to be specified, only qualified teachers should be appointed as heads in new schools, or when there is a change of head teacher.

(iv) In-service courses should wherever possible allow some places for teachers from independent schools. The independent schools themselves should take through their professional organizations to "increase the facilities for inservice training for teachers in independent schools."

The primary schools were giving good value for the inadequate amount of money spent on them, and went on to state that teachers were too few in number and too unevenly distributed to do the job adequately.

The first priority was the establishment of education priority areas; the recruitment of teachers' aides would be an essential and immediate source of help to the schools everywhere, the essential improvement of bad primary school buildings must be undertaken as soon as possible wherever they existed; and nursery education must be extended through increased accommodation and staff. Planning should begin on changes in the national dates of entry, and also on the ages of transfer between the different stages of primary education.

The Plowden Report represents one of the most thorough investigations into any area of education ever produced. Perhaps not least of its achievements was its virtual unanimity, which is reflection on the goodwill and singleness of purpose of its twentyfive members over a period of three years of intensive work and study. Out of every 100 women who enter our colleges of education, only 47 will be in the schools after three years of teaching; and after six years of service only 30 will remain. Perhaps the most sanguine way to look at the figures is simply to argue that 70 women out of every 100 so trained have, at least, qualified in a profession to which they may later return, but in any case they have found one way of obtaining higher education, with often minimum of entry qualifications; and as mothers, in the majority of cases, they will have a better understanding of educational problems.

The Fundamentals

The problems that arose for those charged with managing the curriculum at the school level can be analysed in three discrete categories: curriculum time allocation, teacher expertise, and resources in primary schools. The first reason for unmanageability is the apparently simple matter of time allocation.How much time is needed for each subject and for the whole curriculum. The problem has been commonly represented as the result of the statutory orders and the pint pot of the teaching week. If you are sitting on a national committee inventing or revising the statutory curriculum, it must appear merely a mechanical matter. Reduce the content until the whole curriculum matches, or is slightly less than, the time available.

The second reason concerns the task demands on class teachers attempting to deliver the whole curriculum-most obviously the range and level of subject knowledge required, the pedagogical skills necessary, including differentiation, the sheer detail and number of Statements of Attainment, and techniques necessary for reliable assessment. These have now been seen as unrealistic demands to make upon normal classroom teachers by all save the dismal succession of Ministers of State parading before us to assert that primary teaching, especially at Key Stage 1, is not a particularly demanding job, needing for its successful performance neither graduate knowledge nor long training.

The third reason concerns resources. Primary schools are staffed less favourably than secondary schools, even when the comparison is based on only Key Stage 3, yet the range and demand of their educational activities, and therefore their staffing needs, are almost identical. When Kelly ran a computer model of Stockport's curriculum led staffing, she found that it led to staffing needs that were more-or-less identical across the five to sixteen age range.

The first difficulty faced by teachers was simple; there was too much curriculum for the time available. One reason commonly given for this was that the statutory curriculum had been invented by means of committees of subject enthusiasts who were unable to consider how their subject had to fit into the whole curriculum.

There was some truth in at least the first two of these sentences, but the extent of policy error was substantially greater than Graham and Tytler allow. First, at an early stage Ministers had worked on a broad view that the Education Reform Act would create a curricular framework in which the national prescription should cover substantially less than the whole curriculum. This was because Religious Education and other important curricular areas such as health education and moral development were conceived of as lying beyond national prescription. The consultative document suggested that in schools where there was 'good practice' the National Curriculum subjects would occupy 70-80 per cent of curriculum time.

Three implications arose for curriculum management from the notional time allocations in this table. The most important is that they represented an error that was to have disastrous effects as the curriculum was implemented. The notional time for English and Mathematics combined, was dramatically lower than was conventionally provided by primary teachers, according to every study that had examined time allocations in the post-war period.

A summary covering much of the relevant research in the last fifteen years showed that 50 per cent of time was typically given to English and Mathematics, excluding their application to other subjects. Empirically, the phenomenon of 50 per cent of time on these two subjects-what we might call the 'basic instinct' in the primary curriculum-is firmly established. Indeed, a study by Meyer et al., which is an examination of official elementary and primary curricula world-wide across this century until the late 1980s, argues that the phenomenon has been a global constant-irrespective of region, political economy or state of development.

The second point refers to the time available for the whole curriculum. It relates to 'evaporated time', a term coined in a professional development programme and used by Campbell and Neill to indicate time technically available for teaching but used for non-cognitive purposes such as supervising children changing for PE, moving them from one location in the school to another, lining up and clearing away.

It is important because it is assumed to be available for teaching, but the studies referred to above that took account of this time by excluding it from teaching time, showed that something between 22 per cent of teaching time evaporates in this way, the amount depending upon the age of the pupils and the physical layout and size of the school and the methodology of time analysis. In general, younger pupils and those in open-plan settings experience more evaporated time. It occurs in small units of time in any one day, but in Campbell and Neill's research, based on time logs of over 3000 days from over 300 primary teachers, the average evaporated time per week was calculated at nearly two hours per week, equivalent to nearly 10 per cent of the teaching time available and equal to the notional time allocated for at least one of the non-basic subjects, in the National Curriculum.

Long hours spent on repetitive computation exercises do not necessarily mean challenging learning for bright pupils any more than do long hours spent by low-attaining pupils on tasks too difficult for them. Nonetheless, the conclusion from the research findings on time showed no general problem in primary classrooms about the adequacy of time being spent on teaching and learning the two basic subjects. Evidence after the introduction of the National Curriculum suggested that little had changed, with Campbell and Neill showing 51 per cent and 49 per cent of time devoted to the basics. The reasons for this state of affairs are three well-known ones.

First, as Ashton's research showed, drawing on a national sample of 1500 primary teachers in the early 1970s, the highest curricular priority was given to the basic skills of Reading, Oracy, Mathematics and Writing. Art. PE, Music, Sex Education, Science and Technology and a second language were given low priority. A follow-up study by Ashton with a less representative sample at the end of the 1970s, showed, if anything, higher priority placed on Mathematics and formal language competence. Thus, commitment to the basics has always been at a premium in the professional culture. Second, parents and governors place highest curricular priority on the basics also, as Thomas's investigation of London schools showed, and the Government has required greater teacher accountability to parents and governors. Third, there has been a long tradition, stretching way back before 1988, of formal testing focused on Reading Comprehension and Mathematics, a tradition reinforced by National Curriculum assessment arrangements, though it is now slightly broadened by the inclusion of Science in the core. Such testing washes back into curriculum priorities.

The basic instinct is sustained and reinforced by the workplace culture in primary schools. Thus, it becomes startlingly clear that the National Curriculum in primary schools, introduced by a series of Secretaries of State who had constantly banged on about the need to get back to basics and to raise standards of literacy and numeracy, put in place policy guidance designed to reduce the time typically spent by primary teachers on the basics, and especially on English, where the astonishing reduction of about one-third of existing time was proposed.

With respect to time allocations, the policy guidance outstripped the practice in the schools for liberality and breadth. It offered a fundamentally different concept and ideology of curriculum balance. The guidance given to the working group devising the English curriculum was such as to encourage infant teachers to reduce the time they typically spent teaching children to read and write from about seven hours to little over four hours a week. No wonder there was widespread stress at Key Stage 1 with infant teachers accurately reporting that, against their own professional judgment, they were having to reduce the time on hearing children read in order to fit in everything else. As if to confirm this interpretation of the general policy, the National Curriculum Council issued guidance on planning the Key Stage 2 curriculum in which three presumably recommended case studies of school planning were provided: two of them (year 6 and 5 classes) suggested that the basics should be planned to occupy 41 per cent and 37.5 per cent of curriculum time respectively.

The Year 5 class plan was developed into a yearly programme in which Mathematics and English occupy 316 out of the 846 hours available, some 37 per cent of curriculum time in their terms. Schools are urged by the NCC to review the exercise, including reviewing whether the time allocations are appropriate. In this context, it is interesting, but confusing, to see that in the summer Update from the NCC, the curriculum planning in a Coventry primary school was celebrated; it initially used a plan which involved only 40 per cent of time on basics, but after training, it changed to 50 per cent.

There was thus built into the curriculum at national level a four-pronged problem for every primary school: too much planned prescription overall; too much content in the statutory orders for each subject: not enough flexibility to allow for evaporated time; a pretence or assumption that there would be more time available for the non-basics than there was in actuality. The task demands placed on class teachers by the National Curriculum have been analysed by Thomas, who shows that in the slimmed down curriculum, teachers at Key Stage 2 had to be familiar with about 500 statements of attainment, detailed and confusingly presented programmes of study, poorly defined cross-curricular themes and religious education.

In addition they would have to possess subjects knowledge in the ten subjects up to about Level 6, or to be able to differentiate the planning, teaching and assessment across at least 4 levels or the curriculum in each subject. To achieve all this they would need to be the curricular school equivalent of Albert Einstein. Marie Curie and Lanford Christie rolled into one. The evidence about subject expertise sometimes takes a narrow view of the concept.

Serious Deficiencies

There are serious deficiencies in individual primary teachers understandings, especially but not exclusively in the science and technology areas. Graduate students training for primary teaching provide no greater reasons for being sanguine, if those studied by Bennett and Carre are typical. They brought with them to their PGCE courses rnisunderstandings of everyday phenomena, such as the energy in a sledge moving down a hill, the explanations for night and day, and basic arithmetic competencies such as expressing $18 as a percentage of $120. Bennett and Carre's research used tests in Mathematics, English and Science based on National Curriculum levels 4, 5 and 6, and Assessment of Performance Unit (APU) tests. In some of these latter, the top 20 per cent of primary pupils scored higher than the average of the PGCE students.

Technically, of course, the curriculum demands are placed on the whole school rather than the individual teacher, but in practice for the medium term further, most teachers will remain responsible for teaching most of the curriculum for the pupils in their class. Given the research findings, Alexander, Rose and Woodhead's assertion that 'Teachers must possess the subject knowledge which the statutory orders require' sounds like a plea of desperation.

A major management issue therefore becomes how the specialist expertise in the whole staff group can be deployed to extend the work of class teachers, with the overarching purpose that, as Richards argued, such deployment should 'support not undermine' the class teacher's role. The previous two problems for manageability apply to all schools irrespective of location, size or other factors. Resource issues affect schools differentially, depending upon funding formulae, school size or pupil characteristics. There is however one key resource issue—the level of surfing. The disadvantage for primary schools of historic staffing allocations has been acknowledged for almost a decade, although the difficulty of translating the acknowledgment into staffing resources has been enormous, particularly since the acknowledgment occurred in a period of public expenditure restraint.

If primary schools are to develop more specialist approaches to the curriculum, if class size should rarely exceed 30, and if teachers are to have some time free of class teaching in the school day; if, in short, the schools are to be enabled to implement the National Curriculum without stress and overload remaining a chronic feature of teachers' work, some improvement in the resourcing of schools is required. Acknowledgment is no longer enough. The funding formula at local level and the approval of schemes of devolved management at national level will need to be based on realistic assessment of the work activities now required of teachers in modern primary schools. Without the development of such national or local policies there will remain constraints on the extent to which the curriculum reform policy can succeed.

For the management of primary schools, the Dearing review's interim report appeared to hold out seductive promises to make the curriculum manageable by slimming it down. In terms of the analysis provided so far, however, it was limited to the issue of time allocations, and the evaluation of Dearing start form this recognition; the review had nothing to say about subject expertise or resourcing perhaps more fundamental problems than time allocation. Even the restricted problem-solving of the final report is a sleight of hand in respect of the 'curricular arithmetic' of time allocations, according to Alexander and Campbell.

Dearing's approach was to allocate 20 per cent of curriculum time for discretionary use by the school and to free two weeks of the school from any curricular prescription, and then to offer guidance on time allocation for the remaining time, viz for 80 per cent of thirty-six weeks. In discussing his own arithmetic, Dearing acknowledged that it was difficult to apply it to primary schools: 'Specific time will have to be set aside for work in English, but the full 30 per cent (KS1) and 25 per cent (KS2) does not have to be found in addition to time given to other subjects.' Perhaps too defensively Dearing added, "This is not sleight of hand; it is a statement of fact based on the realities of teaching expressed by teachers'. His own arithmetic was presented in a table in para, 4.20. With the bracketed figures referring to cross-curricular application, and therefore not counted in the total. Added percentages based on the total annual hours of 612 and 675 for which national prescription was envisaged, and these percentages appeared to reflect the historic practices of teachers, at least at KS1, with about 50 per cent given over to the basics.

There was however an assumed reduction in the proportion given to English at KS2. Alexander and Campbell however provide an alternative arithmetic, based on the overall time, not just the 80 per cent. Their arithmetic is given. Expressed this way, Dearing appears to have rendered almost a quarter of the school curriculum year discretionary, and therefore to have solved the manageability problem. However, as Alexander and Campbell show, there are five reasons why this has not really happened. First, the percentages for English and Mathematics are dramatically lower then previous or current practice, and time will have to be taken from the allegedly discretionary time to restore the basic instinct of 50 per cent time on them. Second, there is no educational or research-based justification for Dearing's assertion that as primary children become older they need less time on English.

The DES Primary Staffing Survey found 27 per cent allocated to English in the junior stage, and while it is obvious that the nature of English at KS1 is different from that at KS2 it is not clear why it should take less time. Nor has it done so in practice. Third, time on science has been reduced from what was previously proposed as necessary and the 10-15 per cent of time that was actually needed for the science curriculum. Fourth, national testing remains focused on the core subjects, pressing in on school management to ensure that teachers give priority to them in time allocation.

Alexander and Campbell calculated that all discretionary time would have to go to the core. Fifth, the time remaining for the other subjects will be inadequate, especially for those that are time consuming, such as PE, Music, Art and Technology. Sixth, without good reason, excessive time has been set aside for RE. As a consequence, the only way the curriculum will become manageable is if it is recognized for what it is, underneath the Dearing rhetoric a return to the elementary curriculum of the basic and RE updated with some Science and Information Technology. But manageability will have been gained at the expense of breadth and balance.

Management implications of the argument is based on two assumptions about the relationship between a national quango and individual schools. National quangos are not good at details, and have little competence in respect of the curriculum organization of individual schools. For example, within the space of nine months the National Curriculum Council and the School Curriculum and Assessment Authority could not even agree on the simple technical matter of how many hours per year should be considered as available for instruction.

Second, as Thomas pointed out, the National Curriculum was established by reference to the best practice in each subject. To the Test' or even good at everything is not common in individual human beings or their institutions so that there was and is a certainty that virtually and schools would, to some degree, fail to meet the statutory requirements. He added that 'Schools in other countries commonly fail to meet the requirements of their national curricula'. If these two assumption are confirmed, the first lessons for school management are that it is in the individual school, not a national agency, that will create a curriculum that can be made to work for the school concerned; and that concern to cover the whole curriculum will have to be tempered by consideration of quality and standards in pupils learning. This latter goal might be more readily arrived at by the school establishing its curricular priorities than by attempting to deliver every statutory prescription equally well.

It was, after all, the quango charged with the inspection of schools that first made clear that coverage had been achieved only at the cost of depth in pupil learning. To restore confidence in their own professional judgment, it may first be necessary for teachers to lose faith in the ability of the national agencies to manage the curriculum implementation process sensibly. Dependency on external forces is as counter productive for the whole school staff as it is for the head and is likely to reduce rather than increase empowerment and accountability. On this basis six possible ways forward may be identified, though each will be contested by some teachers because of the value assumptions it contains.

First, in respect of time allocation, there is the possibility that much more of the teaching of English and Mathematics than currently might be planned, delivered and assessed through their application to other subjects. This is a position advocated for at least fifteen years by HMI, but has been found problematic in practice.

The problem is not helped by the framing of the curriculum in single subjects, nor by the tendency for mathematics and English schemes to be subject-specific. It is a good example of how a staff would have to have confidence as HMI had, that standards in the basics would improve by their being applied to other subjects. Unfortunately, it may be easier for staff in schools where pupils already have high achievement to develop such confidence than for staff where pupils appear to need substantial amounts of time on basic skills. Second, schools might consider the use of homework as part of their overall policy, especially perhaps at KS2. If there is shortage of time for English, part of the solution might be to cease to consider the pupils' curriculum time as synonymous with the timetabled school day.

Successful experience at KS1 with parental partnerships provides exemplars for developing similar approaches at KS2. Some opposition might be raised by those who would see such a systematic approach to homework as increasing the disadvantages of pupils who live in unsupportive families or physical conditions unconducive to doing homework. School based provision for facilities for doing homework, while a contradiction in terms, might go some way to mitigating the difficulties, though at a cost in staff supervision time.

A third solution to the problem of curriculum time might be to extend the school day, week or year. This is clearly sensible for those schools who currently spend less than the minimum expected weekly hours on instruction. It will be opposed on grounds of workload and of inappropriateness in rural areas where pupils have to travel long distances. It might also be surmised that while the current assessment and testing policy remains in place, any extra time would be devoted to the core and thus not release time for the non-core, which is the problem. A solution to teachers' lack of confidence and competence in subject expertise could be remedied by a greatly expanded In-service training programme along lines similar to the DES twenty-day courses. This is obviously true, assuming that the courses are effective, and that their effects are long-lived, an assumption that Bennett and Summer's review of research questions in part. However, the problem for primary schools is that extensions of In-service training programmes are also extensions of the times when teachers have to be away from school and their class, so that a substantial programme of In-service Training in the school day may have disadvantages for pupil learning where schools do not have access to good quality supply cover.

A second possibility lies in suggestions that schools should deploy their staff in ways that enable their subject expertise to be exploited more effectively to the benefit of the school as a whole, whether as specialists, semi-specialists or as coordinators. Again, within limits, this might offer gains to some schools, especially those with staffing allocations that permit some flexibility of deployment. For most schools, however there is almost no flexibility, and, as school size reduces, the range of subjects in which there is staff expertise also reduces.

A third possibility is that more use should be made of class texts in which the teachers can have confidence that the intellectual content is reliable, freeing them to concentrate more upon planning for how pupils may learn more effectively from the texts. There may be some reluctance in the profession to the purchase of texts for whole classes, since it is seen as at odds with concepts of good practice which stress learning from first hand experience, building on pupils' interests, and practical investigation. While recognizing that purchasing class texts will not solve all problems, perhaps influenced by past images of whole classes sitting reading class textbooks at the same pace, each pupil being asked to read aloud with the rest of the class following. The way texts are used with primary classes is obviously an important matter, but the adoption of good quality class texts would be the quickest way of helping class teachers cope with both the cognitive demands of the whole curriculum and the time demands of preparing all learning materials for their pupils.

Professional Culture

There is something puritanical in a professional culture which implies that the virtuous teacher is the one who prepares every worksheet herself. One of the few ways that a national quango could make itself useful to teachers would be to issue 'kitemarks' to texts to indicate that the statutory orders were accurately and adequately covered by them and that there were useful assessment activities integrated into them. This is, politically speaking, quite different from requiring that schools use one particular prescribed text.

Little use can be added about the formulate by which, external, resources are allocated to schools, beyond what has been argued earlier. On the internal allocation of the resources when allocated, one further point needs to be raised. In most primary schools lack of time, especially lack of time in the school day, has been a major obstacle to effective delivery of the curriculum. Yet Campbell and Neill showed that teachers spent about eighteen hours a week teaching, and between five and six hours a week on low level routines, such as mounting displays, supervision, moving pupils round the school, registration, and collecting dinner money, etc. Where teacher had more time with a non-teaching assistant, they tended to spend more, not less time on such routines, probably because of the 'collaborative cultures' operating in them.

Yet there is something unsettling about the picture of teachers naming lack of time as the main obstacle to achieving the cognitive objectives of the curriculum while spending so much time on non-cognitive routines. Given that teacher time is the most valuable and most expensive resource available to a school, it is worth the management of the school exploring the advantages of re-thinking the use of time of all adults on the staff of the school, to see whether the non-teaching assistants' time might be used imaginatively to free up teachers' time. Professional groups validate their professional claim by reference to 'expert' knowledge, supposedly hard-won and rigorously tested, but few people are naive enough to believe that in a job as complex as teaching such formal training provides the sole resource for subsequent professional thought and action.

Experience plays a substantial part. 'On the job', teachers develop skills and insights through constant interaction with children; they come to recognise patterns, commonalities and recurrences in behaviours, situations and problems and thereby develop habits of diagnosis and response whose practical effectiveness they can confidently demonstrate. Similarly, to an extent perhaps not sufficiently recognised, teachers draw on their pre-training experience; for, uniquely among professionals, they are engaged in a process with which they have already been involved, continuously and unremittingly, since the age of five or earlier. Their teacher training course is but a brief part of this total, cumulative educational experience and the latter, as much as the specifics of the one to four year training course, shapes the view of the educational process and its purposes within which they operate as teachers. It is a commonplace that many young teachers teach as they were taught in school rather than as they were urged to teach in college. Significantly too, teachers themselves display ambivalent attitudes towards initial training.

In the context of debate and negotiation about salary and status the teacher is a 'trained professional' in possession of expertise denied to all but those who submit themselves to the rigours of Certificate, BEd, or PGCE. But in everyday discourse, good teachers are 'born, not made' and that same expert knowledge may be dismissed as 'irrelevant' theory.

The truth is that it is empirically impossible to isolate initial training from earlier, contemporaneous or subsequent experience for the purposes of demonstrating its precise impact on the way a teacher performs in the classroom. It seems sensible to assume that it does have an impact, but to avoid the extremes of the grandiose strategic claim prepared for negotiation with Burnham on the one hand, and the dismissiveness of teacher folklore and Staffroom conventional wisdom on the other.

Instead, two hypotheses can be supported. One is that by incorporating in its emphasis on certain sorts of knowledge and skill particular views of the teaching role, the nature and needs of young children, the initial training course tends to facilitate some lines of subsequent professional development and to discourage others. Second, initial training influences subsequent development as much by what it omits or does badly as by what it treats positively; or, to use for the sake of convenience some mild jargaon, a course may 'de-skill' as well as 'skill'. This latter point is particularly opposite in the present context, given that we have seen how primary ideology may relate to professional insecurity. The ideology, it will be recalled, is most strongly focused and most forcibly expressed in relation to those aspects of primary teaching where empirical study shows the greatest weakness.

Therefore it is not firm evidence of behavioural casuality—element X in initial training produces action Y in the classroom—so much as a succession of positive and negative correspondences between training and subsequent practice which are sufficiently pervasive and exact as to leave little doubt about a causal relationship of some sort, albeit diluted by the power of experience, circumstance and contingency, and mediated through each individual's unique combination of personality, intellect and worldview. To provide a framework for the analysis which follows it is necessary at this point to give a brief resume of the overall structures and contexts of courses. There are two main routes into primary teaching, the four year BEd and the one year PGCE. The former is a post 'A' level undergraduate course and the latter, self-evidently, is taken by graduates in subjects which could equally well lead to other careers.

Deferred student choice and flexibility were major aspirations; this was the era of the 'container revolution', of courses which students put together from a wide selection of units and modules, and which often meant that professional study and work in schools were deferred until the second or even the third of four years. By the late 1970s, deferred choice, consecutive training and modularity were running into the logistical problems attendant upon contraction, for such courses had to be large to be viable. There were other criticisms chiefly revolving round the continued lack of sufficient professional emphasis, the perceived divorce of theory and practice and the split between subject and professional study.

A large number of institutions had transferred from university to CNAA validation and alternative notions of 'degree worthiness' had begun to be explored. Mark III BEds lasted the full four years, were usually honours only, and included serious attempts to put professional concerns at the centre of the course and at last to break down the barrier between subject and professional study. But by that time, during the early 1980s, there were countervailing pressures.

The Syllabus

Successive HMI surveys, of primary and secondary schools had identified what were regarded as major weaknesses in serving teachers' professional expertise, above all in their curriculum knowledge. First HMI, then central government then ACSET, the teacher education advisory body-less from conviction than recognition of the irresistibility of political dogma backed by landslide election success-and finally the DES again proposed that all BEd students, whether primary or secondary, should spend half their course on main subject study in order to remedy these curricular deficiencies.

The inadequacy of the models of primary curriculum, primary teaching and initial training thereby encapsulated will be discussed. Courses are not disembodied artifacts but events and ideas which acquire their reality from particular institutional contexts. The majority of today's established primary teachers not only trained by the 2-3-4 year route but did so in a distinctive sort of institution, the college of education, which preserved a culture of remarkable homogeneity and historical persistence until the institutional reorganisations of the 1970s forced many of the surviving colleges into a usually reluctant alliance with mainstream higher education institutions.

While the PGCE was located mainly in the universities and until the rude advent of compulsory initial training, comprehensive schools and mixed ability teaching-prepared its students for grammar and public schools, the 3-4 year course reflected the requirements of a less prestigious tradition, that of secondary modern and primary schools. Thus, the two routes embodied and reinforced the mutual exclusiveness of the two central traditions in British education: minority/elitist/academic, and mass/ elementary/utilitarian. Like primary schools, the colleges' origins were humble and impoverished. Like primary schools, they acquired a substantial contrary ideology-idealist, romantic, espousing values of self-actualization, individualism and student/ child. By the 1950s and 1960s, the professionally formative years for the deputy heads, heads and advisers of the 1970s and 1980s, the college ethos was predominantly one, in Taylor's often-quoted words, of 'social and literary romanticism'.

Partial rejection of pluralism: suspicion of the intellect and the intellectual; a lack of interest in political and structural change; a stress upon the intuitive and the intangible, upon spontaneity and creativity... a hunger for the satisfactions of interpersonal life within the community and the small group, and a flight from rationality. The extent to which this incorporates caricature is debatable, but when one considers the institutions into which most of the products of these colleges went-primary schools-the correspondence is irresistible.

Specific manifestations and echoes of these values will continue to emerge from our discussions. We turn now, however, from general background to the first of several specific aspects of initial training; the means whereby it seeks to generate that 'understanding of children' required for primary class teaching and pre-eminent in the class teacher's professional claim.

In most post-war teacher education courses the intending teacher's capacity to understand and relate to children has been seen as the virtually exclusive concern of two elements:

(a) academic-courses in what until the 1960s were termed 'principles of education', subsequently the separate 'disciplines' of psychology and sociology of education, but more recently somewhat disguised within integrated, thematic education /professional courses;

(b) experiential-teaching practice and other school based activity.

Little or no overlap of function is envisaged or, in terms of academic territoriality, allowed. There is assumed to be an exact correspondence between professional attribute and course component so that each becomes the 'property' of a particular department or group of staff. Thus 'understanding of children' is the concern not of anyone with insights to offer but of just two academic disciplines, psychology and sociology.

Psychology is relatively well-established in initial teacher education. The McNair Report's 'principles of education' included; physiology and physical education, psychology, 'great classical writers on education', history of the education system, and appreciation of the 'home circumstances of the pupils'. This approach lasted well into the 1960s: Taylor, Tabble, Browne and others record the dominance of the 'mother hen'-the education tutor dispensing a mixture of 'method', history of educational ideas and, above all, psychology. The 1960s witnessed the coming of age of the 'four disciplines' of education, but this strengthened the position in primary training, where the 'child development' course continued to rule supreme. Despite this relatively long-established pre-eminence in teacher education, it must be recalled that as an academic discipline psychology is young, and sociology younger.

Descriptions and Explanations

Through a combination of empirical research and theory generation they seek to offer descriptions and explanations of individual and collective human behaviour which must be regarded as tentative, provisional and incomplete. Theories and models are frequently put forward, or at least received by students, as unassailable truths about the real world, their status as such apparently confirmed by the strong positivistic orientation of a good deal of the research drawn upon and by the convenient tendency of such work to offer quantified findings. Wilson showed how the very examination questions BEd and PGCE students were required to answer presumed their tacit acceptance of a wide range of concepts and constructs. That claim is readily substantiated.

Equally unsatisfactory, none of the questions invites application to the task of the teacher. Assuming the intending teachers duly demonstrate that they have committed the various theories, facts and arguments to memory,what then? What are they supposed to do with this knowledge? If it is seriously intended that it should inform their thinking about the job of teaching, why is no opportunity given for this capacity to be demonstrated? Or is it more important that they have knowledge than that they can use it? Taking their lead from this style of questioning, essays are peppered with the catch-phrase 'Research has proved that ....' without apparent regard for the need for all proof claims to be probed, for the provisionality of scientific findings. The connection with everyday professional practice is evident.

The same formulae re-emerge in much of the published work exemplified in, and in the written and spoken utterances of some serving teachers. Here, however, their linguistic hardness may be duly softened to match the gentler, familial ambience of child-centred discourse, and with the 'authority' now accorded a hushed, parent-surrogate,almost Messianic reverence: 'Piaget has shown us that...'. In both contexts such unconditional deference, by negating the element of natural scepticism combined with informed critique vital to academic study and the proper use of academic research, effectively invalidates the latter's claim: for it is no longer knowledge-open, provisional, challengeable dogma.

Conversely, the students are exhorted not to trust 'mere opinions', to have a higher regard for academic than common sense modes of analysis and explanation, and to prefer the 'objective' data of the social sciences to their or an experienced teacher's subjective' judgement. Understanding oneselves and others has probably always been a human preoccupation. Certainly from the time when the first written record was produced we have shown a deep interest in human and animal behaviour. Yet our ideas have been almost entirely unsystematic and unrepresentative.

Even now we casually watch others or listen with prejudiced ears to conversation and from this evidence build up distorted rules of thumb about human nature. It is of course highly probable that our 'interest in human and animal behaviour' predates written records, but that is to quibble. More problematic, it seems to me, is the implied dismissal of all but the psychologist's way of doing things as `unsystematic', 'unrepresentative', 'casual', 'prejudiced', and 'distorted': clearly not the author's intention, but open to that interpretation by someone new to the discipline.

Thus, may be generated or reinforced a basic epistemology to which the polarising of 'objective' and 'subjective', of `fact' and 'value', of 'truth' and 'falsity', of 'knowledge' and 'belief', are fundamental. If internalised, this simplistic conceptual map is able and likely to provide signposts for a wide range of contexts: the teacher's subsequent response to educational research and theory most obviously, but also other situations in which knowledge claims are significant-record cards and diagnostic or attainment tests for example, and the wide and crucial range of claims which teachers make about children, their abilities, their potential, their home background, and so on. The other context where this epistemology bears fruit in a palpable way is the primary curriculum. Its most public and assertive face is the view of curriculum in general and knowledge in particular which we explored-for example the way a view of knowledge as brute 'fact' can be used as a justification for rejecting knowledge in any guise.

Less obviously, but perhaps in the end more significant, the framework may influence the way in which different curriculum experiences are presented for the child, and the view of knowledge the child thereby acquires: art at the 'soft',, 'subjective', 'value' and the continuum science at the 'hard', 'objective', 'fact' end. Moreover, by according experientially derived insight lower status an initial training course misses an obvious and significant opportunity. Given that it is at the commonsense, intuitive level that the student/teacher is frequently forced to operate once under the pressure of everyday classroom circumstances, it is precisely these sort of judgements which should be exposed and explored during initial training, with a view to refining them and making them as reliable and reflexive as possible.

The psychologist's rejection of such perspectives is the more emphatic for being made on methodological grounds: personal knowledge is counted not so much less significant as inadmissible. Psychology has sought to replace commonsense theories about mental processes with propositions derived from the application to human nature of the methods of the natural sciences. Pre-eminent in this methodology is the charting of observable behaviours.

The 'introspective' method which seeks to uncover individuals' private knowledge, beliefs, attitudes, and so on by eliciting these by word of mouth, is considered by the behaviourist majority to be inconsistent with the scientific claim. Thus, because by the canons of a particular methodology such date is deemed inaccessible, as the object of study it ceases to be of interest. This raises broader issues concerning the historical development of psychology-its origins in the philosophy of mind, the late 19th century rejection of mind in favour of 'scientific' study of the brain and the central nervous system, the consequent issue of the distinctiveness of psychology vis-a-vis neurology and physiology, and the continuity of the behaviourist/ introspectionist debates.

Such issues are beyond the scope of this book, but what is important for teachers and teacher educators is an awareness of the consequences for the way their task is defined in initial training. For teachers are not neuro-surgeons: their main focus of concern is that elusive entity, which causes psychologists such difficulty, the human mind.

Alternative perspectives on children which would complement the portrayal of the behaviourist psychologist-from literature, drama, philosophy and pre-eminently, everyday discourse-are explicitly rejected. Apart from its tendency to impoverish the teacher's professional development and classroom thought, this monopoly reveals the extent to which the view of teaching as science has pervaded academic and professional opinion, even including groups-like literature teachers and tutors who might be expected to be more resistant. Perhaps, as academics so often do, they fail to make the connection between the claim that the arts offer unique and profound insights into the human condition and the obvious fact that teaching itself is nothing if not concerned with that condition. Three provisos must, however, be expressed, lest it be thought that this chapter's discussion stems basically from an anti-psychology standpoint. The first is that the teacher education community as a whole, rather than its psychologists alone, have to take responsibility for excluding alternative sources of insight into children in general and into their mental processes in particular. There has been large-scale connivance at this needless impoverishment of the training process. Second, arguing for courses as a whole to include addition perspectives not for psychologists to do what artists do.

The third proviso is that the psychology component of teacher education courses, particularly until, in the mid 1970s, it began to be taught by graduates with a broad psychological training, may have been singularly unrepresentative of the parent discipline. It might, for example, over-emphasise Skinnerian behaviourism or developmental psychology; it might neglect study of the unconscious mind or of the social dimension of behaviour. It might fail to develop in students a proper consciousness of the extent to which a psychological model is a metaphor for behaviour, not the behaviour itself nor ever necessarily a particularly accurate representation of it.

Above all it might fail to convey the necessary sense of psychology, as of every discipline, as variegated, contentious and changing. The extent to which psychology of education courses directly reinforce the 'sequential developmentalism' element in primary ideology, which-drawing on King and others-provides a good example of several of the points above, particularly those concerning distortion in content and methodological oversimplification.

The central theme or core of such courses has traditionally been a chronological treatment of child development. Here 'development' is conceived as a matrix with norms for ages and stages providing one axis and various categories of human development-'intellectual', 'social', 'emotional', 'moral', 'physical' etc. This developmental matrix, open to fundamental criticism as it is provides a basic, widely accepted structure for primary discourse, curriculum planning and pupil assessment: the firmly fixed reference points on an otherwise shifting and undifferentiated map.

The ages attached to stages postulated by Piaget are approximate, and that the inevitability of the sequence and the state-independent processes and mechanisms of cognitive development-equilibration, assimilation, accommodation-are more significant than any inferred chronology. Yet it is notable that in student essays, as in professional discourse and teachers books and curriculum materials,the stages as such feature more prominently than the stage-independent theory, despite the fact that an understanding of the latter is essential to using the undoubted insights of Piagetian theory to promote or accelerate learning. A Piagetian approach to HMI's concept of 'match', for example, would demand that children encounter learning tasks which are slightly, but not excessively, more complex than their present understanding, and that without this element of 'stretching' the disequilibration necessary for learning will not be produced. Where students or teachers perceived development in terms of states rather than processes they will tend to wait for learning to occur 'spontaneously' or 'naturally' rather than seek as teachers to advance it, on the grounds that the child has to be 'ready'.

Dominance of Developmentalism

Just as the dominance of developmentalism in everyday practice is matched by the dominance of the developmental 'matrix' in educational psychology courses, so the traditional fare of sociology of education courses corresponds strongly with another element in professional discourse, the family and home as the prime or even sole causes of the child's difficulties or failures at school.

Until the early to mid-1970s sociology of education courses were dominated by the issue of the effect of family and social class factors on the child's attainment at school. Early studies of streaming pointed the way to the possibility that the school itself might be a contributory factor in the under-achievement of working-class children, but research on class-related socialisation practices, parental attitudes, language, and so on, tended to swamp such relatively slender evidence. Only with the 'new' sociology of education, with its two-pronged, ideologically committed concern to explore first the cultural loading of the school and its curriculum in favour of certain groups of pupils and, second, the nature of everyday classroom life, did alternatives to the family/home deficit model present themselves with much credibility.

A substantial literature concerning the effect of teacher expectations on pupil performance, teacher constructs and typifications, classroom interaction and teaching styles, now permits a more balanced appraisal of the relative impact of family and school, parents and teachers, on the child's educational career. Some of this work was referred. The shift, however, is recent, and everyday primary discourse, in as far as it is demarcated and to some extent controlled by senior members of the profession such as heads and advisers, still appears to display fairly unreserved affiliation to family/home theories; certainly the confident professional assertions about 'good' and 'poor' parents and homes are part of the essential fabric of both staff room discussion and pupil record cards. What will be worth monitoring is the extent to which the 'new' sociology of education produces a discernible shift in the way children's learning difficulties or lack of motivation are explained as students of the 1970s gain headships in the 1980s and 1990s and seek to influence their school's 'philosophies'. If, however, the family background theory is such an indispensable element in professional ideology-in that, for the weaker teacher in particular, it is fundamental to the preservation of his self-esteem, we can anticipate little movement overall.

Theories of child development and educability, it will be apparent, not only have ideological potential but need to be simplified, and perhaps even distorted, to achieve that potential. Thus, Piagetian theory may be interpreted as confirming a doctrine of 'readiness' rather than as challenging the teacher's ingenuity to provide the child with appropriately structured and sequenced learning experiences. Similarly, the complexity and tentativeness of, say, Bernstein's work on language and social structure may be ignored in preference for gross polarisations of 'restricted' and 'elaborated' codes which may confirm a student's or teacher's existing cultural stereotypes and prejudices. Both theories exemplified can be invoked to justify low expectations of children-on the 'grounds' of age, or of social class.

In fact, much of the theoretical material regarded as indispensable in initial training is intrinsically extremely elusive and difficult to understand, let alone to apply, and especially so for the 18-21 year old with neither professional experience of schools and children nor a background of introductory study in the social sciences. However, its misinterpretation could be reduced or offset if the typificatory process which it appears to reinforce were itself the object of scrutiny on initial training courses. But it is a characteristic of mainstream education courses in initial training that, more recent sociology and social psychology perspective apart, they tend to devote little attention to the teacher as such. This is particularly true of psychology of education courses: an examination of student texts end course syllabuses will reveal that most deal not so much with the psychology of education as with the psychology of the child, and that child's education is treated only in so far as it can be conceived independently of the person who is its chief architect, the teacher.

The child emerges with an identity shaped by a combination of heredity and environment, having characteristics which are given and immutable. There is little or no psychological analysis of adults in general, or teachers in particular; nor of the teacher's contribution to that classroom character of the child which serves as the basis for the teacher's appraisal of him or her. The child's actions are presented, if only by default, as independent of the teacher's; a conception of the child is encouraged which is somehow independent of the person, the teacher, who does the conceiving. These tendencies can be illustrated by comparing two recent psychology of education textbooks.

The model is not of the interaction of minds and personalities, still less of teaching as dependent on teacher qualities as well as child attributes, but of the operating theatre: the teacher, as complete person and competent professional, works on the child's mind with the detachment of the surgeon working on the anesthetized body of the patient. Skill is presumed; the sole knowledge required is of the mental anatomy of the child. Fontana's psychology for Teachers stresses in its introduction that 'no child's behaviour can be fully understood unless we study also the behaviour of others-teachers, parents, school friends-towards him', and, subsequently argues that within the context of the school the teacher is the most important influence upon the child. Despite this promising beginning, and the author's reservations elsewhere about traditional psychology of education courses, twelve of the sixteen chapters are devoted to the pupil, only three to interaction and teacher-child relations, and just one to 'teacher personality and characteristics'.

The latter is a brief summary of research on the behavioural characteristics of 'effective' teachers, contextualised in an acknowledgement of some of the problems involved in defining teacher effectiveness: about a page each on the teacher's emotional security, attitude,, styles and classroom talk-all crucial issues but far too briefly dealt with.

In the economic climate of recent years, publishers have been increasingly reluctant to take on other than obviously marketable basic texts and course readers in education. The original or unusual is squeezed out and the second- or third-hand comes to rule supreme. Primary education has suffered particularly from the flood of edited 'readers', many of them drawing repeatedly on the same rather limited pool of 'safe' articles. Thus, though one must not overstate the case, the public teachable, examinable face of the educational process is increasingly defined by a combination of academics' personal interests and market forces: the research which, fortuitously, happens to be feasible, interesting, fundable or available, and what publishers and entrepreneurial editors or authors see as likely to sell.

But that is to digress. 'Understanding children' is an attribute not of the object of that understanding but of the teacher who claims it. The teacher will perceive a child in a particular way not only because of the sort of person that child is but because of the sort of person the teacher is.

In the primary school, we remind ourselves, the classteacher system ensures that a child is so perceived for educational purposes for a whole year by just one person: with that much at stake it seems indefensible for initial training courses to neglect the psychology of the teacher. Four shifts are indicated therefore. First, the inclusion, as argued, of a substantial focus on teachers and their impact on those various aspects of the learner conventionally treated as independent of them.

Second, a deeper exploration of the ways individual behaviour-whether the child's or the teacher's, can be understood in the context of, and sometimes explained as a consequence of, interaction, possibly through the use of transactional analysis techniques applies in industrial psychology and psychotherapy, as well as interaction analysis schedules and theoretical perspectives of social psychology and interactionist/ phenomenological sociology. Third, a preparedness to explore the irrationality which frequently characterises human actions and interactions, not least in the classroom; the dominant psychological tradition in teacher education, as we have seen, takes the teacher's total rationality for granted and moreover imposes a sometimes over-tidy, predictive framework- on the child. Fourth, just as theoretical study of children in teacher education is required to be supported by work with children in classrooms, so teachers in classrooms and above all students themselves would need to be the object of practical study.

If self-exploration is now included in the training of other professional groups whose job involves the management of people and relationships, it can surely be justified in the training of teachers. The second major context a course provides for developing the student's understanding of children is school experience. Again, a historical perspective on this part of the course is helpful because its character and purposes have changed in recent years, though not as radically as some current advocates of 'school-based' courses would have us believe.

To make use of schools not merely as a context for practising executive skills but as a prime means for developing the student's capacities to observe, understand and relate to children is a sine qua non of teacher education. It has to be asked, however, whether the opportunities are fully exploited. This is only partly, as we have seen, a procedural matter; what needs closer attention is the teacher educators' and course validators' view of what this 'understanding' might mean.

At present, and certainly during the decade when today's primary teachers and heads trained, the interpretations, explanations and hypotheses of students and serving teachers have been under-valued and therefore insufficiently pursued and tested. And while a somewhat restricted canon of child related theories has been, in comparison, over-exposed, it has been the exposure of obeisance, rather than critique.

Some of the consequences, or correspondences, suggested by this restricted epistemology have been outlined in this chapter and exemplified more fully. There seem to be a number of ways the situation can be improved, of varying degrees of radicalism:

(a) the focus for 'understanding' can be broadened;
(b) better use can be made of existing education disciplines;
(c) additional (academic) sources of insight can be explored;
(d) 'everyday' modes of understanding can be more fully exploited;
(e) different conceptions of professional theory for teaching can be applied.

In an obvious sense, by definition, students are the main concern in a course of initial training: the qualities, skills and knowledge which they are deemed to need are the course's *raison d'etre.*

So while arguing that the course needs to focus more explicitly on the student and on the serving teacher, we are arguing for a specific kind of attention with which this self-evident concern is not to be confused. Courses are premised on the importance of teachers' mastery of certain executive skills, their manifestation of particular personal qualities and their possession of certain kinds of knowledge. Pre-eminent among the latter is that academic knowledge about children which we have explored in this chapter, and which they may or may not make significant use of in practice. What, by and large, are neglected are the many layers or facets beyond these generalised propositions which combine to create the particular ways individual students and teachers actually view, or 'understand', the children they teach in particular classroom settings: teachers' actual and tacit, as opposed to preferred or espoused or idealised, knowledge of children, and the biographies which produce this knowledge: their subjective realities, as opposed to the quasi-objective ideas or the educational situation with which they are presented in training.

Merely to offer to the student a set of propositions from psychological/ sociological theory or research-this is the way children are, this is what they are like, this is the reality to which your decisions must be addressed is to ignore, or at least to fail to acknowledge sufficiently, two basic arguments concerning children in classrooms in which much of this book's discussion has been grounded. First, regardless of generalised principles of child development, motivation, and so on, children are 'as they are' in classrooms, in part at least, because of the actions of the teacher; they respond, as in interaction all humans respond, to personality, to climate, to tacit or explicit signals, attitudes and expectations from a variety of sources, but chiefly, in the educational context, from the teacher.

Second, though individual children are viewed differently by each of those with whom they interact, and their self-concept indeed in part evolves from a consciousness of these various perceptions, in the educational context the teacher's view of them is the most significant. It is the teacher who defines their abilities, their potential, their personality, their attainment and their attitudes, for the purposes of making curricular decisions, evaluations and predictions, and, as we have seen, in a way which is consistent with their ideology. Such is the nature of the educational process, and the classroom power relationship, especially where young children are concerned, that the central assumption in child-centredness, of the child's autonomy, is not only fallacious but dangerously so.

It can never be the case that on the one hand we have the child, about whom there is pre-existing objective knowledge, and on the other the teacher, who simply has to acquire that knowledge. The teacher's knowledge of the child is subjective, it is created by the teacher, its character is therefore as strongly conditional on the way the teacher is as the way the child is. The theme for initial training, which should complement 'understanding children' is 'understanding how teachers "understand" children'. And if it is indeed students understanding that we wish to promote rather than their capacity merely to parrot the prepositions and formulae of others, the source as well as the character of such 'understanding', on the basis of which students and teachers act, needs to be explored; this necessitates attention to the unique individual biographies of each students as well as to the more generalised analysis of the professional, historical and ideological situation of the particular groups of teachers offered. The outcome of this process should be to sensitise the student to the possibility of a much wider range of diagnoses and explanations. The fact that introspective methods are unacceptable to some psychologists is worthy of debate in this context but is not a ground for rejecting the perspective defined. The course aims to train teachers, not professional psychologists, and if a perspective is helpful it should be included, methodological qualms notwithstanding. Thus, the scope of 'understanding children' in initial training needs to be broadened chiefly by taking in teachers' influence on both the children and their 'understanding' of them.

Equally important, and more easily enunciated, is the need to allow existing perspectives on children offered by psychology and sociology to be supplemented by alternatives from within those disciplines. Clearly, given our discussion of the complementary relationship between ideology, professional theory and practical situation, the introduction of less comfortable psychologies and sociologies might be resisted, but perhaps we can begin to accept that our comfort may well be secured at the expense of the quality of the child's education. This shift has already begun in the sociology of education: the sociology of knowledge and of classrooms has provided the needed counterbalance to the family/ home educability preoccupations of the 1950s and 1960s. We now need a 'new' psychology of education which more fairly represents the richness of mainstream psychology.

New Perspectives

The newer perspectives offers both alternative focuses and tools for analysis. Centre-stage are not only classroom processes and the interactions of teachers and children which feature in 'objective' study in the Flanders tradition, but also the meanings which the teachers and children themselves assign to those processes. The underlying assumption here is that human actions can be properly understood only if one uncovers these meanings, since 'action is forged by the actor out of what he perceives, interprets and judges... The "objective" approach holds the danger of the observer substituting his view of the field of action for the view held by the actor.

In studying classrooms it becomes important to understand pupils' as well as teachers' definitions of the situation, and the extent to which the latter are not autonomous but are influenced by the former; at the same time the power differential in classrooms makes the impact of teachers' meanings on children and classroom life considerable. This perspective prominently informs the classic and comprehensive exploration of school interaction by Hargreaves and specific studies of primary classrooms like that of Berlak et al. The study of infants' classrooms by King, to which I have made frequent reference, is eclectic: it is critical of phenomenological, interactionist and Marxist perspectives yet is also influenced by them. It belongs to the 'family' in so far as it is grounded in close and sustained observation which is interpreted by reference to actors' perceptions and explanations rather than observer preconceptions.

At the same time it places these in broader frameworks of ideology and social structure. These developments are recent: empirical study of primary classrooms, of whatever methodological complexion, is still relatively thin. Nevertheless, in terms of what by this book's analysis seems to be needed—far greater attention to how teachers 'understood' children and teaching -the growth points are now significant, diverse and rich.

The last point notwithstanding, we also need to ask whether the monopoly by psychology and sociology of insights into children and classrooms is to be desired or supported. The other two disciplines in the educational studies pantheon are philosophy and history. Philosophy of education-whether so defined or used thematically in an integrated course tends to concern itself with broad non-contextualised questions about aims, the nature of knowledge, the justification for particular educational concepts and activities, the ethics of reward and punishment.

Frequently it is conceived as a tool of encouraging a sharper, more reflexive and considered mode of analysis than the easy, instant judgement, as a basis for critique of teachers' and students' 'commonsense' statements. This is undoubtedly necessary, but it is also the case that by such means, intentionally or unwittingly, is the status of academic thought preserved, for philosophical analysis ought equally to be applied to the statements, judgement and explanations offered by psychology and sociology of education: conceptual analysis should have no boundaries.

Especially, a concern with epistemology ought not to start and finish with the school curriculum, but should encompass the knowledge and truth claims of the teacher training curriculum as well, the ways of making sense of and understanding children, teaching and learning which the initial training course expects the student to internalise and subsequently 'apply' in the classroom. In other words, 'ways of knowing' about educational processes should be subjected to the same level of scrutiny as are the ways of knowing which constitute the school curriculum out there in the school. To fail to do this is to miss an opportunity to give the student a working understandingof epistemological issues; and it could be construed as hypothetical to subject to critique the school curriculum but not that of teacher education. A similar argument applies in the case of history of education.

We saw that how usefully a historical awareness of the institutional and ideational background of primary education both illuminates and provides a basis for critique of present-day ideas and practices, particularly in respect of the ways of the child is viewed and the curriculum defined in the context of the class-teacher system. We also saw how primary professional discourse with its 'cocoon' imaginary and polarising of the child and society, seems resistant to a sense of the interplay of historical events, cultural values and educational ideals.

Conventionally, history of education courses have done little to remedy this. Courses in 'the educational system of England and Wales' can still be as normative, functionalist, systemic and superficial as they were in the years following the McNair Report: presumes of the clauses of education acts and the recommendations of major reports, but rarely interpretations or explanation beyond a sort of sub 'O' level 'seven causes of the Boer War' variety, and certainly little real delving into the pedagogy and curriculum experienced by previous generations of children and the justifications offered by teachers and others in support of these.

Of course academic monopolies are not fortuitous: the one under discussion reflects aspirations to make teaching a 'science' grounded in a set of empirically derived principles and so to demonstrate the 'expert knowledge' basis of the teacher's professional claim. However, we might try asking afresh, with no preconditions, the open question: 'What is the best way to develop the young adult's capacity to understand other human beings, especially pre-adolescent children?'in pursuit of an answer we might attempt to catalogue those ways which humans have learned to understand each other and themselves. On the one hand, and prominently, there is the pervasiveness and potential of insight grounded in individual and collective experience.

Meanwhile, we concentrate more on academic or public modes of personal and inter-personal exploration, we have to acknowledge that the field can encompass, at least, literature, art, music, drama and religion as well as the social sciences; and that even the latter can extend much further than teacher education has allowed. The modes of inquiry we actually make available to the student are from one small spectrum of human knowledge, and, as it happens, they are from one of the newest and-to workers in the physical sciences and the arts alike one of the most suspect in terms of its claims to represent humans as they are. Putting into operation such extended concepts of 'understanding children and teachers' is not necessarily easy, but the issue needs to be faced. As presently conceived, teacher education courses place arbitrary and unnecessary restrictions on this aspect of the student's development.

The most basic reappraisal would concern the academic/ professional distinction, and, as a consequence, the common ground between subject studies and education theory as regards each's capacity both to generate professional insight and to meet 'personally educative' functions might be disconcerting. However, the most substantial and necessary shift in this context is towards the exploration and use in initial training of non-academic, everyday, subjective professional knowledge. The arguments seem inescapable: such knowledge is pervasive, inevitable and influential in everyday practice and therefore requires exploration; it is effective in that it is the basis for teaching of a high quality and therefore may encapsulate ideas worthy of emulation; it is also, conversely, the basis for weak teaching and therefore its limitations as well as its strengths need to be exposed. Where as in this context, the everyday knowledge in question concerns children, it taps, or may tap, insights stemming from one of the most fundamental of human relationships: it cannot simply be disregarded on the grounds of arbitrary stimulative definitions of what constitutes 'science' and 'objectivity'. This is not an argument for rejecting academic inquiry, or for a revival of apprenticeship approaches to teacher education.

Rather, the case is made for recognising the strengths and limitations of any mode of understanding pursued in overmuch isolation-particular disciplines, academic study in general, personal, experientially grounded everyday knowledgeThis includes acknowledging the advantage of using these in combination and juxtaposition, particularly in pursuit of that understanding of ourselves and others which educationists seem happily prepared to lay claim to, despite the fact that the rest of humanity has found it rather more elusive. Such eclecticism as is argued here would be conditional upon courses sensitising students to the epestemological problems raised. It is not adequate to 'raid the disciplines', or rather to 'raid' all available and potentially productive sources of insight, without also understanding the nature of the truth claim each makes and the limitations thereof.

Traditionally courses have tended to treat academic sources as given the experiential sources as suspect or unacceptable: all are problematic, though in different ways. It will be apparent by now that, in combination, the ideas above require not minor adjustment to the content and pedagogy of initial training courses, but a more fundamental shift.

'School-based curriculum development' is a clumsy term, used to refer to activities which, because they take place in the unique contexts of individual schools, are necessarily diverse. This chapter attempts to place some structure on the idea of schoolbased curriculum development by linking material from four relevant areas. First, theoretical concepts are outlined; second, these concepts are qualified by reference to the practice of curriculum development in primary schools; third, contextual factors influencing the nature of such development are examined; and finally, the values underlying school-based curriculum development in primary schools are briefly elaborated.

One of the problems faced by anyone attempting to understand school-based curriculum development as an idea is that it is used very much as a catch-all concept. For example, as illustrated by Miston, it means something as substantial as groups of secondary school pupils, together with appropriate staff training and resources development; or it may be small-scale revision of a language programme in a primary school, such that is described by Timms and Lees.

The DES have stressed the significance of school-based approach, but two writers in particular have helped to sharpen the formulation of ideas about them. Eggleston's introduction to six case studies provides a useful starting-point. Although it is unclear whether Eggleston was describing school-based curriculum development or prescribing a particular way of doing it, four features of his definition are worth picking out:

1. *It is particularistic:* The curriculum-development activity is focused upon the diagnosed, or perceived, needs of the specific school or part of it.
2. *It is process-oriented:* In the terms of 'strategies for the curriculum' intended, the process by which these are developed in important in itself.
3. *It is participatory:* The appropriate style for developing the curriculum is cooperative, that is, staff working together to produce plans for change.
4. *It is preliminary:* The curriculum developed is to be seen as experimental, in the sense that it is open to evaluation and appraisal after its implementation.

One of the interesting things about this definition is the stress, not on the curriculum as such, but on the roles that teachers have to play in the process of its development, and the attitudes that are required to underpin it. This characteristic is also central to the analysis offered by another writer, Skilbeck. He identified three models of school-based curriculum development the rational-deductive, the rational-interactive and the intuitive-and located them within differing politico-educational frameworks.

The first operates in centrally directed educational systems, where the task of the school is to 'interpret central directives' and the role of the teacher is as a mere functionary in a bureaucratised educational service. The second emerges in mixed systems, such as those in England and Wales, which stress the active role of teachers in adapting the curriculum at school level within rather broad general outlines of national policy. Teachers working within this kind of framework have a more complex role than in the rational-deductive model and have more demands made upon them; they 'have to act as course assessors, to help construct syllabuses, to select learning materials and to devise learning systems'.

The third model stresses the individual teacher's decision making and creativity, and leads to great diversity between teachers between schools, and to inconsistency between 'normal policy and individual school programmes'. Although school-based curriculum development may share elements from all three, the rational-interactive model represents the style and values most appropriate to contemporary English schools, especially because of the stress put upon the range of roles expected of teachers, and the assumption that teachers have to negotiate the fine details of their roles by working in partnership with each other. Thus, in this formulation also, school-based curriculum development is as much about changing roles and relationships among a school staff as it is about changing schemes of work or methods of teaching and learning. A major goal of school-based curriculum development in Skilbeck's terms is the continuous adaptation by teachers of externally defined curricula into forms of educative experiences unique to the teacher and learner. We need a system for curriculum development that combines the advantages of national policy making, national centres for the production of materials and for research and development, with the flexibility, adaptability, and professionally satisfying features of local initiatives and creativity.

Thus, school-based curriculum development is predicted upon the concept, admittedly idealised, of teachers who creatively reconstruct the curriculum within a recognised framework of local and national expectations; it is not predicted upon passive acceptance of external definitions of the curriculum, or the myth of the 'autonomous' school, existing independently of its political and economic context.

Given the political development, outlined, of a national framework for the curriculum, the relevance of Skilbeck's model for teachers in England and Wales has increased considerably. Skilbeck's analysis enables us to add two further characteristics of school-based curriculum development to the four identified earlier. These concern the relationship between the school's curriculum and national or local guidelines, and the view taken of the role of the teacher.

The distinctive arena for school-based curriculum development is the staffroom rather than the classroom, and the distinctive discourse is concerned not only with the surface details of curriculum practice, but also with the assumptions underlying it. The theoretical analyses discussed above are necessarily generalised, and need to be qualified somewhat in the light of the practice in the Warwick inquiry schools.

Brief outlines of the programmes have already been provided, which suggest two characteristics that are perhaps distinctive to primary school curriculum development. They can be considered under two headings, namely gradualism and specialism. To dichotomise rather too simply, gradualism qualifies the idea of 'development', while specialism qualifies the idea of 'curriculum'. By gradualism, three related features of the notion of 'development' which stress the limited expectations that may be held for it. These three limitations may be thought of as the problematic, the unpredictable and the incremental qualities of curriculum development in primary schools.

The problematic nature of curriculum development derives from the fact that there is a conceptual difference between development and change. The latter is neutral and implies merely that practice has altered, not that it has been improved. 'Development', 'renewal' and probably 'innovation' imply not merely change, but change for the better. What counts as a change for the better in education is problematic.

An analogy with the practice of medicine may he helpful. If a doctor diagnoses, say, constipation in a patient and prescribes a change of diet as a remedy, there is not much professional or lay disagreement about what would constitute a change for the better in the patient's condition. Not being constipated is generally regarded as an improvement on being so. But the school curriculum is a more difficult area for diagnosis, with less sure a basis for agreement about what constitutes improvement.

A curriculum where there has been, so to speak, little movement for a number of years is not necessarily in a worse condition than one in which there has been a great deal of it. One of the points that follows from this is that, although the term 'curriculum development' is widely used throughout the literature and in this book, in practice it cannot be shown in advance, and often it is not known even in retrospect, whether changes are actually developments. At best it is commonly a matter of belief, intuition and professional judgement of those involve.

Indeed, to return to Eggleston's emphasis on the process of development, it was quite striking to note how frequently the teachers in the Warwick inquiry reported that the major benefit, for them, of school-based development activities had been the experience of being involved in the process rather than, or in addition to, any changes in actual curriculum practice. It was as though they were hedging their bets on the curricular outcome of the initiatives. Second, there is lack of predictability in outcome.

Given the experimental approach characterised by Eggleston as 'discussion, planning, trial and evaluation', there is the built-in risk that the evaluation might show no tangible development in the desired direction. This seems to have been the case in the Oxfordshire primary school reported in a case study for the Open University prepared by Cliff. He reported a self-evaluation exercise by the school staff, lasting over a year, and involving at least seven in-school staff meetings, to prepare a review of the school's policy, provision and practices across a range of activities, including the curriculum. It appears to have been characterised by serious, professional involvement by the staff, and to have been efficiently and yet flexibly organised. It covered, among many other matters, problems or curricular aims and how they should be described, curricular practice, including the grouping of pupils and catering for individual differences, and the provision of curricular guidelines, and was carried out by effective teacher collaboration.

Aims and Practices

The kind of sweeping changes in curricular aims and practices currently being promoted for the 14-19 years-olds, for example, could not easily be developed in the school-based mode precisely because they are predicted upon external intervention fundamentally to redefine curricular aims at least in the innovation period. School-based curriculum development is a more modestly conceived activity, designed to build upon existing mainstream curricular practice, and predicated upon the assumption of a curricular framework about which there is already consensus, or which can be taken for granted. It is incremental, not radical, change in the curriculum, with slow, small-scale, almost routine, benefits, accruing over time from a school staff gradually building upon its collective strengths and, where possible, remedying weaknesses.

There should be little of the heady rhetoric associated with large-scale national projects of the 1960s and early 1970s, not just because such rhetoric tends to lack credibility in the routine of school life, but because school-based approaches are designed to improve the normal curriculum, not graft abnormal practices on to it. Discussions with teachers in the Warwick inquiry illustrated the incremental quality in an interesting way, showing the mundane and highly pragmatic nature of what was involved. In School 1, a staff group met to review their curricular policy in social studies, and attempted to revise an existing scheme by constructing it around some basic concepts and skills, drawn partly from some Schools Council curriculum materials and partly from their experience with the previous scheme. No grand claims were made, or were felt necessary to be made, about either the changes that might follow or the process itself. Many frameworks were tried in private and rejected; it was felt important to demonstrate that the content could be organized-conceptually.

To test this we developed a matrix, setting four broad conceptual areas of Environmental Studies across four conceptual themes from 'Home and Family'. When we did this, we simply jotted down in the matrix what we thought would work, given that had worked before, and the overall conceptual scheme we were developing. And then we met and looked at what we'd written down and tried to sort it out from there.

What strikes one about these statements is their very ordinates, their tentativeness and the absence of extravagance is what is being claimed. They are the voices of routine improvement not radical, or even substantial, change, expressing the gradual, incremental quality of school-based curriculum development at primary-school level. They embody the view of HMI that: A slow but steady build up from the points of strength of individual teachers is probably the only way forward.

Specialism refers to the exploitation of expertise in a subject or, more accurately, in a curriculum area. This exploitation took a variety of forms in practice but three can be distinguished: specialist teaching, subject teaching and subject diffusion. Specialist teaching occurred in two cases, with teachers used to teach a number of classes and having no class responsibility themselves. The two cases provide ambivalent evidence, limited though it is, for the idea of specialist teaching as a basis for in-school development. Both teachers taught their subject to all the older children in the school, but non the less needed to influence the quality of work with the younger children, who were taught by class teachers. They exercised responsibility for raising the quality of work done throughout the school, though they also acknowledged a reduced impact upon the younger classes. They appear to have experienced little of the conflict and strain that other postholders felt, as reported. This was probably because teaching one subject and not having class responsibilities dramatically reduced the range of the other demands made upon specialists.

On the other hand, as suggests, the two teachers used as specialists tended to have involved their colleagues less in the process of curriculum development than did other postholders. Furthermore, the specialist teachers did not involve colleagues in evaluation of their programmes. This suggests, accepting that these are two cases only, that specialist teaching, whatever its merits in classroom practice of the specialist, may, in terms of initiatives of a school-wide kind, tend to produce leadership of a more isolated, less collective style than would otherwise be the case. Subject teaching occurred when teachers with specialist subject knowledge taught one or two other classes on a regular basis, while retaining a generalist class-teaching role with their own class. This occurred in two cases.

A related version of subject teaching was when a teacher irregularly, and for limited specific purposes, taught alongside colleagues, or swapped classes, in order to teach a specialist topic or skill or to demonstrate a skill and show the quality of work that could be expected. This happened in three other cases. Subject diffusion occurred in all the programmes, when teachers with expertise were consulted by others who needed advice, or when they took a lead in curriculum planning and review groups. It was the main mechanism for spreading specialist knowledge from the post-holder to the other staff. It was what the Inspectorate meant when they talked of postholders' having an 'influence' on the work throughout a primary school. With organisational arrangements reflecting the class-teacher principle, even where some subject teaching occurred, this diffusion model was the dominant style of in-school development.

The stress on the use of teacher specialism in the curriculum development programmes is largely explicable in terms of the political analysis. All the programmes were focused on issues raised in the Primary Survey, which stressed the need to provide for greater progression and continuity, to cater for able children, to fill the gap in science, to extend advanced reading skills, and so on. Although it may not be a permanent characteristic of primary school curriculum development, it probably provides quite strong evidence of the impact of the survey, an impact followed up in two later surveys by HMI in which 'specialisation' and its contribution to curriculum development in first and middle schools were further examined.

There is an ecology of curriculum development. Just as certain kinds of plant and animal life flourish in favourable conditions of soil, light, temperature and the balance of relationships in their overall environment, so the context of primary schools inhibits or encourages the growth of the kind of curriculum development discussed above. Factors in this context can be considered as external to the school or internal to it, although the distinction is not clear cut.

External factors are those derived from the educational system itself, from its administration, finance, demography and from teacher career opportunities. Internal factors include the role relationships of teachers and the ways in which authority is exercised by the headteacher.

More important, however, overall staff expertise may be affected, because the impact of falling rolls will lead to loss of flexibility in the ways that staff can be used, and sometimes to arbitrary loss of specialism. Even if staffing is reduced in line with pupil numbers, a school's ability to deploy teachers in ways that can effectively exploit their skills and expertise will become limited and, most crucially perhaps, the opportunities to free teachers for necessary curriculum development activities in school time will be lost. It is for this reason that some local authorities have developed what they refer to as 'curriculum-led' staffing policies.

Although there is a suspicion that such policies could be used primarily to decide that small schools are not viable, an interesting consequence of them is that the local authority has to make clear what its conception of an adequate primary school curriculum is, for curriculum-led staffing policies in effect move from a ratio as an index of staffing policy.

The minimum number of classes that each type of primary school ought to be able to form if a satisfactory curriculum is to be available to pupils. It went further towards defining the curriculum by which its staffing policy should be led. If an adequate middle school curriculum is to be provided... then the staffing must provide some who are capable of specialising in science, craft, foreign language and music. Thus, in theory at least, staffing allocations, and curriculum-led staffing policies, can be seen as supporting school-based curriculum development. Precisely because, having broadly defined the curriculum provision thought to be appropriate, they highlight the need to identify, develop and exploit staff expertise in order to maintain and renew the local authority, conception of the primary school curriculum. This still obtains as a principle, even where teacher-redeployment strategies adopt criteria other than curricular specialism. At the present time it is unclear whether decisions about which teachers should be redeployed are based on curricular demands, degree of seniority or local political pragmatism; probably all three are involved to differing degrees. There is no logical reason why redeployment of staff should in itself reduce curriculum development possibilities, assuming that the nettle of curriculum led staffing priorities can be grasped. Put at its most basic this would mean that a teacher with essential specialist curricular expertise would not be redeployed simply because he or she might be the youngest, or the most vulnerable, or the least likely to cause a fuss, or a part-timer.

Equally, it might mean that a teacher with expertise in a shortage area might work in two schools rather than, as is normal, only one. In the recent past the real value of capitation resources allocated to schools has fallen quite substantially, and in some local authorities the reductions were regarded by HMI as endangering educational standards. Although it is a truism to say that such reduction adversely affects the potential of a school staff to improve their curricular provision, the effects will vary greatly according to the nature of the particular curriculum development programme.

Impact of Resource Expenditure

There is a great difference in impact of resource expenditure upon a programme requiring for its introduction in a school the purchase of new sets of materials and equipment and one requiring different applications of existing materials and approaches. It has been argued earlier that school-based approaches in primary schools tended to be developments of existing practices, and resource reductions may go some way towards explaining that feature. If so, it suggests that such reductions will influence the nature of school-based development, rather than stifle its growth entirely.

The objective experience of contraction may not necessarily be the most powerful constraint upon development; the ways in which such contraction is perceived subjectively by teachers may be a far more important determinant. Put crudely, curriculum development depends much more upon the ability of a staff to harness its collective energy and enthusiasm than upon marginal reductions in staffing, or even real reductions in resources. It is upon teacher morale that the progress of innovation hangs, and morale itself has been damaged by contraction.

In part, the impact of contraction has been cumulatively routine, with teachers coming in each morning to uncleaned rooms, dusty desks and other evidence of reduced expenditure, which has nothing directly to do with the curriculum, but which effectively eats away at teacher enthusiasm. But the dramatic impact is upon the teachers' perceptions of reduced career and promotion opportunities, which are real enough and may help to discourage innovation amongst career-minded teachers. This is, however, very much a two-edged sword.

Under an expanding system, teachers were sucked up into senior posts by a kind of capillary action and, having obtained their promotion, would demonstrate their merit afterwards. They would be given their special-responsibility allowances and then earn them. In a contracting system such promotion as there is will have to be earned in advance. As a local-authority adviser put it. Previously we promoted Mrs X in order that she would develop science in a school; now we may be able to reward her if she has developed it. And this has to apply to Scale 1 teachers as well.They will have to learn to lead other teachers in an area of the curriculum before they get a responsibile post.

Of course the degree of certainty of promotion differed in the two situations. However, the point about shrinking career opportunities is that they too will be perceived differently; some teachers will doubtless be confirmed in their view that there is no point to curriculum development if it is not certain to be rewarded, whilst for others it will at least be a surrogate for, and at best a precursor to, promotion. It would be unrealistic to ignore such a factor in examining the context of primary school curriculum development, and it may be for that reason that a number of recent commentaries have included the notion that it should help to raise morale and channelise the professional energies of teachers who would previously have been promoted more easily. There is, however, a small irony in the situation.

Whatever the general disadvantages of reduced promotion opportunities, from the point of view of school-based development there is one advantage. For development of this kind to be originated, implemented and above all maintained requires, a relatively permanent, or at least stable, staff group. Frequent and widespread teacher mobility is not conducive to schoolbased approaches to curriculum development.

The impact of the external factors, even in a contracting system, upon a school's ability to develop its curriculum is not overwhelmingly and inevitably adverse. Perhaps the most optimistic element is that primary pupil rolls are expected to stabilise in the mid1980s and arbitrary loss of specialist skills within a staff group will occur less often. A further issue in the next decade, currently being canvassed in some local authorities and nationally, is the idea that it could become part of the contractual obligation of teachers. If this were to be successfully negotiated it would give considerable impetus to school-based curriculum development, especially if, as is also being considered, it is allied to earmarked resources and a realigned career structure for teachers.

Much of the discussion in the literature about school-based curriculum development is implicitly about secondary schools, so that internal issues raised are problems of relationships between subject departments, of development 'across the curriculum' and of managing large institutions. For primary schools the internal factors pressing upon change are different.

Recognised authority, in respect of the primary school curriculum, is nearly always perceived as residing in the office of headteacher. There is a legal basis for this, but in an age when a broad liberal curriculum in mathematics, English, Science, art, music, craft, physical education and social and moral understanding is expected to be offered to all children, the notion of the headteacher as an authority in all these fields is no longer credible, if it ever was. There is therefore a mismatch between authority and responsibility for the curriculum in primary schools, with teachers who are responsible for developing aspects of the curriculum in which they are the 'expert' having little in the way of formal authority ascribed to them, and the headteachers, who have the authority, lacking the expertise.

Lack of formal status is compounded for postholders by lack of informal recognition from their colleagues, according to HMI, who found few primary schools in which the postholders had a school-wide influence in their subject. It is disappointing to find that the great majority of teachers with posts of special responsibility have little influence at present on the work of other teachers. There are some practical implications of this comment for the primary school post-holder's workload, but the major issue concerns the attitudes of primary school staff toward curricular authority.

Some shift towards a kind of collaborative decisionmaking about curriculum matters has been proposed by a number of commentators on primary schools, including Coulson and Razzell, although the latter appears, as Harling shows, to understate the obstacles to such an approach being adopted generally. The problem may not be so much about the attitudes of headteachers as those of other teachers. When headteachers delegated responsibility and authority to their deputies, according to Coulson and Cox, the problem was that other teachers did not accept the transfer of authority as legitimate. This brief review of the internal factors has been deliberately uncritical of them in order to report in summary form the prevailing view of the internal culture of primary schools. This internal culture is seen as structuring both teacher relationships in primary schools and teacher perceptions of curricular authority in classrooms and schools so as to provide a major constraint on postholder-led curriculum initiatives development.

8

School Administration

The Administration

The history of educational administration in India has its formal beginning in 1775. The East India Company administration had set up three schools, for the running of which a sum of Rs.l lakh had been approved. This sum was not utilised for twenty years. In 1853, Lord Macaulay formulated an educational policy, and a year later, in 1854, Sir Charles Wood introduced the system of aid for educational institutions. At the same time, the Directorate of Public Instruction was established. In 1882, the Hunter Commission came forth with a number of suggestions for the improvement of administration in education. In 1921, because of the dual administration set up in the country, state legislative assemblies and the ministry of education came into existence. At this stage,. the Indian ministers had great and burdensome responsibilities, but of rights and authority they had almost none. In 1929, the Hertog Committee recommended the setting up of an Educational Advisory Council, and this was done in 1935. In 1944, the Sargent Commission, defined national development as the goal of education, and also recommended that greater liberality should be introduced into administrative matters. In 1948, the University Education Commission, too, recommended a number of improvements in the administration of higher education in the country. In 1952-53, the Secondary Education Commission laid even more emphasis upon the improvement of the administrative structure concerned with education, because, according to the Commission, in any attempt at educational reconstruction, under any kind of scheme, the administrative sphere is of particular significance because it is the administrative machinery which is responsible for the growth and improvement of various educational institutions. Hence, it was felt that the goal of education could not be achieved without the necessary improvements in educational administration.

Focal Point

The Central government formulates the general educational policy and is also responsible for the growth of education in the Union Territories and the areas governed by it. At the central level, the following is the structure of educational administration:-

1. Education Minister
2. Minister of State of Education
3. Deputy Minister of Education
4. Education Secretary
5. Advisor, Deputy-advisor, Programme Department
6. Director
   (i) Project
   (ii) Adult Education
   (iii) Statistics and Information
7. Joint Secretary
   (i) Programme Controller
   (ii) Education Advisor
   (iii) Deputy Secretary (school division)
   (iv) Deputy Secretary (UNESCO division)
   (v) Assistant Educational Advisor (Publication unit)
8. Director (Internal Finance)
9. Joint Secretary.
   (i) Director (Administration)
   (ii) Deputy Secretary (Book improvement)

(iii) Deputy Secretary (Hindi section)
(iv) Special Officer (Sanskrit)
(v) Sub-education Advisor, Deputy Secretary (Youth Services)

10. Joint Educational Advisor
    (i) Sub-advisor (higher education)
    (ii) Deputy Secretary (foreign scholarships)
    (iii) Sub-advisor (union territories)
11. Educational Advisor (Technical)
    (i) Sub-advisor (technical education division)

At the central level, the direction of the educational policy is in the hands of the Central Education Advisory Board, which is headed by a famous educationist and educational administrator. The central government has also set up some specialist institutions for encouraging education in the country. They are

University Grants Commission. Its function is to maintain harmony and balance in the sphere of higher education, and to nourish it by giving the necessary grants. It came into existence in 1953.

National Council of Educational Research and Training. This body was founded in 1955. The institution has many other bodies under its control. Article 48 of our Constitution speaks of providing free education to all children upto the age of 14, and the task of achieving this objective has been entrusted to this institution. In the sphere of primary education, this institution performs the functions of educational planning, administration, preparation of literature, collection of statistical data and making arrangements for directing the development of education.

Thus, we can see that the central government has accepted a part of the burden of education. For this reason, mutual and cordial relations between administrative institutions is essential, though the greater responsibility of administration lies with the States, since education is, constitutionally, a state subject. The departments of education of the states are the main agencies for preparing educational plans and implementing them. It is very unfortunate that proper attention has, so far, not been given to their development. During the British period, these departments were set up for the implementation of a very limited number of projects. Even today, the structure which was then created has not be modified. Their methods of working and programmes are generally similar.

We must also keep in mind that administration implies confidence, direction, courage, enthusiastic leadership and ability to maintain human relations successfully. For this purpose, sufficient stress can hardly ever be laid upon the fact that suitable employees must be recruited. Most of the major shortcomings of the education departments of our states are directly related to their employees. Some of these shortcomings are: dearth of officers at the highest levels, untrained employees, unsatisfactory scales of pay and conditions of service, unsatisfactory modes of recruitment, inadequate arrangements for in-service education, and an inadequate number of workers.

Government's Role

At the state level, educational administration is structured thus:

1. Education Minister (2) Deputy Minister of Education, (3) Educational Secretary, (4) Joint Secretary, Education, (a) Additional Secretary, (b) Deputy Secretary, (c) Assistant Secretary (5) Educational Director, (6) Additional Director of Education, (7) Deputy Director of Education, (8) Assistant Director of Education, (9) Regional Director of Education, (10) District Inspector of Schools, (11) Deputy Inspector of Schools. (12) Sub-deputy Inspectors.

There are Regional Inspectoresses for the education of girls. The accompanying chart will clarify the nature of educational organisation suggested by the Secondary Education Commission. These days separate directorates are being establishment at almost every level. The necessary steps in this direction have been taken in Uttar Pradesh.

Role of Municipal Bodies

The function of the Education Secretariat and Directorate is to ensure that the government's educational policies and schemes are implemented. They offer recognition and affiliation, maintain the strength of the educational administration, give grants and aid, formulate the curriculum, recommend text-books and inspect schools. The following table will clarify the local administrative structure in the educational sphere:-

	Local Level
District Board	Municipal Board
	Education Supdt.
Dy. Inspector	
Sub deputy Inspector	Sub-deputy Inspectors
Panchayat Samiti	
Education Expansion Officer	
ADO (Education)	
Basic Education Officer	
Adult Education Officer	

The basis of local administration is decentralisation, and what is needed is that the local administration strengthened and made effective.

Outline of the State Educational Administrative Mechanism Suggested by the Kothari Commission

	Ministry of Education	
State Board of Vocational Education	Education organisation	State Board of Education
		Higher Secondary Board
		Examination Board
	District Education Office	District Education Board (District Level)
	Block Education Office	Block Education Committee Block Level

Major Hindrances

The faulty administration of education in India is responsible for the failure of education in achieving its goals. The administrators have formed a class of their own, a caste which has become a symbol of the growing alienation between education, the educator and the process of education. According to the Kothari Commission educational administration in India lacks many things which it ought to possess. This administration is burdened with administrative and financial work, in the main, and it limits itself to collecting statistical data about finances and education, and preparing reports about them.

The following are the problems of educational administration in India-

1. Various ministries implement different educational programmes falling within their jurisdiction, for instance, medicine, engineering,, social planning, etc. Because of this many difficulties arise in achieving harmony and unity of purpose with the ministry of education, which then faces problems in implementing a particular educational policy or directing activities of teaching institutions.
2. Because of the fact that different educational programmes fall within the purview of separate ministries, much duplication is often the result, and this becomes the cause of stagnation and wastage in education.
3. The administrative structure is such that a balance cannot be maintained between secretaries and directors of education.
4. The administrative unit wishes to direct educational activity in a general and normal manner but it also seeks to remain indifferent to the actual problems of education.
5. In this administrative structure, democratic values are almost invariably neglected and frequently violated.

Suggestions for Solving Problems. The Secondary Education Commission has suggested the following solutions to the problems outlined above:-

1. The Director of Education should also hold the office of the Deputy Secretary of Education so that he may, in consonance with the minister of education, be able to discharge his duties efficiently.
2. Ministers of various ministries should organise a council under the chairmanship of the education minister. This council may then formulate policies for the educational activities of different ministries.
3. A secondary education council should. be set up, with the director of education as the chairman, for the formulation of general educational policies.
4. The Central Educational Advisory Board must make periodical studies of the problems of education in India and offer its suggestions, which should be implemented.
5. The school has an important function in educational administration. Hence, the inspectors of schools should be conscious of the problems of education. They should also have sufficient staff to carry out their functions effectively.

The Kothari Commission has put forward numerous very significant suggestions for vitalizing educational administration. These are as follows:-

1. 50% of the employees of the education ministry should consist of individuals promoted from the departments of education so that knowledge about the actual problems of education may be obtained, because these individuals will have personal knowledge of such problems.
2. At the State level, Education Councils should be created to evaluate the working of the education ministries.
3. At the national level, an Indian Educational Service should be organised, within whose cadres there should be such posts as Directors, officials of the directorate of education, district level officers, and posts of principals of the state and central schools.
4. A similar State Education Service should also be constituted. In this service, the first class posts should

include the secretary of the district schools council, district inspectors and teachers. 75% of the appointments should be direct, while 25% of the appointments should be by promotion.

5. In service curricula or courses should be introduced for the non-gazetted staff.
6. It is important to enact educational laws in the states as well as union territories. In accordance with these laws, the educational administration should be restructured.
7. Staff colleges should be established for the training of administrators in education.

In this way, we can note that wherever there is laxity in administration in the educational sphere in India, it is due either to lack of adequate staff or indifference towards the problems of education. The Kothari Commission has accepted national development as the ultimate goal of education, but this goal cannot be achieved as long as the administrative structure, which frames educational policies arid implements them, is not suitably modified.

Various Schemes

Education can achieve its objectives only if the administration is sound, because in the absence of an able administration, nothing. can be done correctly. The Kothari Commission has offered the following suggestions about administration:-

Planning. The Kothari-Commission points out that the existing mechanism of educational planning lacks many desirable elements. It has neither an adequate staff nor is this staff suitably trained. At the district level, there is hardly any educational planning anywhere in the country. The planning units in the offices of education directors are inadequate, and they are staffed by men lacking training in this field. Their work is mainly administrative and financial. It is limited to collection of educational and financial statistics and preparing reports based thereon. Hence the following suggestions are being given for making educational planning more effective:

1. Formulating a comprehensive anal effective policy for the development of education.
2. Introducing programmes designed to avoid wastage.
3. Where the budget is small, there is greater need for economy and growth.
4. Universities, professional institutions, training colleges, etc., should assist in the evaluation of work.
5. The Asian Institute of Educational planning should work upon educational planning in various states.
6. The U.G.C. should establish centres for advanced studies concerned with educational planning, administration and finance.
7. There should be cooperation and sharing of responsibility in school education, local organisations and states, while higher education should be sustained by the co-operation of states and the Centre.
8. The states must shoulder the responsibility for providing educational facilities.

Private Enterprise. The work of education and its spread has taken place more through private institutions, hence the following principles should be observed in the setting up of private institutions-(a) state governments should extend all possible aid to such institutions. (b) state governments should make available all facilities necessary for the spread of education.

Local Administration. The process of education gains momentum through local administration. The suggestions in this regard are - (i) the local administration should maintain a good educational administration, (ii) all the educational committees of schools should always maintain awareness of the process of education, (iii) local conditions must always be kept in mind, (iv) District School Boards must be established to look after the local schools, and to implement the state's educational policy; in addition, such boards should also formulate local educational policies, (v) in large cities, the municipal boards should take up programmes of the kind described above, (vi) appointments and transfers should be decided upon by a committee, (vii) the school board should, in the initial stages, not be burdened with excessive administrative load.

Work of the Central Government. The responsibility of the Central Government lies in the creation of administrative efficiency and skill. Hence, the following arrangements should be made: (a) making arrangements for education in the centrally administered territories, (b) taking the assistance of reputed and brilliant persons in the work of national development, and inspiring educational growth in the country, (c) making changes in the budget only with the consent of the Planning Commission, (d) since the direction of education has been put in the hands of the central government by the Constitution, it should maintain flexibility and freedom in conducting experiments in the sphere of education.

Ministry of Education. The administrative structure of the ministry of education should take the following form: (i) a tradition should be created for appointing a renowned educationist as the secretary and advisor of the ministry, (ii) 50% of the appointments to the ministry should be made by promotions of individuals from the state departments of education, while 50% of the posts should be reserved for well known educationists. (iii) Committees should be constituted for the performance of various tasks. (iv) The Central Advisory Board of Education should perform its functions effectively and forcefully. (v) The statistical department of the ministry of education should be restructured so as to give concrete shape to the suggestions of the Commission so that education may be planned in the most suitable manner.

National Council of Educational Research and Training. At the national level, the NCERT bears a heavy burden of responsibility for the development of education. In this context, the following suggestions have been mooted- (i) For the departments of education of the various states, the national board of education, the NCERT, etc., should function as a technical agency. (ii) The non-governmental representation on the controlling body of the agency should be taken from every class and part of the country. (iii) It should have full time directors and joint-directors, who should be employed for a period of five years, which may, if necessary, be extended. (iv) The Central Institute of Education should be handed over to the Delhi University.

Administration at the State Level. At the state level, the administration of education should be improved in the following manners: (i) Educational councils should be constituted at the state level, and these should implement evaluative programmes at regular intervals. (ii) There should be a standing committee of officials under the chairmanship of the secretary of education. (iii) The secretary of education should be an educationist, and his main function should be to reflect upon the problems of education. (iv) A statutory council of education should be constituted in each state, consisting of representatives of universities, with the minister of education as its chief. The annual report of such a council, along with its suggestions, should be put before the legislative assembly. (v) The secretariat of education should keep an eye on the financial and administrative problems of education, and implement the government policy liberally.

Indian Education Service. The introduction of an Indian Educational Service at the national level is a very fine suggestion. It has been suggested that-(1) An Indian Educational Service should bt introduced. (2) One third of its posts should be filled by direct recruitment. (3) For the remaining two-thirds of the posts, the policies of promotions and direct recruitment should be adopted. (4) Some of the posts should be reserved for teachers also. (5) This service should have the following posts- (a) A Director, and officials of the directorate, (b) Officials at the district level, (c) Principals of state and central- institutions. (6) High scales of pay should be given in universities and colleges, so that high standards may be maintained, (7) 50% of the I.E.S. officials should be allowed to remain in the regions to which they belong.

State Education Services. At the state level, too, a state education service should be established in the manner outlined below:-

1. Even in the states, an education service at the state level should be set up. 2. Kinds of Posts-

(a) Class 1

(1) Secretary of the District School Board
(2) District Inspectors
(3) Teachers

(b) Class II
(1) District Inspector
(2) Teachers.

75% of the appointments should be direct while 25% should be through promotions. It must be kept in mind that teachers must have the same scales of pay as the officials of the administration.

Training of Educational Administrators. For the proper training of administrators in the educational sphere, a staff college should be set up in the following manner - (i) the State Institute of Education should run courses with the help of colleges and universities for the training of non-gazetted staff so that this staff may be properly trained. (ii) Administrators should be given leave to enable them to study the problems of education. (iii) Administrators should also be given opportunities for improving their qualifications and skills through in-service courses. (iv) A national staff college for educational administration should be set up. (v) The staff in the departments of education should be increased.

Method. The methods of educational administration are, at present, lacking in uniformity. Hence it is suggested that (1) the attitudes of the administrators should be changed. (2) methods, work and achievements should be subject to periodic evaluation, and (3) inter-state exchange of views should be made possible.

Education Act. There are varying acts on education in the country. In order to end this confusion, an ideal act should be formulated. The following suggestions have been given- (a) Education Acts should be enacted in the states and centrally administered territories, (b) the Central government should enunciate an educational policy, and the state governments should implement it. (c) The possibility of enacting a national education act should be considered.

On the whole, we can clearly see that the Commission has given all possible thought to the total reform of education in the country.

The purpose of school organisation and the administration is to raise the standard of education. Many factors have contributed to the decline in the standards of school education in India, but the main ones among them are the administrative difficulties of inspection or supervision and survey. Hence, the Education Commission has offered the following suggestions for improving the standard of education at the school level:-

1. A common method of public education should be evolved.
2. School education should be organised at the national level, with their distinct objectives- (a) bringing all institutions to a certain minimum standard, (b) giving each institution the opportunity to develop to the highest level of which it is capable, (c) taking each institution to the ideal point within the next ten years.
3. The office of the district education officer should be made effective.
4. The state institute of education should be made more effective and powerful.
5. All kinds of programmes should be organised in the centrally administered territories.

The Education Commission has sought to solve education's administrative problems on the basis of the principles outlined above.

Common School System of Public Education. Our country lacks a uniform educational policy. Education is conducted through governmental, non-governmental institutions, schools run by local bodies, and public schools. The accomplishment, of these different kinds of institutions vary greatly. Because of this, it is essential that a common school system of public education be evolved. Its prime function is to evolve uniform educational standards at all the three levels. No guardian should feel compelled to send his child to a different school. In order to ensure this, the Commission has suggested the following steps for the evolution of such a system:-

A. All teachers without any discrimination should get the same facilities.

B. Teachers should get equal pay for equal work and similar qualifications.

C. Provisions for retirement and the corresponding benefits should be the same for all teachers.

D. Conditions of service should be the same despite differences in management.

E. Rules for the appointment of teachers should be the same.

The major feature of this system, as well as its objective, is the provision of free education. At the primary and secondary levels, all education should be free. Each institution should work for the progress and improvement of the community. The policy of neighbourhood school should also be implemented to make this system a success.

Schools Run by Government and Local Bodies. Despite the availability of all facilities, the actual achievements of government schools are common place and there are very few schools which can boast of any exceptional achievement. The main reasons responsible for this are the maximum exploitation of security of service by the teachers and their negligent attitude towards their duties. Schools managed by local bodies suffer from similar shortcomings. Hence, a change in the system of education is essential. The Commission has offered the following suggestions for raising the standard of achievements of these schools- (i) Making provisions for the construction maintenance and repair of school buildings, school gardens and playgrounds. (ii) Providing the necessary resources. (iii) Distributing books and writing materials to the children. (iv) Introducing uniformity in the award of scholarship and prizes. (v) Making arrangements for compulsory education in each region. (vi) Strengthening the relations between the school and the community. (vii) providing lunch to the students. (viii) Making provisions for the spread of school education in each region.

A School Committee, should be constituted to look after the schools managed by the government or local bodies. This committee will help bring the school closer to the community. Half the members of such a committee should be selected from the village and officials of the municipal organisation, while the other half should be composed of those individuals who are interested in education and be nominated by the District School Council.

As far as the question of this council's expenditure is concerned, (i) it should have adequate funds at its disposal, and the funds should be created by the municipal organisation and village panchayats, (ii) From time to time, the funds should be replenished by donations and collections, (iii) grants should be given by the district school council. The council should aim at removing the laxity and indifference found in schools run by local bodies or governments.

Private Schools. Private schools are run by diverse private groups. They can generally be classified into three groups- (i) Recognised institutions which receive aid. (ii) Recognised institutions. (iii) Non-recognised institutions.

Of these, the number of recognised and non recognised institutions is much smaller than those of the first category. Despite the private management, these schools are an inseparable part of the system of public education. Most of their expenditure is borne by the government. Where scholarships are offered to students, the expenditure thus incurred is also compensated by the government. Such schools have intimate links with the community. They are free to act as they wish, and this is true even today, despite the increased departmental checks upon them. These institutions are found suffering from two major drawbacks- (i) bad financial condition, (ii) inefficient or corrupt management.

It is found that the standard in very large institutions is low while in smaller institutions it is high. Privately managed schools also suffer from the problem of arbitrary appointments of teachers, irregularities in payment of salary, misuse of financial facilities, etc. The teachers teaching in these schools do not get the same scales of pay, facilities or respect as the teachers in the schools run by government or local bodies. All these factors adversely affect the teachers.

In order to overcome these shortcomings; the Commission has suggested that- (i) The discrimination between private and governmental teachers must be ended. (ii) By the end of the fourth plan, education should be completely free at the primary level. (iii) By the end of the fifth plan, there should be free education at the lower secondary level. (iv) Necessary facilities for good education must be made available. (v) The government should inspect schools which receive governmental aid. Badly managed schools should be taken over by the government. (vi) Privately managed schools should enjoy the same facilities as the government schools.

With reference to the schools which has not been given recognition, the Commission have clearly said that these generally include the pre-schools or preparatory schools in urban areas. Most kinds of coaching classes cause more harm than good. For such institutions, the first legal step can be to compel them to seek registration. Those which fail to do so will be regarded as committing a crime. The state government should have the right to cancel the registration of any institution which it finds functioning in an unsatisfactory manner. The criteria for such a decision may be : (a) lack of proper grounds in the school, (b) improper location of the school in view of the age, ability and sex of the students, (c) absence of proper teaching arrangements, (d) the owner or teachers of the institution being unfit to hold such office.

Neighbourbood Schools. The Commission feels that our schools are found to be suffering from distance or a sense of separation. Hence, the mechanism of education should be such as to encourage social and national unity. For this purpose, the Commission has recommended the concept of "neighbourhood school". Elaborating the concept, the Commission points out that the concept of a neighbourhood school means that no student of the neighbourhood should be refused education on the grounds of caste, community, class or religion. This will have two advantages: (i) these schools will provide good education because of the normal life and atmosphere in the school, and (ii) when such schools are established the rich and powerful classes will begin to take an interest in public education. This scheme will put an end to the alienation which exists at present between different kinds of schools. For this, it is necessary (i) to bring all primary schools to the same standard, and (ii) to implement in practice the concept of neighbourhood schools.

Scholarships. All the children in the country should receive their education under the system of public education, which should give them the opportunity to develop their talents. In order to develop interest in nationhood, it is necessary to make education free and to grant scholarships to all brilliant students. Scholarships should not be available to students studying in schools which have separated themselves from the mainstream of public education.

School education is a partnership between local and state administration, since the responsibility for it falls upon the local community as well as the state government. It is directed by the District School Board and the local committee. In the opinion of the Education Commission, the entire responsibility for school education is upon the state government. There is no doubt that the local community does take interest in education, and it would be desirable if the state government helped these local institutions. Local institutions perform the function of agents in the spread of education. The department of education should perform the following tasks:

1. Formulating an intensive scheme for school development, and making periodical preparation and revisions of curriculum, text-books, teacher's guidance materials, and also improving evaluative as well as teaching techniques.
2. Determining the standards in schools with the assistance of the State Board of Education, the State Evaluation Organisation, etc., and providing the necessary financial aid for attaining the requisite standards.
3. Supervising the training of teachers, their pay-scales, their facilities regarding vacations and retirement, and also organising in-service training through training colleges.
4. Fulfilling the responsibility of inspecting and supervising schools, which may be done by the officials of the state education department or state board of school education, or both.
5. Making arrangements for a state evaluation organisation.

6. Improving the administration of local committee and institutions.
7. Organising a state institute of education.
8. Making provisions for vocational and technical education at the school level.

Many efforts must be made to give a proper form to educational administration. 'Till the present, schools have generally been found lacking in the facilities necessary for proper administration. At the local level, many deficiencies have to be made up. Administrative and organisational improvement can be achieved by taking the following steps:

Organisation of Offices at the District Level. The district educational officer and his assistants play an important role in the organisation of schools. In the district, he performs the same functions as are performed by the director. of education in the state. This official belongs to the class I category in many districts, while in many others, he is of the class II category. He has deputy and sub-deputy inspectors to assist him. The nature of his work differs according to the nature of the state, but in all states he has at least one common function, which is to get recognition for the schools in his district. His main function is inspection and supervision.

Nowadays, the importance of district has increased, with the increase in population. Hence, in order to strengthen the organisation at the district level, the Commission has suggested the following steps:-

(i) The district education officer should be given a suitable grade, and this can be done easily if this post falls within the purview of an Indian Educational Service.

(ii) The district education officer should be liberally endowed with rights or powers so that he may be able to fulfil his functions effectively. The district office should function as the directorate for the local schools.

(iii) The inspecting staff suffers from three defects- (i) their number is inadequate; (ii) because of their low salaries, they are usually not suitably qualified, (iii) the inspecting officials, instead of being specialists, are generalists. These defects have to be overcome. Hence, according to the Commission-(a) better pay scales should be offered to attract more talented and qualified individuals, (b) at the district level, the staff should possess specific qualifications, and (c) the number of workers should be in proportion to the number of students.

Principal. The function of inspection and supervision, as a part of administrative activity, is not limited only to the district offices. The principals of local institutions also play an important part in it. As a class, principals are being neglected at present. In this context, the Commission has pointed to the scales of pay of principals. It has suggested that special courses should be prepared for the training of principals. Principals of governmental institutions are treated with even greater indifference. The members of their staff are often transferred without their consent. Hence, it is essential that - (1) principals be given the necessary powers, (2) they should have full freedom in their work, (3) in private institutions, the management committees should give the principal the necessary freedom.

School Complex. In many schools in India, the means of teaching are not available. Hence, the Education Commission has suggested the idea of setting up school complexes through the co-operation of local institutions, so as to bring about a general improvement in educational standards. It has said that the school complex programme should be developed as a national programme and under it, conditions should be created to encourage each school to strive for the highest results which it is capable of achieving.

The Commission's suggestions with regard to 'school complex' are :

(i) Each school should be treated as a unit and assisted to move towards progress at its own pace.

(ii) There should be more emphasis upon human resources instead of upon material or physical resources.

(iii) In the next 10 years, at least 10 primary and secondary schools in each such complex should be raised to the limits of their development.

'The School Complex' is an organisation of educational institutions, of similar or different standards, in which the institution strives for their educational improvement through co-operation. It gives rise to mutual goodwill, co-operation, healthy exchange and mutual encouragement. These factors are helpful in bringing about an acceleration in the pace of progress at various levels for the better achievement of educational goals.

In the Education Commission's opinion, supervision is, in one way, the basis of educational development, but unfortunately, the supervision of schools has been neglected for many reasons. These reasons are - (a) The proportion of supervisory staff has not increased in the same ratio as the schools. (b) The functions of inspection and supervision have to be performed by the same officer, and thus, because of an excess of administrative work, supervision is often hindered. (c). Members of the supervisory staff have to engage in non-educational work as members of Block Team Work, and thus they get little time for their own real work. (d) Prescriptive methods are used for supervisory work whereas, in fact, creative or developmental techniques should be employed in this activity. (e) Inspecting officials also do not have the requisite qualifications or even abilities.

To overcome these shortcomings, the Commission has made the following recommendations—

***Separating Administration from Supervision* .** In order to simplify supervisory work, it is necessary that the district education council should perform the supervisory function while the district education officer should function as the inspector. Both these institutions should work in consonance with each other. The advice of the district education officer can be sought in such matters as evolving new methods of teaching, guidance of teachers organisation of in-service training, organisation of extension services, etc.

Giving Recognition to Schools. Nothing would be better than making it possible for the schools to get recognition themselves. However, at present, a school is able to get recognition only when it fulfils certain conditions and complies with certain rules. This is the situation in every state. The Commission's view is that recognition is an opportunity, an achievement, which the schools should seek to attain. It has expressed the hope that every local and private group should request the government. to grant recognition to their schools. The department should grant recognition only when the school fulfils certain minimum conditions. Periodical inspections should also be carried out.

Kinds of Inspection. The existing practice is to carry out annual inspections, and they are more nominal than factual. For the future, the Commission has recommended the following two kinds of inspections for each school:-

Annual Inspection. This inspection should be conducted by officers of the department of education. Primary schools should be inspected by officials of the district education council, while secondary schools should be inspected by officials of the state's department of education.

Quarterly Inspection. Every school should be inspected thoroughly every three or four months. The primary education officer should inspect primary schools, while secondary institutions should be inspected by a panel.

At this point, it should be clarified that supervision has a flexible base since it aims at helping and guiding schools and colleges. It should guide the general schools to improve and progress, and also provide facilities for the better schools to conduct experiments. The entire nature of education can undergo a radical change if supervision is effectively implemented by qualified and able supervisory officers. This can be achieved through the following means- (i) improvement in the abilities of inspection staff, (ii) possession of specific qualifications by them, (iii) in-service training. But the establishment of a national staff college for educational administrators is essential.

Problems related to school organisation and inspection have always had a profound impact upon the standard of education. However, it is also true that the solution to all these problems can be found through a single step, which is the proper organisation of the mechanism for administration and inspection. The following are the Education Commission's recommendations regarding improvement in school administration:-

Preparation of Institutional Plans. In order to improve school administration, it is essential that each school should prepare its own plan. The characteristic feature of our educational system has been the fact that its schemes have been thrust upon schools from above, without ever reaching the base. Some guidelines can be provided for guidance, and such schemes may be concerned with reduction in wastage and stagnation, development of teaching techniques, assistance of sub-normal children, special attention to the brilliant students, improvement in the effectiveness of the curriculum, organisation of instructional programme in the school, improvement of the teacher's qualifications under scheme of self-study, etc. They may also include schemes for the improvement of the local community and the school. Praiseworthy work in this direction has been done in Tamil Nadu.

Intelligent Planning and Continuity of Efforts . Every scheme for improvement depends, for its success,- upon skilful planning and continuous efforts at implementation. For any such scheme, it is essential to orient the educational officers at every level. The Centre as well as the States should make efforts in this direction. In the Commission's view skilful planning and continuity should be integral parts of our educational programmes.

Experimentation and Elasticity. Teachers as well as institutions should be encouraged to experiment, but the existing system of teaching does not allow such freedom to either teachers, or schools. Decentralisation will have to be introduced if we wish to try out new ideas and methods, and the government will have to accept each school as a separate entity in itself.

Classification of Schools. The success of many an educational programme depends upon the continuance of certain teachers in those institutions in which the experiments are being conducted. Hence, in order to create contact with the community and to win its co-operation, it is essential to classify institutions. This classification can be based on the following foundations-

(a) Institutions conducting various kinds of scientific experiments, such as the NCERT.

(b) Institutions which put forward the minimum and ideal qualifications for good schools, such as National Board of Education.

(c) On the basis of their achievements, schools can be classified thus -

  (i) Schools with a standard higher than the expected standard.

  (ii) School with a standard falling between the minimum and the maximum expected standards.

  (iii) Schools with a standard lower than the expected minimum standard.

Programme for Action. Work should proceed on the basis of the following points if the programme is to achieve success: (i) Quality schools should be established at every level. The number of good schools should increase. (ii) The Work should start by first strengthening the existing good schools. (iii) At the primary level, there should be a proper distribution of schools and neighbourhood schools in the rural and urban areas. (iv) At the primary and secondary levels, an adequate programme of scholarships should be introduced. Scholarships should be distributed on the basis of geographical as well as communal factors. (v) The minimum standards should not be allowed to fall further. (vi) Students achieving distinctive results in periodic assessments should be given prizes.

State Institute of Education. A state institution of education should be established in each state for the progress of education. These institutes should do the same work as the NCERT is doing for the Centre. Their functions should be as follows:-

(i) Arranging for the in-service training of departmental officials; for this, in-service training programme should be introduced for the training of both officials and teachers.

(ii) Teacher's training should make progress, and for this purpose a state board of teacher's education should be established.

(iii) Preparation of curricula and text books, giving of guidance and carrying out evaluation should be pursued. Vocational work should be done on 'no profit, no loss', basis.

(iv) With the co-operation of universities and colleges, programmes for research and evaluation should be prepared.

(v) Work related to educational problems should be published.

State Board of School Education. The prime function of the department of education is to bring about steady improvement in the standard of education. This standard of education is of three kinds- (i) the potential educational standard which is determined by the teacher, the curriculum, the text-books and guidelines for teachers, and which the teacher aims at attaining ; (ii) the standard which becomes apparent from the achievements of the students through evaluation; and (iii) the standard determined by periodic educational planning for the future.

In order to attain these standards at the state level, it will be necessary to establish State boards of school education in each state, which will help the state to attain the national standards in the educational sphere. It will examine and evaluate the work of the existing educational councils. It must also perform the function of formulating the curriculum and granting recognition. It will also look into the working of the department of education, and organise public examinations. There should be a sub committee to look after the Board's work. The Board may also be divided into a number of small units so as to ensure that examination results are declared on time.

State Evaluation Organisation. The Commission has suggested the establishment of a State Evaluation Organisation for improving the standard of education in the states. This organisation should get the co-operation of the state's department of education. Its functions will be as follows- (i) rendering assistance to the district education officials in improving the existing modes of evaluation in primary and secondary institutions ; (ii) developing and improving the external examinations for classes 10, 11 and 12, organised by the State Board of School Education.

Thus, the programme of working of such an organisation will be as follows:

1. Collecting and preparing standardised evaluation material.
2. Emphasising the adoption of novel techniques of evaluation and examination in training colleges.
3. Acquainting the inspection officials with new techniques of inspection.
4. Conducting research into the problems of evaluation.

National Board of School Education. It is necessary to set up a National Board of School Education in order to maintain the standard of education at the national level. It should be entrusted with the following functions-(a) defining the various standards of school education ; (b) making necessary change from time to time in the national standards ; (c) evaluating the standards achieved; (d) advising the state governments about curricula, text-books, preparation of teaching materials, etc., (e) advising the state governments about improvements in the standard of education. Such an institution should be organised in the following manner- (1) Chairman. (2) Two representatives from the NCERT and the ministry of education. (3) Two representatives from the UGC. (4) Chairman of the State Boards of School Education. (5) Four teachers, of whom one must be from the primary level. (6) Three teachers from universities interested in school education. This board should have a secretariat possessing all necessary facilities, and it should perform diagnostic and developmental functions.

Programmes in Centrally Sponsored Sectors. In order to bring about an improvement in the standard of school education, it is essential that comprehensive programmes should be taken up in the centrally sponsored sectors also. These programmes can be of the following kinds-(1) development of vocational education, (2) establishment of good secondary schools in the centrally administered territories, (3) making adequate provisions for scholarships, (4) organising the public examinations for classes 10 and 12 with the national board of school examination.

The reality is that standards of education both at the state and at the national levels have to be improved. Qualitative and quantitative improvements are essential for achieving the highest objectives of national development. And this is possible only when the administrative machinery in education is changed. Educational planning and administration lie at the root of a potential revolution in the field of education. In this sphere considerable thought has been devoted to each level of education, within the framework of a national policy. As a result, the following problems of planning and administration have come to light. Solutions to these problems have also been suggested.

Lack of Harmony, Dearth of Able Workers. For the development of education in the desired direction, it is necessary to have an effective mechanism, a fact to which sufficient attention has not been given so far. At present, all that educational planning and administration mean is-putting together the educational activities of various departments and harmonizing them. This synthesizing is done by the State Planning and Finance Department. In the context of the fifth plan, the notation of educational planning is gradually evolving in the states, but in spite of this, educational planning becomes difficult in the absence of necessary information. At the district level, there is also lack of adequate staff for planning. And, whatever staff does exist is lacking in professional expertise.

Ineffectiveness in Transmission. We are lacking in an effective mechanism for providing necessary information and thereby making possible the implementation of schemes. This mechanism, or its absence, is responsible for the failure of implementation of schemes, the reasons for which are presentation of schemes in a general way, without laying the necessary stress on their special features. The result is that the individual as well as the institution has great difficulty in implementing programmes. Hence, what is needed is that educational plans should be prepared in an intensive and comprehensive manner.

Inefficiency of the Information Gathering Mechanism. It has also been observed that the existing mechanism for collecting, consolidating and transmitting information is inefficient. The information that is gathered is either not adequate or is unsuitable for the preparation of plans and the achievement of their objectives. Individuals responsible for collecting educational statistics also lack training, besides which they are not able to devote their undivided attention to this task. Statistical information collected in a systematic and regular manner is useful; in its absence, the best kind of educational planning is inconceivable.

***Absence of a Mechanism for Formulating Plans*.** At the state level, there is an absence of any institution for the formulation of complete plans for higher education, with the result that a balance between general and technical education, in the context of enrolment, finance, etc., is not maintained. The colleges affiliated to universities do not raise any voice regarding educational planning although these colleges provide the entire enrolment for their respective universities. Besides, the state governments also do not have any representation on the Visiting Committee of the University Grants Commission. In consequence, many obstacles rise in the way of balancing expenditure and obtaining matching grants.

Steps for Betterment

The Steering Group of the Planning Commission has offered the following suggestions for strengthening educational planning and making it effective-

Organisation for Educational Planning. For the implementation of educational plans, it is essential to have effective organisations at the various levels of administration. Besides, there is also need for synthesis and harmony among the various governmental and non-governmental institutions working in the educational field. Hence, a Human Resources Development Board should be established at the national level. It should be looked after by the Prime Minister. A similar board, composed of the representatives of various departments, universities, colleges, private managements, industry and other professions should also be set up at the state level.

Organisation in the Education Department. The department of education of each state should have a developmental or planning wing in order to make educational planning more effective and to bring about harmony in educational and training matters. This wing should direct the institutions of school education, college education and technical education agriculture, health, labour and employment. This work should be performed at the level of the secretary of education of the state, and the planning wing should be under the charge of the director of education. The officials of this wing may have different qualifications in view of the differing needs of the states.

Planning Mechanism for Higher Education. In each state, there is need for a separate planning mechanism for higher education so that balanced growth may be achieved. For this purpose, a University Planning Board can be set up in each state, consisting of a Chairman (the Chancellor); Secretary, Director of the State Planning Organisation, the vice-chancellors of every university in the state, secretaries of the education, agriculture, health, planning and finance departments, representatives of the Planning Commission, the University Grants Commission, and the teacher representatives of affiliated colleges and universities. This body should formulate a comprehensive plan for the improvement and spread of higher education, with the help and co-operation of governmental and non-governmental agencies. The plans thus produced should not be merely repetitive or imitative, instead, they should seek for originality and benefits in hitherto unexplored regions. This body should also keep in touch with the other plans of the state.

Decentralisation of the Planning Process. Decentralisation of the planning process is very essential, because in educational planning and administration, the district has its own individual and unique importance. The Kothari Commission's suggestion for the establishment of a District Education Board is an important step in this direction. In view of this, the following suggestions have been offered:-

(a) There should be a district education committee in each district, with the district education officer as its chairman. Its members should include those representatives of governmental and non-governmental institutions who are concerned with or interested in educational planning and harmony. This committee should be responsible for implementing the state's educational policies in consonance with the needs of the district.

(b) There should be an educational planning wing in the office of the district educational officer. This wing should redefine and clarify matters pertaining to the condition of local schools, selection of teachers, teaching materials, resources and plans.

Local Cooperation. Successful implementation of educational plans necessitates the enthusiastic co-operation of local individuals. Teachers and the officials of the department of education should be allowed to perform their functions without interference from local, Panchayat-raj institutions. Institutions should also have the freedom to implement plans, though the department of education should exercise technical and administrative control. Representatives of the local unit should make use of local resources for implementing such schemes as provision of lunch, ensuring regular attendances, winning the co-operation of teachers and guardians, etc. This kind of democratic decentralisation should be evaluated with a view to introducing effective evaluation of educational requirements.

Inspection and Supervision. The main function of the department of education is the educational supervision of schools. In this activity, the attitude should now be modified. The purpose should be advice and guidance, not fault-finding. But this is possible only when able individuals are available for inspection of educational institutions. General inspection and educational supervision differ from each other considerably, and hence, for the latter, a professional method should be evolved. It is desirable that at the state, district and block level, institutions should have the services of specialists, who should remain in continuous touch with students and teachers and provide information about the latest techniques to both.

Classroom Teaching. The actual teaching in the classroom depends entirely upon the teacher. Hence, it is desirable that the teacher's teaching ability and capacity are developed and improved, something that can be achieved by giving the teacher opportunities for in-service training. The teachers should themselves be prepared for self-training for improving their abilities. For this purpose, Subject Associations should be organised.

Administration at the District Level. The administrative mechanism at the district level must be strong if success is to be achieved in the implementation of educational plans and the educational process. Because of negligence and indifference at this level, suitable individuals are not appointed to key posts at various levels. It is also essential to make the most efficient and effective use of the available fmancial resources. Through extension services, the school should be kept in effective touch with training colleges, state educational institutions and the NCERT. For this, it would be best if secondary colleges maintained contact, on the one hand, with primary schools, and on the other, with training college. The secondary school should receive help from the neighbouring college. In this way, a complex of many institutions, starting from the lowest and reaching the highest, can be created. In this scheme, work should be entrusted to the NCERT college teachers and school teachers for short periods of time.

Provisions of the Fifth Plan. The following schemes were proposed under the fifth plan -(i) Rs.13.32 crores were allocated for strengthening the school inspection and supervision machinery. (ii) Rs.15 crores were allotted for improving the planning, administration and statistical mechanism at the central, state and district levels. (iii) Rs. 63 lakhs were provided for organising state boards of teacher education. (iv) Rs. 2 crores were provided for the improvement of state education institution. In addition, a separate allocation of Rs. 15 crores was made for programmes under the first three sections.

9

Technical Aspects

Growth and Development

The Rigveda indicates that, since the very emergence of Indian culture and civilisation, the people of that ancient period had learnt to make dams for irrigational and other purposes. The ruins of Mohanjodaro and Harappa are concrete proofs of the fact that India had always been the leader in the technical and vocational spheres. Even Alexander the Great took many objects made of iron from India, a fact that proves the excellence of this industry. Not merely this, concrete products of the Indian industry and profession are to be found in every part of the world. However, with the passage of time, India fell behind in the race for progress, and, as a result, the countries which used to be considered backward in cultural terms, are today giving advice to India in the technical and vocational fields.

The modern period in the history of technical education has its beginnings in the administration of the East India Company. It began when the company felt the need for some workers and technicians. A few schools were set up to train skilled workers for; certain specific tasks. Although the Christian missionaries repeatedly emphasised upon the company administration the need for setting up technical education institutes in India, the company failed to pay much attention to it.

The history of technical education in pre-independence India can be divided into three periods.

From 1800 to 1857. It was proposed that in the educational field, the organisation should be such as to offer practical benefits to the people of India. The administration did not attach much importance to this statement, but the Roorkee Engineering College did come into existence in 1847. Later on, in 1857-58, two engineering colleges were established at Madras and Calcutta. A mechanical school came into existence in Poona in 1854, but considering the situation of the country during this period, this progress can be termed negligible.

From 1857 to 1902. Although Mr. Wood was deeply influenced by the- arts and sciences departments in England in the preparation of his famous despatch, he did lay very deep emphasis upon vocational education. He proposed the introduction of technical education in his Despatch, but the British government, adopting the policy of laissez faire, unburdened itself of this responsibility. Only such institutions were set up as could be of use to the administration. In consonance with this policy, the Poona Engineering College (1886) and the Victoria Jubilee Technical Institute (1887). Bombay, were established. Most of the work was done by the Christian missionaries because it was necessary to provide employment to the new converts to Christianity. In their schools, the apprentices were trained in wood-work and smithy (iron-mongering). By 1902, the total number of students studying in technical schools was 4105.

On the 18th of June, 1888, the government published a proposal, pointing out the need for and importance of technical and vocational education, along with literary or liberal education. Besides, it made clear the fact that such education should be specialised according to industries, for instance, the cotton textile industry etc. It was stressed that this kind of education should be organised with the help of the local administration, and according to local needs. Besides, some thought was given to providing technical education in colleges and universities.

From 1902 to 1947. During this period, the Indian National Congress took birth, and it soon pressed the government to make prompt arrangements for technical education for the development of the country. In addition, it suggested that students should be given scholarships for studies in America and the Commonwealth countries. It was with this object in view that in 1904, the Association for the Advancement of Scientific and Industrial Education was established. By 1905,103 scholarships were granted to Indian students for studying abroad. These scholarships were meant for training in such industries as consumer goods manufacture, mines, pottery, tanning, match-making, glass-work, pencil, paper, etc. At the same time, an Institute of Mines was set up at Dhanbad, and an Institute of Textile Industries at Kanpur, and an Engineering College at Bombay were also established. This progress, of course, touched only one aspect of the advance in technical education, and hence it never became available to the masses in general, despite the fact that the College of Engineering and Technology, Jadavpur, the Tata Institute, Jamshedpur, and the Banaras University had already come into existence to provide technical education.

Out of many other, two factors in particular have influenced technical education- (1) the unemployment resulting from the spread of education, and (2) the need for skilled workers after the World War I, and in preparation for the World War II.

Both these factors were responsible for bringing technical education to India. After the World War I, the British government had come to realise that it could not fight another: war successfully by confining itself and its resources to Britain alone. Consequently, it set up Ordinance factories at a number of places. In 1941, a polytechnic school was set up at Delhi, and, in 1945, a committee was constituted to' study the possibilities of technical education in India, based on the working of the Massachusetts Institute of Technology, England. This committee was referred to as the 'Government Committee'. On the basis of its suggestions, institutions were set up in all parts of India, though these institutions were set up primarily to meet the requirements of war.

On 30th November, 1945, the government set up the All India Council for Technical Education, while in March 1947, the Scientific Manpower Committee was constituted, and entrusted with the task of estimating the need for scientifically trained manpower in various spheres in the coming years. This committee projected that

54,000 engineers and 20,000 technicians would be required by the end of 1947.

In 1947, after independence, India possessed 38 technological institutions providing education to 2,940 students annually. There were 53 polytechnic schools educating 30,670 students every year and giving them diplomas. These educational institutions were made capable of playing a constructive role in the country's five year plans. In the First-Five Year Plan, many new courses were introduced at the degree level, particularly the courses which the country was in dire need of. The following was the nature of technical education in free India:-

Administration. Technical education has generally been directed jointly by the central and state governments. The All India Council for Technical Education, set up by the central government, has done much to encourage it. The centre's purpose is to provide for the technical development of the whole country, to make arrangements for higher technical education, to provide finance for these institutions, to give grants to universities and states, and supervise the functioning of all these various institutions. All these functions come within the jurisdiction of the ministry of education. The aforementioned council created four regional councils, and entrusted them with the tasks of constituting boards of studies,- introducing national diploma courses, part-time courses and post-graduate courses. At the state level, too, technical education is supervised by the relevant departments within the departments of education. This department provides for technical education through a council consisting of 17 members and the education minister as its chairman.

Institutions. Institutions providing technical education can be divided into three main categories-

A. These are institutions which provide education through degree and post-graduate courses as well as research. The subjects covered by them include Mining, Metallurgy-cum-Engineering, High-way (Roads) Engineering, Irrigation, Soil Mechanics, Foundation Engineering. Production Technology, Chemical Engineering, Electrical Communications, Advanced Electronics, Geophysics, Petroleum Technology, Textiles, Architecture, Leather technology, Aeronautical Engineering, etc.

B. Institutions of this category include those which conduct diploma courses, and they provide training extending from 1 to 3 years in a variety of courses. They are called polytechnic institutions. Some of them have been established primarily for girls.

C. Institutions of the third kind provide vocational and industrial training. They conduct two kinds of courses-

(a) The first include courses connected with art and handicrafts, such as - domestic industries, weaving, dyeing, printing, metal-work, leather dyeing, leather working, metalwork, iron-mongery, jewellery making, carpentry, pottery, utensil making, weaving of cane furniture, etc.

(b) The second kind of courses are intended to produce partially skilled and semiskilled workers, and for admission to them students require knowledge only of reading and writing. In 1947, the country had 53 schools and 38 colleges of this nature, providing diplomas to 3670 students, and degrees to 2940 students. By 1962, these numbers had swelled to 221 schools and 114 colleges in which 38,826 students received diplomas and 17,074 degrees. For the third five plan, it was proposed that the engineering profession should be expanded. Consequently, Regional Engineering Colleges were established at Warangal, Bangalore, Nagpur, Bhopal, Durgapur, Jamshedpur, Allahabad, Delhi and Srinagar.

New Schemes. Among the new schemes was the provision of post-graduate education and research at the Indian Institute of Science at Bangalore, while the institute at Kharagpur was converted into a research institution, conducted on the lines of Massachusetts. Besides, Indian Institutes of Technology were established at Bombay, Madras, Delhi and Kanpur, in which education in a variety of courses is provided, with the purpose of developing technical education in the country. In the technical field, new courses in publishing, printing, town and rural planning, printing technology, and diplomas in management were introduced. The Council has also made arrangements for providing scholarships ranging from Rs. 50,75,150 and 250 for students studying under various courses.

Temple of Science. By 1964, the ministry of education, with the cooperation of the ministry of community development had set up 'temples of science' in various parts of the country. In these, students residing and studying in rural areas were kept in touch with the latest scientific information. However, for a variety of reasons, the government has now closed down these institutions.

Research. The Council has given even more encouragement to the existing institutions to encourage research in the technical sphere. These researches have proved fruitful for technical education in such matters as progress, improvement guidance and maintaining liaison. The Council has also sought to ensure that the knowledge produced by these researches should find actual use in workshops. For this, there are provisions for attractive scholarships.

In the light of the progress of other nations, we, find that our country is quite backward. Even today, our country stands in great need of vast developments in technical education, and the need will be met only when the government decides to spend at least 7 per cent of the national income upon education.

Fundamental Difficulties

While the British government failed to take adequate interest in the spread of technical education in India because of its own vested interests, the government of free India has come to feel need for it. The existing government wishes to put India on the path to progress through five year plans, proof of which lies in the various technical schools polytechnics and engineering colleges, etc., established in various parts of the country. The skilled individuals produced by these institutions have played some role in the country's development, but, the sphere of technical education is riddled with certain problems which are preventing the desired progress. The main problems of technical education are outlined below:-

Need for Technical Manpower. India has generally suffered from the lack of mobility of manpower. The rising needs have necessitated an increase in the demand for both quality and quantity in technical education. But, because of hampered mobility, our trained. manpower has not developed as rapidly as in other countries. Wood's view was that it was India's great misfortune that, despite receiving technical education, an Indian does not get the opportunity to apply it in practice, and consequently, he lags behind individuals of other countries. The people of India begin the chapter of their development at which the people of other countries complete the process of their growth.

The conflicts with China and Pakistan, too, have further highlighted the dearth of technicians. Today, apart from the other spheres of activity, the work of security and defence also requires skilled technicians, but their shortage can be overcome only when condensed courses are introduced.

Demand for New Institutions. Another reason for the shortage of trained individuals is that we could not establish a sufficient number of such training institutions. At present, the country has 120 such colleges. The setting up of one college means that Rs. 4.15 lakhs are needed for buildings, Rs. 0.08 lakh, for recurring expenses, and Rs. 3 lakhs for materials, but unfortunately our country cannot afford to spend so much in this one sphere alone. Hence, the Technical Education Council set up 9 Regional Colleges and 27 Polytechnic Colleges, which provided a variety of courses. Even today, continuous efforts are being made to procure more and more trained individuals.

Dearth of Technicians at the Lower and Middle Levels. In technical education, it is possible to obtain individuals at the middle and higher levels in adequate numbers, and, unfortunately, most of them get into the habit of getting the work done by mechanics. The outcome is that, when there is a dearth of mechanics, these individuals just sit idle. Hence, it has become necessary to provide training for semi-skilled technicians also. Such individuals can develop skills for working in various spheres, such as starting an engine, fitting machines, carrying out electrical repairs, etc.

Efficiency of the Administration. In India, it is being increasingly felt that if an administrative department takes interest in its work, it usually shows satisfactory progress. Administrative departments face two major obstacles- (i) in some spheres, individuals have an excessive workload, which prevents them from increasing their efficiency; (ii) in some cases, more than enough staff is provided for a single piece of work, with the result that they pass the responsibility to the next man, thus ensuring that nothing actually gets done. Hence, the Planning Commission has suggested that, in the entire sphere of technical education, the work-load and the responsibility should be collectively and individually put upon the workers. Statistics show that, in the administrative sphere, the real need is for workers actively working in the field rather than in the office. Hence, the administrative departments should be revamped in such a manner that the emphasis shifts to the creative work in the field. There should be more creative and active workers in every department.

Narrow or Limited Curricula. So far, people have generally assumed that the purpose of technical education is to produce an educated manual worker or labourer, while in reality, technical education induces profound respect for labour, and awareness of the dignity of labour. Hence, it is necessary that, technical education everywhere should be accompanied by general education so that the curriculum of technical education should not remain rigidly stuck to training in a particular field of technology. The Council too has been making efforts to overcome this narrow approach, and also to achieve an increase in the number of skilled and semi-skilled technicians.

Medium of Education. Pandit Nehru had recommended that English should be the medium of technical education, since he felt that almost all the literature in this sphere was available only in English. But, the question, is, how many Indians know English? Not very many. The result has been that the common man has been kept away from technical education. It is possible to evolve a technical terminology in the various Indian languages, and it can be argued that rapid progress can be achieved in the sphere if technical education is available in Indian languages, just as education in law is available in them.

Lack of Teachers. There has usually been an acute shortage of teachers in technical and engineering education, because of the fact that the demand for engineers and technicians is very high in the country. Teaching does not offer very attractive scales of pay, and besides, it offers very little scope for working with one's own hands. Besides, the teacher does not enjoy a very high social status. For instance, even at the national level, the engineer is given more importance than a teacher, although the former is the product of the teacher. The dearth of teachers can be overcome if teachers are given better scales of pay, more attractive facilities, more importance than engineers, and importance at the social, economic, cultural and national levels.

Proper Arrangements for Practice in Workshops. The absence of well equipped workshops in engineering and technical colleges has, for long, been a sore point. This problem manifests itself in two ways -(i) lack of good workshops, (ii) presence of excessive trainees in the workshops. Thus, even if the workshop is itself satisfactory, the number of trainees is so large that the workshop cannot achieve its real objective. If workshops are organised on the following bases, technical education can progress more rapidly- (a) workshops should not depend upon imported machines. (b) New workshops should be established and equipped with Indian materials and machines. (c) Industrialists should be induced to cooperate in this collectively. (d) As in the case of the USA, cooperative programmes should be taken up, and students learn to produce the maximum quantum of goods through the most modern technology.

Post-school Education. After emerging from the engineering school or college, the student finds himself backward when confronted with the real work situation. His knowledge once again takes a backward path. In order to confront this problem, it is necessary to introduce morning and evening classes to provide the latest information. The benefit will be that the students will keep in touch with the latest progress in their field, and also make the best use of their time. In-service training courses should also be organised at regular intervals.

Research. India spends only 0.2% of its national production upon research, whereas Russia and America spend as much as 2.8%. And, in fact, it is India which has the greatest need for research into such spheres as improvement in the quality of goods, production of new goods, re-cycling of waste products, reduction of costs, reduction of the risks in productive processes, overcoming difficulties, and determination of basic standards, etc. For this purpose, through engineering design, structure, method of working, etc., research can be made capable of developing techniques which will help the country to create international markets for its goods.

Absence of co-operation between State Industries and Technical Education. Occasionally, our newspapers report that thousands of overseers are unemployed in a particular region. In planning for the spread of technical education, the state must keep in mind its manpower needs, since it is being observed that engineers and overseers are being produced without any planning. It would be far better if the state first conducted a survey of its manpower needs and then made arrangements for the training of a sufficient number of engineers and technicians.

Role of Commission

After reflecting upon the problem of unemployment, the Kothari Commission has expressed its view on technical and vocational education in the following terms-

1. By 1986, 20% of the lower secondary students and 50% of the higher secondary students should receive vocational education.
2. Vocational courses should be introduced at the school level. Brilliant and talented students must get adequate opportunities in this sphere.
3. Arrangements should be made for training skilled and semi-skilled workers. For this, the following kinds of institutions should be established:-
   (a) I.T.I.
   (b) Junior Technical School
   (c) Technical High School.
4. In the courses for skilled workers, the courses below class 10 should be included in the polytechnic.
5. The rigidity of the present curriculum should be abandoned.

Technician Training. According to the Kothari Commission, in our educational system, the second level of skill which exists at the secondary level produces a middle level specialist whose functions are understood very little in our country. Hence, the following suggestions have been offered:-

1. Technician training should be restructured in the light of modern knowledge, and training should be based upon professional differentiation and specialisation.
2. Diploma training will be particularly useful for institutions.
3. Polytechnics should be established in industrial areas.
4. Teachers in polytechnics should be recruited from the industries, and there should be flexibility in evaluating their academic or educational qualifications.
5. There should be different kinds of courses for girls, including diploma as well as certificate courses.
6. In polytechnic schools, wastage and stagnation should be prevented, in view of the labour and power involved in training students.
7. Some selected polytechnics should provide post diploma courses also.
8. Keeping in mind the mobility of labour in the country, polytechnic schools should have courses based on local needs and available resources, but special emphasis should be given to the teaching of science and mathematics.

Other Vocational Education. Today, an almost unaccounted variety of vocational courses have emerged. For their best development, it is necessary to be cognizant of the following facts:- (i) Commercial, clerical, and scientific education should be imparted in classes 11 and 12. The interests and aptitude of girls should be kept in view. (ii) Students emerging from polytechnics, etc., should be encouraged to set up their own enterprises.

Engineering Education. In the opinion of the Kothari Commission; the progress of industrialisation depends upon the proper understanding of science, and, it also necessitates the best possible training for engineers. It is suggested, therefore that- (i) in some subjects of engineering, students with B.Sc. degree, for instance, in electronics, should be granted admission. (ii) The differences in the pay scales of teachers in various institutions should be eliminated. (iii) Practical training should be given for one full year, after the third year of education. (iv) Mixed courses should also be introduced. (v) More productive work should be done in the workshops. (vi) There should be variety in the courses so that they may meet the changing needs of changing times. (vii) The curriculum should be edited and reviewed from time to time, and the various subjects should be given a progressively more scientific shape.

Teachers. The attractions in the engineering professions are so powerful that hardly any engineer is attracted towards teaching. Private firms offer better scales of pay as well as better working conditions and facilities. To overcome this difficulty, the following steps should be taken- (i) Teachers should be allowed to take up consultancy work for industries. (ii) Summer courses institutions should be introduced. (iii) The scale of pay should be made more attractive. (iv) Teacher training courses should be introduced to overcome the present shortage of teachers. (v) The policy of transferring teachers should be suitably modified.

Resources. The best possible education in engineering depends upon the availability of necessary resources. For this, the following suggestions have been offered- (a) Facility of utilising foreign exchange should be given. (b) Machines of the best quality should be installed so that they may be utilised for longer periods. (c) Post-graduate courses should be introduced. (d) The training and education should be practical (e) There should be close co-operation with industries.

Medium of Education. At the secondary, polytechnic and other levels, the medium of instruction should be the regional language. It is suggested that (a) vocational education should be given via the regional language, and hence the literature needed for the course should be prepared in the regional language. (b) Postal coaching or teaching should also be introduced so as to spread vocational education rapidly.

Administration. Good administration is needed for the proper running of engineering institutions. For this, it is suggested that- (i) There should be an organisation similar to the UGC for technical education. (ii) IIT etc. should be granted the status of universities. (iii) Technical education boards should be set up at the state level. (iv) Principals of institutions should have complete powers regarding administration.

The Kothari Commission has thought extensively and deeply about engineering and technical education, and as a result, it is hoped that our country may soon be free of the spectre of unemployment. This Commission has made complete provisions for manpower planning for vocational education. It has also stressed specialised studies. However, what we have before us is only a plan. This alone will tell us how much success it has attained.

Role of Planning

First Five-Year Plan. Rs. 23 crores were spent upon the development of technical education. In this plan, the Indian Institute of Science, Bangalore, was enlarged and arrangements were made for imparting training in crafts, Polytechnic, technical, high schools and industrial training schools were increased and enlarged, while more scholarships were also provided.

Second Plan. The allocation for technical education in the second plan rose to Rs. 48 crores. During this period, the number of institutions offering degree and diploma courses was doubled. New institutions were set up and more scholarships provided.

Third Plan. In this plan, Rs.142 crores were provided for technical education. The new institutions were set up, while the curricula of 12 institutions were reconstructed and enlarged.

Fourth Plan. A sum of Rs. 253 crores was allocated for technical education in the fourth plan, and arrangements were made for the appointment of teachers; creation of hostels, establishment of new institutions, and introduction of correspondence courses.

Today, our engineers are faced with unemployment. This is obviously a very grave problem, and it is reflected in the fact that the enrolment in technical institutions fell to 64%. In the fourth plan, emphasis was laid upon the consolidation of the existing institutions. Besides, the curricula of technical education was remodelled in the light of the requirements of our industries.

Differences in the Rate of Progress. The pace of progress of technical education has continued to vary. The work in technological institutions was started after delays, besides which, the state governments, too, showed little interest in the consolidating and strengthening the existing institutions. The outcome was that even the allocated sums were not fully expended.

Difference in Certificates. Many states committed the folly of issuing different kinds of certificates. Sandwich courses were initiated. The polytechnic method was revaluated, and efforts were made to see how these courses could be made more practicable.

Educational Plan. The need for an educational plan for post-graduate education and research was soon felt. At the same time, management studies were also introduced. The consequence of this progress has been that technical institutions are now capable of offering enrolment to 74,000 students, while this figure was only 2000 a few years agro.

In view of the existing facts, an effort should be made to formulate a plan for the next 15 years, with the object of creating a technical society. For this, the objectives should be clearly defined, so that the necessary flexibility in the method of education may be maintained. In the fifth plan, the following aspects were considered, in the light of the need for rapid development in this sphere—(i) Technical education should be directly linked to economic development. (ii) The curriculum should be restructured so that primacy is given to the generation of skills in addition to imparting of knowledge. It is also necessary to develop practicability and enterprise. (iii) Technical extension services should be introduced, because these services will bring about co-ordination between the masses, the institutions and industries. (iv) For the growth of technical education, state, regional and institutional plans will be prepared. (v) Provisions will be made for the Continuing Education so that, even after the completion of training, the trainee should maintain his contact with knowledge and new skills. (vi) Provisions will be made for every kind of technical education in the light of the need for technically skilled manpower. In this context, thought is being devoted to (a) joint centre state responsibility, (b) blue-print of a plan, (c) an enrolment policy, and (d) Multiple Entry Points.

In the fifth plan, the following provisions were made for technical education, keeping in view, the points elucidated above:-

Programme. Thought has been devoted to various programmes with a view to achieving long-term goals and objectives. Every technical institution was consolidated in terms of its needs for buildings, resources, aid, etc. A detailed plan was prepared for the reorganisation of polytechnic education.

Qualitative Development. Efforts were made to bring about a qualitative improvement in technical education through the development of faculties, curricula and preparation of teaching materials. It was opined that the workshops and laboratories. should be equipped with the latest machines and tools. Besides, such varied courses as practical art, commercial conduct pharmacy, etc., were also developed.

Training of Teachers. The training necessary for teaching technical courses is in itself a serious problem, and hence much thought was given to the training of teachers. According to the recommendations of the All India Council for Technical Education, it is necessary to provide at least short term training to teachers.

Post-graduate Education and Research. For the fifth plan, arrangements have been made to ensure that, in the various institutions, advance study centres should be set up and activated in a planned manner. In the Regional Engineering Colleges, practice workshops and industrial orientation courses have been introduced, with the co-operation of local industries. It was also proposed that in certain selected institutions, there should be arrangements for higher studies and research.

Management Education. It was proposed in the fifth plan, that management education, instead of being limited to merely four management institutes, should be made available through university departments also. Besides, there should be provisions at many centres for training of foremen and supervisors.

Establishment of Specialist Institutions. Institutions related to specific industries should be established, along the lines of such existing institutes as the National Institute of Foundry and Forge Technology, the National Institute for Training in Industrial Engineering, the Central Institute for Industrial Design, etc. The Regional Training Institutes should introduce courses for the training of teachers of training institutions through such courses as pedagogies, creative programmes and industrial experience.' Teachers of polytechnic institutions must also be trained.

Scholarships. The number of scholarships based on ability and resources was increased in the fifth plan. It was suggested that the Apprentice Act should be amended and individuals holding certificates should be taken within the purview of this Act. Archives would be set up in selected institutions while text-books of a superior standard would be produced, and thus science will be brought close to technology.

Administration. It has been felt that there is need for a good administration for effective planning and organisation at the state and national levels. It was suggested that boards of technical education should be set up in state by legislative acts, and in addition, the ministry of education should set up a department for manpower planning, monitoring and evaluation.

The Economic Aspect. Rs. 300 crores were allocated for all these programmes. 2200 crores were provided for all educational programmes, but it was not possible to accommodate technical education within the general education budget. The Working group suggested reconsideration of the plan, pointing out that the expenditure on construction could be reduced. Thus, it suggested the allocation of Rs.190 crores.

The Sixth Plan. In the sixth plan (1978-83), the emphasis was mainly upon a continuation of the programmes of the fifth plan. It was felt that the existing system of technical education was adequate for the forthcoming decade. At present, 25,000 students gain admission to degree courses and 50,000 students to diploma courses. The sixth plan provides that technical education may be revaluated in case of need. Five centres for advanced studies into energy, materials, oceans, etc., will be set up. The plan provides Rs.150 crores for this purpose.

Some of the proposed programmes are - (i) Setting up institutes of management at Lucknow and Bangalore, to be run by such institutions as the NCERT and UGC (ii) Establishment of a national council of science education, similar to the NCERT and UGC (iii) Introducing R & D projects. (iv) Providing for Apprenticeship. (v) Modernizing the new programmes such as Archives and Laboratories.

10

Environmental Science

Bharat H. Desai rightly points out in an article "We are in the midst of a deepening environmental crisis triggered off by unprecedented growth and development of the human race. The unbroken history of rapacious exploitation of natural resources and the continued neglect of the need for regeneration and conservation have begun to boomerang", observes a High Powered Commission in its report submitted to the Government of Gujarat recently.

The twelve-member High Powered Commission (HPC) headed by R. Parthasarathy, Chairman of Vadodara Urban Development Authority (VUDA), was constituted "to study the problems of people affected by large undertakings in Gujarat". However, the findings reached and the recommendations made by the Parathsarathy Commission have wider ramifications, meriting attention for environmental protection in India as a whole especially its recommendation to set up a statutory environment protection agency.

In the post-independence era, urbanisation in the wake of large-scale industrialisation has brought about widespread environmental degradation. Industries sprang up all over Gujarat in the sixties in an unplanned fashion which uprooted hundreds of small and marginal farmers following land acquisition. "The plight of the land losers", according to the HPC, "has been aggravated partly by inadequate negligible compensation and partly by the failure of existing policies and programmes to rehabilitate them adequately, economically and socially." Apart from this, most of the villages affected by land acquisition are suffering from inadequate or near absence of basic minimum needs. The rapid felling of trees, disappearance of greenary, destruction of village forests, indiscriminate disposal of solid and semi-solid wastes by industries in and around affected villages are leading to serious health hazards for the people. "There has been nearly no rehabilitation worth the name of the land losers' families", laments the HPC.

The world is facing or rather passing through many crises but the most dangerous crisis is that of gross and constantly increasing pollution of the environment. Needless to say that if immediate attention is not paid, ways are not rooted out; plans are not implemented in their right direction to put a check on the growing hazards of pollution, the entire humanity may be in the grip of destruction, devastation and it maybe a sign of doom and loom for all of us. For this, proper environmental education is inevitable if we are to attack the problem, not only at the roots but also with a view to have a final solution to our growing gigantic problems of the devilish pollution.

Let us, first of all, see as to what is meant by Environment. In an article-Crisis of Environment-Environment is explained as under:-

Environment refers to surroundings - those natural things around us, from the essentials which sustain human life, such as the earth's atmosphere or healthy air or drinkable water, to the non-essentials that nevertheless make life sustainable, such as wild animals, clean places or human living space.

Thus, the environment is not just pretty trees and tigers, threatened species of birds, animals and plants and the eco-systems. It includes the entire entity on which we live and on which our agricultural and industrial development depends. Saving or preservation of the essential ingredients of life and of the rich natural diversity of the planet is consequently necessary for healthy existence.

The compulsions and complexities of life sometimes require us to make a dent into natural wealth; but everyone now agrees that the fewer such dents human beings make, the better for them and for the coming generations. Certain actions become inevitable, but several others are advisable for man. Continuous destruction of the vital environment certainly robs us, and also the succeeding generations, of variety and beauty in nature.

Undeniably, the environment has become the world's common problem. The environmental health of a country is in fact an indicator of the quality of life of the people. The need for an environmental ethic is now universally accepted. The environment is in grave danger, but it can certainly be saved. Conservation has necessarily to be adopted as a long-term strategy : it must be made a mode of life.

We need air, water and adequate land of sufficient quality to sustain life. Continuous research and monitoring have to be done to ensure that these precious resources are preserved. The importance of their preservation is apparent from the fact that air, water and land are finite, limited sources, and can be exhausted. To use a Term of economics, air, water and land must be regarded as capital, not as income. Even the Vatican and the Holy Sect, representing the Pope, said: "Stewardship of the resources of the physical world has always been a key concern of religion."

Besides this, it will be worthwhile to note that broadly speaking atmosphere that implies both-natural as well as social-in natural atmosphere generally, air, water, trees, vegetables are included. Again it is divided in two parts-biological and non-biological. There may be further sub division-such roots of bio-atmosphere in the forms of generator, consumer and destroyer. Under natural atmosphere all the living beings fall under the head of consumer. The second atmosphere takes into its compass—social, economic, political and family relations.

The History

Balanced use of Natural Resources. There has been a prevalent misconceived notion that more use we make of available natural resources, more the progress of the world. Actually there becomes an imbalance in the nature if there is an unrestricted exploitation of available natural resources. Y. Nondumma is right when she points out that this mis-conceived notion of the exploitation of the natural resources under the pretext that they are meant only for exploitation by and for human being, will take the entire humanity to a point of destruction. As it will lead to the entire change in the environment.

Control over the Waste Material. In every industry there is left enough material which is nothing but waste. This waste is either thrown into the water or somewhere on the ground. In both the cases the atmosphere becomes polluted either through water or through air. To have a control over such a waste material is inevitable if we want to preserve the environment or face pollution.

Check on Industrial Development. Industrial development brings with it environmental degradation and may be a menace for the humanity if no check in the right direction is made on this. Industrial development adversely affects the community and surrounding atmosphere all around.

Proper Utilization of Natural Resources. Nature has given us coal, gas, oil and many other minerals, etc. As there is no limit to the greedy nature of the human being, he has started extracting every thing mercilessly and putting the same at his disposal without caring for its proper utility and the limit to which the same should be exploited, according to need and limit. The result is explicitly clear. At certain places there is drought while at other place there are heavy rains and floods. It brings untold miseries but man has still not learnt a lesson to make a balanced use of natural resources.

Pollution : A World-wide Problem. The United Nations has repeatedly expressed deep anxiety over the ceaseless pollution all over the world and the innumerable problems it creates. In the initial discussions on environment there were wide differences on the issue. The UN Conference on Environment, held in Stockholm in 1972, became known for controversial approach. Two leading US environmentalists openly contradicted each other over whether too many people or too few resources were responsible for the world's deepening ecological crisis.

The Eastern bloc, led by the Soviet Union kept aloof because the UN had not fully recognised the German Democratic Republic. The Third World accused the industralised nations of using the "pollution problems" as an excuse to keep it underdeveloped ; and well-known anthropologist Margaret Mead warned of the need for a "Copernican Revolution" in thinking if we were not to irreversibly damage the natural world.

Since the Stockholm session there have been the UN Habitat Conference on Human Settlements in Vancouver in 1975 and the UN Desertification Conference in Nairobi in 1977. In 1972 only 10 nations had environment programmes ; today the number is nearly 100. Third World attitudes have changed dramatically. As the concern has mounted, so has the Doomsday syndrome.

Scientific agencies issue urgent warnings to emphasise the gravity of the population crisis-four births and two deaths every second; 10,000 new chemicals a year are being introduced into the world some deserts are encroaching at the rate of 30 kilometres annually; a century ago 96 per cent of all energy used was either human or animal and now the figure is 1 per cent ; the oceans are dying and the earth's protective ozone layer is being broken up by aerosols and supersonic aeroplanes. The list of disastrous deeds is endless.

The need to teach people about the environment has become increasingly obvious. In October, 1977, nearly 400 delegates from 74 countries gathered in Soviet Georgia for a major intergovernmental conference on environmental education organised by UNESCO in collaboration with the UN Environment Programme (UNEP). They heard UNEP Executive Directors' blunt warning: "Environmental education is now a matter of life and death." Dr. Amadou Mahtar M'Bow, UNESCO's Director-General, cautioned that the problems of the environment were "jeopardising the development of mankind."

There is a growing number of hopeful examples : 15 out of 18 nations surrounding the Mediterranean signed a "Save the Mediterranean" agreement ; Tanzania had invited international environmental experts to advise on the design of the country's new capital; the USA and Canada were co-operating to revive the Great Lakes. The Chinese have been conserving energy by the widespread use of bio-gas collectors, which produce gas for cooking and generators, and the Soviet Union is minimising the effluence from the pulp plants around Lake Baikal, which contains one-tenth of the world's entire fresh water supply.

An international conference to consider the question of saving trees and forests was held in Paris in January, 1986. The meeting was convened by President Mitterand and brought together for the first time Heads of States and senior government leaders from 36 nations to discuss forestry issues.

Because the pollution envelops the entire world and as such no country- remains aloof from its evil effects, there is an awakening throughout the world to save it from the fatal clutches, of the fearful dragon of pollution.

Elements in Action

Y. Naidumna has rightly stated that the unlimited exploitation of the natural resources has lead to dangerous consequences and now there are only two ways left before the entire human race for its existence-one is to make the environment useful keeping the needs of life while the other is to put a check on waste material along with the use of natural resources. Following are causes of pollution:

Rapid Rate of Development. The editor of *Competition Master* rightly says :-

"The irony of the situation is that the more the economic and industrial development in the world, the more the danger to the environment". At many places, "development" has acquired a sinister dimension—pollution. It threatens forests and farms, human health and aquatic life. Disposal of hazardous wastes is another allied problem.

The United Nations Economic and Social Commission for Asia and the Pacific (ESCAP) warned early in February, 1985, that the Asian environment, already in a critical state, is likely to be burdened with additional load resulting from development activities. Statistical data compiled by this U.N. agency indicated that from 1970 to 2000, the volume of-solid wastes will increase five times- dissolved solids, pesticides, bio-chemical oxygen demand, and particulates.

These statistics mean that every environment has what is termed "carrying capacity", or the amount of pollution or damage an environment can sustain or "carry" without further degradation. A lake that is ten times larger than another one can carry roughly ten times the pollution load. If the loads are not minimised or the environment upgraded to an extent that it will be able to carry them, the environmental degradation will inevitably worsen. As for the size of the expected future loads, solid wastes refer mostly to garbage, there is hardly any Asian city where garbage collection is efficient enough to avoid piles of refuse on the streets.

Bio-chemical oxygen demand (BOD) is a measure of the quality of oxygen required in the natural decomposition and recycling process. BOD is expected to increase four times by 2000, but there are no more sets of clean rivers, lakes and seas to accommodate the additional waste. Many Asian water resources are already at, or past, their carrying capacities.

Chemical Pollution. The editor again throws light on the evil effects of chemical pollution- "There are even more dangerous chemicals in use in India than MIC which caused havoc in Bhopal in the world's worst disaster of this kind. The plastic industry uses a chemical closely related to MIC known as toluene di-isocynate (TDI) to make polyurethane foam. TDI is used more extensively than MIC and is far more dangerous to human beings.

"A group of chemicals called polychlorinated biphenyis (PCBs) are highly toxic. These are widely used in the electronics industry and there is no control on PCB use in India. But only when these chemicals are discharged into water can the Water Pollution Act apply to them.

"There are other equally hazardous chemicals which are being manufactured, sold and used in India, and about which there is no information at all.

"Oddly enough, there is no law in India authorising the Government to collect information on the number of chemicals imported or produced in the country. In terms of tonnage at least 70 per cent of the pesticides used in the country have been classified as highly toxic or hazardous by WHO. Protection and improvement of the environment became a priority issue only in the Fifth Five Year Plan (1974-79)".

Acid Rains. Out of the smoke and other waste material a by product of mills and factories, there is a lot of acid rain which not only damages the outer surface of earth but gives birth to many fatal diseases -amongst human beings and life on this earth.

"Acid rain", which contains 65 per cent sulphuric acid, 30 per cent nitric acid and 5 per cent hydrochloric acid, is caused by pollutants which fossil fuel-based industries emit. It has destroyed considerable vegetation. Sweden and Canada are the worst victims of acid rain which is no respector of national boundaries.

Disturbing the Nature. The pollution caused by machines, motor vehicles, mills, factories, petroleum products, etc., the felling of trees, the digging of the hills and such other fearful devices have given birth to a lot of problems such as soil erosion, the presence of dangerous gases and compounds the layers of smoke and dust prevalent all around are some of the major problems we are facing under its impact.

Population Pressure. In 2000 A.D. there will be 3.4 billion people to feed instead only of 2.6 billion in the early eighties. It is clear, therefore, that if current tends are allowed to persist, Asians will face a grim future-not just zero development, but regression. Undeniably, population pressure is the root cause of virtually all pollution and environmental damage. A realistic national timetable for population stabilisation is clearly indicated.

Major Hindrances

"Surveys have revealed that India has suffered greater havoc by destruction of natural wealth and pollution of the environment than other countries. India as a whole is adding about 4 million tonnes of sulphur dioxide, 7 million. tonnes of particulates, one million tonnes of carbon monoxide, besides nitrogen oxide, hydrocarbons and several other toxic substances. Bombay illustrates the catastrophic dimensions of air pollution in the country: With all its industries, it emits daily 1000 to 1700 tonnes of pollutants. In Calcutta about 1300 tonnes of pollutants are discharged every day.

Because of the three thermal power stations and massive burning of domestic fuel, Delhi has suspended particulate matter as high as 640-1000 micro-gram per cubic metre one of the highest in the world. Delhi is a topper in respiratory diseases. The other badly affected towns are Kanpur, Ahmedabad and Coimbatore.

Dr. S. Dillon Riply, an eminent environmentalist from Smithsonian Institute, said at a seminar in Delhi last year that in India "massive exposure of land, the soil and water and the air to the fruits of technological advance and development without regard for essential biological precepts can only hasten the degradation of what has been a fair land and a marvellous one for all manner of life."

Grim evidence of this came through the well-documented World Conservation Strategy prepared by the International Union for Conservation of Nature and Natural Resources in co-operation with the United Nations, Environment Programme and the World Wildlife Fund. This revealed that more than half of India suffers some form of soil degradation.

A recent study of the Doon Valley indicates that the once beautiful area is fast becoming an ecological disaster. The region's 2000 mm rainfall has percolated into its limestone belt-a vital cog in the ecological cycle of hills. Thoughtless limestone mining over the past 20 years has resulted in a 50 per cent drop in agriculture productivity and the drying up of several perennial streams which once watered the land. Very few commercial concerns have benefitted from the "rape of the land", but thousands of residents continue to suffer.

Life and Death Issue. An even more ominous warning was given in November, 1985, through the Second Citizens, Report on the State of India's Environment (1984-85) released by the New Delhi based Centre for Science and Environment (C.S.E.). The C.S.E. has a high reputation. Its first report in 1982 was hailed by the United Nations Environment Programme as "a model for other countries to follow."

The rapid pace of environmental destruction in India through soil erosion, deforestation, pollution and urban decay is already affecting the lives of millions of poor people ; the country faces social, economic and ecological disaster if its environment is not properly managed. The report seeks to establish a link between environmental destruction in rural areas and urban decay. Many slum and pavement dwellers in India's cities are 'ecological refugees'.

A five-year study of air pollution in Bangalore city has shown that pollution due to automobile emissions and domestic firewood consumption (cars and kitchens) pose a greater danger than industries.

The construction of dams and power stations, the growth of the mining industry and the destruction of forests and grazing land have displaced large numbers of people. The World Bank financed Narmada Valley Project involving the construction of 329 large dams at a cost of 3.5 billion will displace a million people.

The report is not merely a catalogue of catastrophes. It points out that, proper environmental management can provide India with opportunities to tackle poverty. Government-controlled waste-land, which covers between one-third and half of the country, has enormous agricultural potential. But where wasteland development is taking place, few attempts are being made to involve the landless. Most afforestation schemes, for example, are designed solely to meet the industrial requirements of paper mills and fibre manufacturers.

In a signed statement at the end of the report, the authors call for a new 'social order' for resource management. Government policies have served to create' a strong sense of alienation' among village communities which should be left to manage forests, grazing lands, rivers and lakes themselves.

'Environmental activism' has increased dramatically in India. The building of two dams has already been stopped as a result of public protests-the Silent Valley Project in Kerala and the Bedthi project in Karnataka. The Munda people of Chhotanagpur are fighting against a third project-the massive Koel Karo Scheme in Bihar. A co-ordination committee and the participation of local leaders of various political parties from probably the strongest popular anti-dam movement in India."

Many dangerous chemicals are used in India. The Plastic Industry uses chemicals Toluene-diiso-Cynate which is closely related to MIC which caused havoc in Bhopal Gas tragedy in 1984.

Needless to say that this (TDI) is more fatal for life. Similarly a group of chemicals called Polychlorinated biphenyis (PCB) which are highly toxic are widely used in electronic industry. Besides this there are other hazardous chemicals which are being manufactured sold and used in India. In terms of tonnage at least 70 percent of the pesticides used in the country have been classified as highly toxic or hazardous by WHO.

Role of Education

Before we discuss the role of education in the eradication of pollution let us keep in mind a few things like its impact on health, the radio active waves, rise in respiratory and eye diseases, the growth in diseases caused by virus, the gastroenteritis diseases, various diseases relating to noise resulting in deafness, and other diseases of lungs and heart. The growing adverse effect on all types of vegetation cannot be ignored.

Now it shall be worthwhile to discuss the role of education in the eradication of pollution. Following are the measures if adopted in letter and spirit in the right carnest, may bear fruitful results.

1. New ways of looking at the environment so that its value can be reflected in the national accounts, better planning and legislation, more careful and wider use of existing and new environmental technologies, including the all-important environmental impact assessment-a way of appraising the effect of any proposed project on the environment before it is launched.
2. The new Environment (Protection) Act, 1986, is far better in approach than the earlier laws. The Water (Prevention and Control of Pollution) Act, 1974, and the Air (Prevention and Control of Pollution) Act, 1981, were weak and merely regulatory in character.
3. The aim of the new measure is stated to be: 'To provide for the protection and improvement of environment and for matters connected therewith.' The Act contains provisions for tackling the inter-relationship between nature and human beings and the diverse kinds of pollutants. Section 6 (b) empowers the Central Government to make rules for

'the maximum allowable limits of concentration of various environmental pollutants (including noise) for different areas'.

4. There is a section on hazardous industries and environmental disasters. Thus, hazardous industrial pollution is also covered. A hazardous substance is defined as "any substance or preparation which, by reason of its chemical or physio-chemical properties or handling, is liable to cause harm to human beings, other living creatures, plants, microorganisms, property or the environment.
5. There are stringent measures to check hazardous pollution. Section 8 of the Act states clearly: 'No person shall handle or cause to be handled any hazardous substance except in accordance with such procedure and after complying with such safeguards as may be prescribed.' Section 6 (f) empowers the Central Government to make rules for 'the procedures and safeguards for the prevention of accidents which may cause environmental pollution and for providing remedial measures for such accidents.' Moreover, it is now mandatory for a person responsible for the discharge of any hazardous substance in excess of the prescribed norms to immediately inform the concerned authorities and to render all possible assistance. Earlier there was no such responsibility.
6. Vigilant citizens can initiate proceedings against an establishment that is polluting the water supply or otherwise ruining the environment. The penalties for defaulters have been made more stringent. The Water Act provided for a maximum imprisonment of six years and/or a fine upto a total of Rs. 5000 ; in the Air Act the limits were a maximum imprisonment upto three months and/or fine upto a total of Rs. 5000. The new Act provides for imprisonment of defaulters for upto a total of seven years and/or a fine which may extend upto Rs. 1 lakh.
7. However, there are some flaws even in the new Act. One, all power and authority is vested in the hands of the Central Government.

8. (i) There is no provision relating to forests, even though it is open knowledge that in India about 50 per cent of the energy consumed is non-commercial or collected from fields, trees and bushes.
   (ii) Secondly, supplementary legislation in respect of enhanced penalties and for tightening the enforcement of the provisions has yet to be brought up. Nor is it clear whether the new Act supersedes or supplants the two earlier laws. The enhanced punishments may or may not be deemed applicable to cases which fall under the purview of the other Acts. The areas of jurisdiction have not been clearly demarcated.
   (iii) Thirdly, there is no clear provision for public participation which is vital for preserving the environment. The relevant issues are left to official bodies (Air and Pollution Control Boards) and other regula-tory agencies. Any individual can file a complaint with the Government against a factory management, but it requires the complainant to give 60 days' notice, which permits the offending management to bring its emissions within control. The role of the public, especially voluntary bodies, needs to be enhanced considerably under the Act.
9. Section 6 (e) of the Act empowers the Government to make rules for "the prohibition, restrictions on the location of industries and the carrying on of processes and operations in different areas". But there is no mandatory provision for the industry to prepare and submit to the concerned authorities a suitable environmental impact assessment report before the location is approved. The US National Environmental Policy Act, 1969, requires that an environmental impact assessment must be prepared prior to any federally financed project. In India all that a government-financed industrial unit needs is a simple "no objection" certificate from the concerned Pollution Control Board.

10. Addressing the first meeting of the National Land Use and Wastelands Development Council on February 6, 1986, Prime Minister Rajiv Gandhi called for a nationwide "people movement" to protect the country's ecological balance. He suggested a time bound land reclamation and afforestation programme. The approach to this problem could not be departmentalised or compartmentalised but had to "respond to the differing needs of every section." An integrated approach, not hemmed in by internal contradictions, would ensure sufficient food, maintain nutrition levels, meet fuel and fodder needs and raw material requirements of industry and help preserve natural habits. 'We will have to mobilise not just the Government, but we will have to mobilise absolutely everyone. Stressing the need for decentralisation of nurseries, tree growers' co-operatives, he called for the involvement of farmers, youth and women in the programme. The landless and the marginal and small farmers should be the key elements in the programme.
11. Having experienced the ill effects of industrial development, it is high time a long-term strategy for environmental protection is evolved. In this respect, the Parthasarathy Commission has strongly pleaded for a Regional Development Strategy and a National Urban Development Policy with a view to contain metropolitan chaos, for developing secondary cities and to ensure development of existing small and medium towns as well as establishing new ones, as part of a regional strategy generating employment and promoting decentralised urbanisation. In addition, a clear industrial location policy will ensure setting up of specific large industries at specific locations with a predetermined time-frame. It will ensure not only syste-matic industrial growth but also facilitate in taking measures for environmental protection economically and in a coherent manner.
12. All State governments, semi-government bodies and municipalities as well as social organisations have been propagating "grow more trees" campaign. To boost the

idea of growing more and more trees, the government has taken up the project of "social forestry" on a large scale. The project aims at planting trees singly or in groups wherever they can be grown.

13. Apart from increasing the forest wealth, the programme generates additional earnings to the Panchayats, more employment to labour, and it provides cheap fuel to the village poor. In Dhanoli, a village in Valsad district of Gujarat, social forestry has achieved remarkable progress. By adopting the scheme of raising village forests in only four hectares of land a net income of over Rs. 43000 was generated.
14. Social forestry not only prevents felling of trees but also tries to distribute the produce of the project directly to the people of the area. The scheme also aims at growing more trees and forests on unused land and promotes research in the science of trees and their varieties.
15. Community lands in villages are wasted and used only for grazing village cattle. This unproductive use of land yields the village panchayats hardly Rs. 4000 to Rs. 5000. But the same land, if utilised for a cluster of trees for which the Government provides free seedlings, can fetch a much higher income to the Panchayats. The Gujarat Government has decided to give 50 per cent of the net profit realised from the sale of village wood-lot to the Panchayat. Crores of trees are required to strengthen and support agricultural and animal husbandry, to combat pollution and to attract adequate rains and also to stop erosion of fertile soil.
16. But social forestry, especially the growing plantations of eucalyptus, has been criticised by several ecologists, sociologists and economists. The environmentalists claim that social forestry is encouraging monoculture, and in particular the plantation of eucalyptus, which makes up 80 to 90 per cent of all the trees planted so far under these programmes: Eucalyptus, it is contended, degrades the soil and permits nothing to grow beneath it. It is a heavy consumer of water and lowers the water table.

17. The Government of India has launched a Rs. 292-crore project to clean up the mighty Ganga, which has been greatly polluted as a result of the inflow of effluents and dirt from various sources. There are about 100 cities situated along the banks of the river, in the States of U.P, Bihar and Bengal. Nearly 4200 small and medium units are responsible for polluting the holy river. The Ganga Project is the largest and most ambitious of all the environmental protection plans launched in the country.
18. The cleaning up work began at Rishikesh and Hardwar in September, 1985. Cleaning the Ganga is also in progress at Varanasi waterfront, which is heavily polluted. A Central Ganga Authority had been constituted under the chairmanship of the Prime Minister himself.
19. The wanton destruction of natural wealth, including forests, and the indiscriminate setting up of chemical industries endangers the lives of both human beings and animals. The greed for personal gain, the general decline in values, the knowledge that one can flout the laws with a vengeance and get away with it, or at worst to pay a small fine, have cumulatively rendered ineffective the agencies entrusted with the duty of protecting the environment. There are poachers galore, but it is only rare that legal action is taken against such offenders.
20. Besides, there are wide variations between official data and the actual position. For instance, the Forest Departments in the States have been spending crores of rupees during the past 30 years and claiming that a large area has been brought under forest cover. The Union Minister of State for Environment and Forests Mr. Z.R. Ansari, said in the Lok Sabha that only 13 per cent of the country's geographical area is under "forest cover" according to satellite pictures, whereas the revenue records show the area to be 22.7 per cent.
21. In February, 1986 the Supreme Court directed the Union Government to examine the possibility of setting up environment courts. The court judgement in the Shriram Foods and Fertiliser Industries case may well provide a

basis for action by the Government to safeguard the environment in areas where potentially hazardous industries are located. The court has in fact set out a framework for appropriate governmental action. It has also set up a monitoring committee to ensure that the expert bodies recommendations are implemented. Even more significant is the suggestion that measures should be taken to educate the workers and provide early warning systems for the public.

While the increasing awareness and rethinking about the importance of preserving all aspects of the environment, including forests, clean air, and wild life is welcome, there is an urgent need for earnest implementation of declared policies. So far, the implementation has been poor and, consequently, the environment has been deteriorating; forests, in particular, are disappearing at a disconcerting pace. It is time to recall the farsighted Chanakya's observation in the 4th century B.C. that "the stability of an empire depends on the stability of its environment:" Strong and committed machinery is needed and it must have sufficient resources.

Ecology also has some effect on poverty. Undeniably, an ecologically and scientifically sound afforestation programme can provide a solution to the problem of India's poverty, if it is not based on the profit motive alone. More research is undoubtedly needed to evaluate the costs of monoculture based social forestry. Unless afforestation programmes are linked with the basic needs of the rural poor, they will prove economically counter-productive and ecologically disastrous.

Obviously, the plunder of what nature has built over billions of years has to be stopped. We need a new life-style with environmental ethics as an integral part of it, not only for this generation but also for the future generations to live and enjoy the freedom of this planet and beyond. It is important in this regard to reduce the rate of population growth to one per cent from the present 2.2 per cent, as China has done. Industries generating high pollution should be moved out of the perimeters of cities. Environmental education should be made compulsory at every level of learning.

For the rapid protection of environment the following measures should be adopted:-

1. Aesthetic sense among the citizens be developed.
2. Attitude towards cleanliness be evolved.
3. Civic sense must be prevailed.
4. Social forestry be adopted.
5. Religious attitudes towards trees be scientifically developed.
6. Eco club be established.
7. Research in Environmental Studies in every subject be promoted.

11

Awareness on Population

The population explosion is the most potent cause of the crisis which the world is facing. This explosion has come about through a natural and automatic process, but it has been implicit in its very farreaching consequences. The increase in material resources and every individual's right to live have created an upheaval in the world of education. When we forget the international arena, and think of this problem in the context of India, we find the situation even more pitiable and disheartening. In every five year period, the addition to our population is more than the existing population of England, and if this situation continues, there can be no reason to doubt that problem of foodgrains will assume truly alarming proportions.

The Perceptions

The notion of remaining constantly aware of the increase in population and its future consequences arose in 1960. Efforts were then made to define and clarify the concept to relate it to education. Stressing the importance of this, Philip M. Hauser remarked that "It is about time for twentieth century school curricula to comprehend and understand twentieth century demographic findings in the context of their 20th century implications."

In India, it was Prof. Sloan Wayland of Columbia University, who gave concrete shape to the notion of population education.

According to him, irrespective of the nomenclature, we are concerned with the fact that the public policy on family planning, nation and family, the desirability of family planning, etc., should be comprehended under the counselling system in formal education. At the same time, studies should be conducted into the economic and social development of education, size of the family, and the dynamism of the qualities of a nuclear family. Hence, it is necessary to develop a special method of education at the school level under the linguistic provisions in a particular society.

Burleson has conceived of population education as population awareness. In his view, the increase in population brings about an increase in the already increasing expenditure on education. Education can modify the problem by arousing a population awareness among teachers and students. Population education is the awareness of knowledge relating to population. It has two objectives(1) Educationists and others concerned with them should understand the importance of population, the disadvantages of its nature. (2) Teachers and students should understand the nature of their own tendencies.

Objectives and Purposes

Population education is essential for the reconstruction or restructuring of our modern, rapidly changing society. The NCERT has set up a special wing entitled Population Education. It has set out the following objectives of population education-

1. Orientation of the school teachers towards preparing training units on which students will obtain information about the increasing population and the problems created by it and also take interest in finding solution to the problem.
2. Conducting experiments in extra-curricular courses in selected schools, and implementing similar experiments on a larger scale if successful.
3. Preparation of suitable teaching material for population education in schools.
4. Making provisions for research and study concerning population education in schools and making the programme more effective.

5. Evaluating the productiveness of students covered by the programme and developing the necessary skills.

It is evident from these objectives that in the programme of population education, it is necessary to keep in mind the ecological complex. According to Duncan, Ecological complexes are built up out of changes in the environment, changes in the structure of population measures for fighting the problem of population and the mutuality of factors, and an account of these complexes amounts to population education.

In the same way, Chauls has expressed the following opinion on population education. He says that population education should comprehend the culture of the students, the population situation of their society, their own views about the existing situation, their logical, reasoned and organised ideas on the situation of the population and its effects.

The UNESCO workshop defined population education in the following terms- "Population education is our educational programme which provides for a study of the population situation in family, community, nation and world with the purpose of developing in the students rational and responsible attitudes and behaviour towards coping with the situation."

Due to Rise in Number

It is only natural to ask why we should have population education. The answer is very obvious. Today, population is increasing at such an alarming rate that material resources have completely failed to keep pace with it. There is a complete imbalance between material resources (food, clothing, housing and the size of the population. The existing situation naturally encourages exploitation and misery, thus leading to increasing social injustice.

In order to face and overcome these conditions, educationists and demographers have come to feel that the problem must be given the form of a revolution in ideas. This implies that the problem of population must be given the form of a revolution in ideas. This implies that the problem of population must be integrated with education. In India, the task of educating people about the problems of population is being done by the governmental agency, NCERT, and the informal agencies-Family Planning Association, All India

Federation of Education Association, etc. These programmes are directed at - (1) schools, colleges and other educational institutions, (2) those who have left school or have not received any education, (3) those imparting training to teachers, teachers themselves and those who impart education through training, counselling and guidance.

State of Affairs

In India, the concept of progress means industrialisation, exploitation of resources, improvement in the standards of living through material progress, and acceptance of education as the medium of the foregoing. Population is the focal point of the fulfilment of these objectives. The co-operation of all possible agencies is essential for understanding the problems likely to arise in the future and for promoting this programme of population education.

Various Schemes

The Family Planning Association of India has prepared the following for population education -

1. Family and the individual focal points of population education at these levels, determination of scope and syllabus.
2. Nation
3. The World

The following elements will be comprehended under these objectives-

Population, Factors and Results. (Rates of birth, death, life and increase).

Human, Situation and Environment. (Population, reduction in consumption and production).

Social, Economic and Development Aspects. Production, national production, health, education, housing employment.

Family Life and the Individual Aspect. (Family and social institutions, education for family life, sex education, position of women).

Fundamental Values and Qualities of Life. Objectives of society, techniques, a consumer's society, utilisation of resources.

These programmes will be implemented through studies, discourses, regional schemes and research.

1. The objectives outlined above will be achieved with the help of the ministries of education and health and other ministries, administrators; educationists, principals and teachers.
2. Arrangements will be made for discourses, contact with the people, publication, guidance cells, training syllabi, etc.

New Plans

(Syllabi, extra-curricular activities, etc., in village/city).

1. This programme will be implemented through the medium of schools, colleges, social education classes, adult education classes and classes for the employed.
2. For this purpose, arrangements for reading class units, context books, hand-books, audiovisual material, information centres and library facilities will be made.
3. Studies into marriages in villages and cities, sex, family life, population problem, awareness of the population problem and the attitudes towards it.
4. A survey of guardians of school-going children for an understanding of begetting of children, sex, family life, population awareness and study of problem.
5. A study of the knowledge of teachers with a view to introducing population awareness, marriage, family life, sex relations, begetting of progeny, etc., into the syllabus.
6. A study of the leaders of education in the contexts outlined above.
7. Active research into teaching methods and techniques, pertaining to sex, family planning, population education, problems, etc.

For all these programmes, close contacts will be established with educational research institutions, teachers' training institutions, social welfare institutions and voluntary agencies so as to impart speed to the programme.

At present, the Population Education Department has taken the following steps under the Fore mentioned programme-

(1) preparation of context books, hand-books and publications, (2) preparation of teaching material, (3) publication of a monthly magazine, (4) establishment of libraries and information centres, (5) issue of teaching materials to schools at low prices, and (6) preparation of kits for population education.

Future Hopes

At present, all of us are being swept onwards by the inexorable flow of an ever-increasing population, but we must try to escape from this flood and also forestall it for the sake of our own existence. Today, the crowds in universities are growing larger, colleges lack even an inch of spare space. Our population annually increases by 13 millions, which is equal to the entire population of Australia. In the next twenty-five years, our population will double itself. In order to solve the problem of the future, we should adopt the following programmes:

1. Departments of education should make arrangements for in-service training, research and programme implementation.
2. Various departments of universities should conduct research and prepare desirable literature.
3. Departments of science should conduct factual experiments into the evil consequences of rise in population.
4. Various programmes of population education should be implemented through seminars, discourses, exhibitions, etc.
5. This programme should be made a part of education at every level.
6. The United Nations Fund for Population Studies has been set up at Bombay with the co-operation of the World Health Organisation and the United Nations for the purpose of combating the problem of education at the international level.

It is hoped that through the implementation of this programme, the increasing population will be brought under check, and our future generation will be freed from the spectre of a gigantic problem.

12

Social Goals

Growth and Development

Education is a life-long and a never-ending process which continues throughout life. As time passes, changes keep on occurring, and every individual has necessarily to pass through these phases of change. The criterion of success for any individual is the extent to which he can adapt himself to changing circumstances. Keeping in mind this viewpoint, the Education Commission has opined that, in a democracy, the function of adult education is to give to every individual the opportunity for obtaining the kind of education he wants, the kind of education which can contribute effectively to his individual prosperity, professional progress as well as his social and political life. The Education Commission has greatly enlarged the scope of adult education by saying that the field of adult education is as vast as life itself.

India has, for a long time, suffered from a very low percentage of literacy. During the British period, Lord Macaulay's educational policy did much to alleviate this illiteracy, and though, during this period, the British government did, in theory, accept the importance of public education, in practice it did little to achieve this goal. Whatever little was actually achieved was the result of the following three forces- (i) Rise of a middle class in urban areas. (ii) The cooperative movement in the villages. (iii) Growth of political consciousness among the people.

Of these, it was the third factor which contributed the most, and it is. the same political consciousness which has made the future of adult education bright. Till the end of the World War I, satisfactory progress was made in this direction. Adult classes were run exclusively as night classes, and the teacher working in these classes was given an additional allowance.

The co-operative movement was started in 1905, and people felt that it was impossible to make it successful without becoming literate. Hence arrangements were made for creating libraries, and stress was laid upon the reading of newspapers. Gradually, universities set up adult education sections in their extension departments.

The growth of adult education can be divided into four periods:-

During this period, adult education suffered a blow because of the economic depression. The political movement raised the demand for adult franchise. The soldiers in the army were also infused with a strong national spirit when they returned home occasionally from their duties. By 1926, the number of cooperative committees had risen to 80,182. They conducted 100 night schools. In the Punjab, there were 3,784 adult schools in 1926-27, in which 98,414 students were enrolled. In Bombay,. there were 27 schools in 1922 while in Uttar Pradesh, 6 municipalities managed night schools for providing adult education. Similar efforts were being made in the other provinces also.

This was a period of political turmoil, but many new schools came into existence during the time. Some missionaries, such as Dr. J.J. Lucas, Dr. J.J.H. Lawrence and Mr. Daniel prepared new books for adults in the Roman script. During this period, not much progress could take place in Punjab, because in 1936-37, it had only 189 schools with an enrolment of 4,988 students. Two experiments, however, were carried out in Punjab. (i) Normal school teachers were inspired to organise libraries in villages for adult education ; and (ii) Cultural centres were set up in villages.

Similar experiments were also carried out in Bombay, Madhya Pradesh, etc., and many new institutions took birth, among them the Rural Reconstruction Association, Adult Education League, Literacy Association, Seva Sadan Social League, etc. The Travancore University began to send sets of books to rural libraries from its own collection for the purpose of adult education.

Rapid Rise

During this period, nationalist governments were set up in the provinces. Dr. Sayad Mahmood, the education minister of Bihar, himself went to villages, equipped with a blackboard and chalk, to educate the villagers. Dr. Rajgopalachari himself wrote text-books and ran a strong movement for literacy over a period of three months. Teachers of primary schools made valiant and commendable efforts to spread literacy in villages, and as a result, 12,000 people were made literate within these three months. In this way, for the first time the responsibility for adult education was grasped by the Indian mind, and the government took this onerous task into its own hands. New curricula were formulated. The medium of teaching was changed. Books, posters, film shows and other things were recognised as instruments of adult education.

At this time, literacy movements were launched in Assam, Bengal, Bihar, Uttar Pradesh, Orissa, and Jammu and Kashmir, keeping in mind local conditions and needs. New text-books were prepared for the neo-literates in regional languages, and a separate department for adult education was formally created. After 1942, the urge towards education and literacy grew even stronger in the country, the outcome of which was that by 1947 as many as 9,50,002 adults were made literate, and 6,33,896 books were distributed among them. The Talukka Library and the Bombay City Adult Education Committee were set up in Bombay, An Education Expansion Department was established in Uttar Pradesh, while comparable organisations quickly sprang up in other parts of the country also.

The period 1942-47 was a very difficult one for adult education because it was buffetted on the side by the nationalist movement, and on the other by the instability and indecision of the government. Despite this, the movement continued because the people were keen to receive education.

After independence a central education advisory committee was constituted. The committee then set up a council to reflect upon the potential for adult education. This council took adult education out of the limitations of a knowledge merely of letters and raised it to the level of authentic knowledge, and, as a result, adult education was rechristened social education. A plan for social education was put before a committee of State ministers of education on February 19-20,1949, and the Government of India distributed Rs. 60 lakhs to the States for adult education.

Social education centres were established in Bihar, where, in order to speed up the pace of social education, such programmes as touring drama troops, troops of folk dances and hymn singers, etc., were organised. In Madras, libraries were developed, and a training camp for teachers was organised under the auspices of social education. Similar work was also done in Bombay. In Madhya Pradesh, literature was prepared in Hindi and Marathi. In Uttar Pradesh, Etawah a project was initiated. It was later assimilated with the development programme and social education officers came to be appointed. The Government of India, too, has played an active role through such organisations as the Institute of Audiovisual Education, the All India Radio, the Institute of Social Education, which became involved in preparing literature and discovering new techniques of adult education as well as the training of teachers.

The Kothari Commission, in particular, is extremely conscious of the need for and the importance of adult education. In one of its statements on this subject, it says that though, to its observation, the history of adult education in India is not an old one, literacy had risen to 29.3%, a fact which clearly implied that the movement should be suitably accelerated. In the sixth plan, the programme of adult education is being implemented on a national scale.

Objectives and Aims

Adult education must be looked at from a new perspective. In planning for education in backward areas, it must be remembered that the adult has already gained experience of life but in receiving education he consciously regresses to his childhood stage. At the same time, he has many memories of family responsibility and of his contribution to the economy of the family. He has to discover and form social, political, constitutional and mutual relationships. Though he may be illiterate, these elements form his background. He does not possess extensive knowledge of society, but he has the requisite ability to learn all this. He can easily learn reading, writing and counting. Hence, it is essential that the adult should be properly understood before an attempt is made to teach him.

Social education is corrective or remedial education. Those who never got a chance to go to school, or could attend school only for a short period, find that their social education has remained incomplete. The deficiency can be made up through social education.

Today, many terms have become prevalent in the sphere of social education:- Adult education, social education, informal education, continuous education, etc. Each one of these terms is indicative of adult education, but they differ conceptually from each other. The general and obvious meaning of adult education is the teaching of adults. Bryson has said that education, in every situation and in every condition for the individual is what constitutes adult education. Organ and Bundy define it as the adult individual's conscious attempt to learn. Rheins, Fenster and Hadley believe that adult education implies the education related to the individual's professional, individual and social life. The concept of a social education is a more comprehensive one in as much as it comprehends reading, writing, counting, etc., and even more, becoming a skilful and useful citizen. The term social education has been coined because the purpose is to arouse civil awareness in the individual. Humayun Kabir believes that it is a means to develop civic consciousness and social solidarity. In it, attention is paid to literacy, the creation of an educated mind, and the growth of a powerful citizenship for the nation.

S.N. Mukerjee. Social education is roughly inclusive of all the informal education that is given to adults. In India, it has two aspects- (i) adult literacy, i.e., the education of those adults who have not received any kind of education in schools, and (ii) continuous education for literate adults.

Barker. His view is that adult education constitutes that education which an individual receives on a part-time basis while continuing in his occupation.

Bryson. According to him, adult education comprehends all those activities which are related to the normal life of the individual, which have some importance for education, in the doing of which the individual has to utilise only one part of his total intellect.

K.G. Sayyidain. He sees adult education as inclusive of education of politics, of citizenship and also of morality.

Humayun Kabir. His opinion of adult education is that it aims at the development of an educated mind in an illiterate individual.

Implied in the concept of social education is the fulfilment of the needs of adults-economic efficiency, increased knowledge and the growth of cultural possessions. The objectives of social education can be pinpointed as follows:-

Remedial. Here, the purpose is to increase the individual's original or innate talent.

Vocational. In this case, the purpose is to impart commercial and industrial knowledge in urban areas and knowledge pertaining to agriculture and domestic activities in rural areas.

Health. Social education aims at acquainting adults with the basic principles of good health and the various means of maintaining hygienic conditions.

Social Skill. The objective of social education is to train the individual in maintaining harmonious relations with friends and companions, leading a satisfactory family life, and becoming conscious of one's rights and duties in society.

Recreational. In order to raise the mental level of adults, adult education seeks to develop the habit of healthy recreation. The varied means of entertainment available today have not had a desirable impact upon the minds of the people, but healthy recreation helps the individual develop his life along the right path.

Self Development. Social education aims at enabling the individual to bring about his own harmonious development by developing a thirst for knowledge, forming an individual philosophy of life and evolving a creative and aesthetic approach to life. Thus, it becomes apparent that the foregoing objectives of social education fulfil four important goals of our- national life:-

Growth of Civic Sense. Through social education, those who have been left behind in the race of progress are enabled to overtake others and to march in step with them, thus, being enabled to perform their tasks with the cooperation of others.

Utilization of National Resources. Having been influenced by adult education, adults are enabled to fulfil national objectives in their own respective spheres. Lenin said that socialism can never come through an illiterate populace because the illiterate is isolated from politics. Lenin's opinion may, or may not, apply truthfully to socialism, but it is certainly an axiom in the field of good citizenship.

Creation of Cooperative Associations. Through social education, the adult individual achieves economic as well as social progress, and thus becomes enthusiastic about the creation of cooperative associations.

Growth of a Social Viewpoint. Society as a whole cannot evolve a particular social viewpoint if its members are uneducated. For instance, the realisation that "we are Indians" can be developed and rooted deeply only when the people are educated.

On the whole, it can be said that our country needs adult education for a social and political revolution. It can, on the one hand, develop emotional and national unity among the people, and on the other, develop self-confidence, fearlessness and skill in the individual. In fact, the success of democracy depends, to a very large extent, upon social education.

Various Streams

Social education is the responsibility of society. In a democracy, every educated individual contributes to the shaping of society in his own individual way. And, the greater the extent to which society shoulders this responsibility, the better is it for society itself. Thus, (a) the government, (b) private institutions, and (c) universities and training institutions contribute to the spread of social education. At the governmental level, many ministries perform this task through a variety of programmes. Social education is imparted to the masses through (i) correspondence courses, (ii) vocational adult education, (iii) training of adult educators, (iv) agricultural and other professions, (v) public libraries, and (vi) museums, etc.

Execution of Schemes

Social education is an educative process that continues through life, and hence its field is very vast. It is inclusive of spread of literacy, knowledge of rules pertaining to the safeguarding of health, vocational training for improving economic condition, feeling of citizenship, awareness of rights and duties, and healthy entertainment. In determining its scope, the following points are kept in view:-

1. Social education comprehends those subjects which are not taught in schools or those which are neglected.
2. It brings about a change in human attitudes.
3. It either reduces or eradicates the differences in social and individual progress, something which should be done through (a) knowledge, (b) deeds and (c) determination.

The Important Aspects

Every individual today is a useful part of society. The purpose of social education is that the adult population should be educated in such a way that it may be able to improve its own life, develop the desire to create a better and a modern society instead of adhering to the traditional society, and also have faith in, the future of its nation. The responsibility for the field work in social education, including adult education, rests with the state govern-ments and the administration of union territories.

In view of this, the importance of social education can be specified in the following terms:-

1. Social education provides the foundations for the success of democracy.
2. It is the lamp of hope for the uneducated.
3. It brings about the political, intellectual and social development of adults.
4. It inspires the aesthetic development of adults.
5. It strengthens the cultural aspect of community life.
6. It prefers new media of expression and forms of recreation.
7. When all other facilities are available in society, the existence of illiteracy is a blot.

13

Role of Planning

In the first five year plan, the education ministry provided financial aid to various projects to ensure the progress of the social education programme. Ideal community centres were set up and some special primary schools were given the form of School cum-Community Centres. Under this scheme, 116 Modern Community Centres and 454 School-cum-Community Centres were created, in addition to which many libraries, rural libraries, service centres and public colleges came to be established.

During the second plan, the National Fundamental Education Centre was set up with the assistance of UNESCO. Its objectives were the following:-

(i) Training workers of noteworthy importance for social education, for example, district social education organisation.

(ii) Conducting research.

(iii) Creating audio-visual aids and teaching materials.

(iv) Performing the functions of an information centre.

At the same time, the Social Education Institute was established at Indore. New literature was produced for the neo-literates and literary camps were organised. The Delhi University and the National Book Trust undertook the task of training librarians to man public libraries.

By the third plan, literacy had risen from 16.6% to 24.0%. In different states, different kinds of programmes of social education were implemented. In addition to the public or Janata colleges, six Vidyapeeth institutions were set up in Mysore State. A social education department was set up in Rajasthan University. 205 district libraries were created in 13 States, and States also gave financial aid for distributing books in rural areas.

The three preceding plans had not given requisite importance to social education. In the fourth plan, a sum of Rs. 3.6 crores was allocated by the Central government for this purpose. The sum was invested on the following activities:-

(a) Organising and strengthening the social education administration.
(b) Establishing labour Vidyapeeth institutions.
(c) Creating suitable literature for the neo-literates.
(d) Developing and expanding the library service in Delhi.
(e) Developing a central institute of library science.
(f) Training librarians.
(g) Implementing other services related to libraries.
(h) Giving aid to voluntary educational institutions.
(i) Initiating practical schemes, setting up Janata colleges, and organising continuous education and adult schools.
(j) Developing social education institutions for the workers.

New literature was got prepared for the neo-literates with the assistance of UNESCO. 419 books were given awards, and an adult encyclopaedia was published under the title '*Gyansarovar*'. A book entitled '*Hindi Vishwabharati*' was published in ten volumes. Workshops were organised as a part of literary camps. Among the non-governmental organisations which do praiseworthy work in the sphere to social education are Indian Adult Education Association, Social Adult Education Committee, and the State Adult Education Council.

The Central Education Advisory Council, at its 31st meeting, laid down the following standard or criterion for adult education:-

(i) Recognition of about 350 words.
(ii) Ability to write numerals upto 100.

(iii) Ability to read simple charts, posters, etc.
(iv) Knowledge of objects of daily utility.
(v) Ability to write simple sentences and names.

Again, relatively less importance was attached to social education in the fifth plan. The movement that was initiated in 1937 for the total eradication of illiteracy among the masses remained a failure then, and because of this, adult education came to be modernised in the form of social education. This programme was implemented throughout the country through the medium of community development programmes, but, for a variety of reasons, even this programme remained ineffective. As a consequence, the social education programme continued to function primarily through local institutions, with the assistance received from the State and Central governments. However, many important ideas and schemes came to light. The Vidyapeeth of Mysore, the Gram Shiksha Mohim of Maharashtra, the Bombay City Social Education Committee, the Literacy House of Lucknow, and the Rural Library Movement of Lucknow, etc., are the main forums of social education. The Farmers' Education and Creative Literacy Movement initiated in 1961 has proved of great significance. By the end of the fourth plan period, it was expected that ten lakh farmers in 100 districts should have benefited from this movement. In addition, departments of adult education were set up in some universities for giving impetus to continuing education. Through social education, efforts were made to provide information about the various aspects of life through programmes concerned with agricultural extension, handicraft training, family planning, child and family welfare, nutrition programmes, etc. However, the total impact of these programmes has not succeeded in bringing us near to the national goal of eradicating illiteracy.

With the expansion of primary education, the percentage of literacy, which was 24 in 1961, rose to 29.6, but the equally bitter truth was the fact that the number of illiterates rose from 333.6 million in 1961 to 386.7 million in 1971, which was obviously due to the rise in population. However, if the age groups 15 to 25 years or 25 to 45 years are taken into account while considering the above statistics, the situation appears to be a little better.

Continuing education is that form of adult education, or social education in which educational opportunities are provided to those who have given up education prematurely. In the sphere of higher education, continuing education is required most in the sphere of technical education, a fact indicated by the surveys and conclusions of the Scientific Manpower Committee (1949), Engineering Personnel Committee (1956), the Working Group on Technical Education and Vocational Training (1960), and the Technical Manpower Assessment Committee (1966), etc. Technical education points to the path for the future plans. Hence, it becomes necessary to provide opportunities for education through correspondence courses, part-time courses or self study courses so that abilities may be developed and people may remain in touch with the latest addition to human knowledge. For this purpose, it is desirable to formulate a general policy.

For the fifth plan, the allocation of funds for adult education is illustrated in the following table:-

Adult Education Plan

	Plan	*Expenditure Rs. in Crores*
1.	State Adult Education Council	1.00
2.	Literature for adults	2.00
3.	Functional Literacy	4.00
4.	Aid to Voluntary agencies	1.00
5.	Research and Experiments	2.00
6.	Capable Schemes	10.00
7.	Continuing Education	30.00
	Total	**50.00**

Considerable thought was given to bringing adult education into the list of the nation's priorities. In the first place, social justice cannot be made available, and democracy cannot succeed in the absence of training in productive techniques, knowledge of fundamental economics and creation of the right attitudes. And, the success of democracy and social justice were the foundation stones of the fifth five year plan. And it was generally accepted that even the success of such a vital programme as the Green Revolution depended upon the success of adult education.

The various experiments conducted so far in social education have brought to light many important activities and ideas. All such programmes must have the in-built quality of attracting adults towards themselves. There is necessarily an intimate relationship between the adult's routine activity and social education. It should be closely related to introductory education, expansion of agriculture, cooperation, etc. Social education must be linked with the national service scheme, and even the predetermined curriculum will have to be linked to national as well as local requirements. It is also inseparably related to research and the creation of suitable literature. We must lay down a variable network of libraries in rural areas, and our aim should be to make illiteracy a thing of the past within the next few years.

1. Linking creative literacy with such nation-wide and productive programmes as the extension of agriculture, animal husbandry, reclamation of land, irrigation and drinking water schemes.
2. Linking creative literacy with such important national programmes as family planning, child and family welfare programmes, etc.
3. Initiating programmes for health and nutrition, literacy, recreation, social organisations, etc, wherever the density of population is high.
4. Laying stress on the programmes that proved successful in the past ; organising adult schools and polytechnics, etc.

Of the allocated sum of Rs. 28,750 crores for social education, 20 per cent was spent upon these programmes. Rs. 580 crores were to be spent upon the training of employees. According to the plan, the States and the Centre could make provisions for Rs.100 crores, while Rs. 20 crores were set aside for setting up departments of continuing education in various universities. At the same time it was also true, that, of the total educational budget of Rs. 2,200 crores not even Rs.120 crores could be set aside for social education, and hence a provision of only Rs. 50 crores was made for this purpose.

Adult education has been given national importance in the blue-print of the sixth five year plan. In India, about 20 crore people are illiterate. In addition, about 70% of the children opt out of schools by the time they reach the fifth class, and so they also fall within the categories of illiterates or semi-literates. For this reason, the sixth plan lays special emphasis upon the eradication of illiteracy, and creation of universal primary education and industry-centered education. There is a scheme for introducing a nation-wide educational programme for the illiterates in the 15 to 35 years age group. For this, it is intended to seek the cooperation of universities, labour unions, public service planners and voluntary organisations. It is hoped that the scheme will benefit 10 crore individuals.

Under this plan, importance has been given to the speeding up of earlier programmes, which include - (i) creative literacy of farmers in rural areas, (ii) setting up of labour schools and multipurpose adult education centres in urban areas, (iii) search for adult education centres in universities, setting up of Nehru Youth Centres, (iv) national service scheme. The plan aims at activating all these schemes, and it is hoped that literacy will be brought to 15 lakh people in the first year, 45 lakhs in the second year 90 lakhs in the third year, 180 lakhs in the fourth year, and 320 lakhs in the fifth and final year of the plan. This objective can obviously be achieved only through a powerful, effective and committed administrative mechanism. Some of the special features of this plan are as follows:

Attention to Weaker Sections. The plan provides for the education of the weaker sections in rural as well as urban areas, with special attention to providing literacy to the people in the 15 to 35 age-group. Special attention will also be given to women, Scheduled Tribes, landless labourers, farm labourers and other weaker sections of society.

Society and National Development. The plan envisages that special efforts should be made to ensure that the poor and illiterate individuals develop the necessary awareness about themselves, become conscious of the social reality surrounding them, organise themselves to overcome the difficulties of daily life and become partners in the process of social and national development. Apart from literacy, attention will also be paid to the fact that mixed programmes catering to the needs of the poor are initiated, comprising of general education, health education, family planning, development of vocational skills, science in relation to daily life, knowledge of technology, physical education and cultural activities.

Inspiration to Adults. The success of the adult literacy programme depends upon the motivation of the adults, and for this purpose particular attention is to be devoted to the selection and training of workers, production of good quality teaching materials, introducing developed methods of learning through the medium of doing and living, surveys and facilities for guidance.

Co-operation of Voluntary Organisations. In order to make the plan a success, the co-operation of voluntary organisations, youth and others interested in social service activities as well as organisations engaged in commercial activities will be sought. Labour unions, retired teachers and those engaged in formal education will also be made use of as far as possible, and adult education will, again as far as possible, be linked with other developmental activities envisaged in the plan.

Stress on Decentralisation. In order to make adult education a success, emphasis has been placed on decentralisation in the sixth plan. A National Board of Central Education has been established at the centre, and it is planned that similar agencies will be created at the state, district, block and local community levels.

Programme. In the sixth plan, the programme for adult education is spread over the entire plan period. The first year is to be devoted to preparation. It is hoped that this programme can be given suitable momentum by making schemes at the block and district level after consulting all related agencies, motivating voluntary youth workers, retired employees, other agencies, the adults themselves, establishing resource centres in every region, preparing suitable curricula, preparation of teaching materials, devising methods and materials for training, training of instructional personnel at the district and project level, etc. All these activities can be regarded as preparation for the programme.

Co-operation Schemes. In this programme attention has also been paid to the state agencies, centres for national development, industry, service planners, entrepreneurs, labour organisations, and the specific qualities of particular areas and groups. The programme has been kept free from the formal modalities of the department of education. In order to achieve the desired progress, the administration, cooperative units and the inspection machinery have also been mobilised.

Finance for Adult Education. In view of the national importance of the problem of adult education, a sum of Rs. 200 crores has been allocated to it. This amounts to 10% of the education budget, whereas in the fifth plan, the allocation for adult education amounted to only Rs. 18 crores, or 1% of the education budget. This budgetary provision is only one source, and it is planned that other resources will also be exploited for this purpose. For example, the various service planners and project officers will provide finance for their own adult education programmes. In the tribal regions adult education will also be financed from the budget for the agricultural and rural development, there will be provisions for providing functional literacy to the agriculturist. Thus, the provisions for adult education within the total educational budget is only one of the provisions. Once the scheme is implemented and experience gained, more funds will be made available, as need arises.

Fundamental Schemes

The National Education Commission has opined that education does not end in the school. It is a life long process. The adult today seriously needs to understand the rapidly changing world and the increasing complexities of social life. Even those who have obtained considerable education should start learning once again because its alternative is isolation from the present reality. The objective of reconstructing our nation can be fulfilled only when each individual continues to receive the latest education so that he may use his intellect skillfully and determinedly in order to bring about economic development, social change and social security. The Education Commission has rightly pointed out that the farmer who turns over the soil or the worker who manipulates machines must understand the nature of the soil or the machine. He must be aware of the scientific process inherent in productive activity so that he may be able to make full use of new achievements and bring about progress.

Maulana Abul Kalam Azad expressed his views on the importance and function of social education by saying that social education means total human education. It grants the individual literacy so that the knowledge of the world may be available to him. It teaches him how to adapt himself to his environment. This implies giving him education in advanced skills and modes of production so that he may achieve the highest economic level. Its purpose is also to give knowledge of the basic principles of hygiene so that our domestic life may be healthy and prosperous. This will benefit the individual as well as society. Through this education, we should impart to him the lesson of citizenship so that he may obtain some knowledge of the world and also be enabled to participate in those decisions of the government which are conducive to peace and progress. However, the path to adult and social education is littered with many concomitant problems, that is, those problems which always raise obstacles in the path of social education. These problems are described in the following paragraphs.

Vague Policy on Adult Education. Ever since the achievement of independence, our policy on adult education and the programmes formulated for it have invariably been vague and undefined. An effort was made to achieve clarity in the community development programme, but even that was partial or biased, since it was intended only for rural adults. It has no provisions for adults in urban areas.

Lack of Finance. The finance so far invested in adult education has proved inadequate, with the result that this programme, which should have been given the highest priority in national development, fell behind. At least Rs. 27 crores should be spent annually upon this programme.

Absence of a Comprehensive Plan. This programme was accepted in principle, but it was never implemented in a suitably comprehensive manner. Had this been done, the problem would have been over come a long time ago. Dr. Frank went as far as to say categorically that if one literate Indian makes another Indian literate, the problem will be overcome within five years.

Problem of Curriculum. The curriculum of adult education has itself proved a problem, because adults were imparted a certain amount of literacy, but no knowledge of anything else, though this can be done. The method adopted for adults is the same as the one used for teaching children, though the needs, attitudes and abilities of adults are completely different. The curricula designed for them must necessarily take into account their particular needs.

Methods of Teaching. The curriculum should fulfill the needs of adults while the methods of teaching should be such that they help in the achievement of this goal. For the spread of literacy, sentence-charts, diagrams, stories, simple words, radio, television, libraries and the drama stage, etc., can be used successfully. But, in reality, because of a paucity of resources, the techniques of adult education are not brought into use in our country to any noticeable extent.

Problem of Teachers. The problem of teachers for adult education has existed from the very beginning. Under these circumstances, an experiment was made by using teachers of primary schools for this purpose, but it proved a failure because the additional allowance given to the teachers was too nominal. In addition, the extension officers, social educators and rural service workers exhibited complete indifference.

Problem of Continuing Education. Continuing education obviously refers to an educational process which always goes on, and in the sphere of adult education, it refers to the education imparted after literacy has been achieved. If facilities for such education are available after literacy has been imparted, some benefit can be derived from it.

The Agencies of Social Education. Apart from the official agencies involved in social education, some voluntary agencies, are also usually, engaged in this programme, but in India, there is a dearth of such agencies. However, the Literacy House in Lucknow and the Adult Education Council in Delhi are doing this work. These institutions aim at producing trained social educators. Only when there is a growth in the number of such agencies can we hope that social education will make rapid progress.

Administration. Social education has a very vast field and there is no uniformity in administration. The various ministries of the government of India have made efforts to train and educate their employees. The Central Education Advisory Committee has organised conferences and seminars from time to time.

Social Education Institutions. Institutions engaged in social education do not get help at the right time and consequently their enthusiasm dies out prematurely.

Training of Workers. There has also been, in general, a dearth of trained workers in the sphere of social education, because of which the Education Advisory Committee has recommended that such workers be trained.

Post Social Education. It is necessary to make arrangements for further education of adults after making them literate.

The Education Ministry of the government of India has suggested the following measures for overcoming the difficulties:-

(i) For individuals of 13 or 14 years of age, primary schools should arrange classes of two hours each at least three or four times a week. This work should be apart from the regular teaching programme of these schools.

(ii) Teachers should be trained for imparting education to the 14-15 age group. The following programmes should be taken up simultaneously:-

   (a) Regular classes should be arranged for men and women over a five month period.

(b) The Neighbouring Group Method should be adopted, under which the teacher should educate groups of people in his neighbourhood. Experience has shown that adults show laziness and unwillingness in coming to teaching centres, and hence, it may be more practicable for the teacher to go to their centres instead.

(c) A Home Class movement must be initiated for the education of women, which can be made an integral part of the Rural Education Programme. Students and teachers should offer their co-operation.

(d) Teacher training establishments should formulate and implement programmes of adult education in their respective communities.

(e) Voluntary organisation should organise adult education schemes.

In the opinion of the Indian Adult Education Committee, the important work of literacy must not be lost sight of in the broader perspective of social education. Literacy should remain an important element in social education because, through the written and spoken work, it affords the adult a powerful medium for becoming educated.

What is needed today is that the various programmes of social education must be organised and harmonised. The objective, should be clear, and the adults must be strongly motivated to receive social education. Success in this endeavour depends upon local leadership and local agencies.

Gandhiji said that illiteracy was a blot upon India's fair name. This blot must be wiped out with all expediency. The objective of adult education is not merely literacy, it must be linked with the daily life of adults. From this view-point, the literacy programme must have three elements- (i) it should be based on work so that it may impart skills to the learner, (ii) illiterate individuals should be able to think about the nation's problem, and (iii) adequate skills in reading, writing and mathematics should be developed so that informal education can then be continued indefinitely.

The Four Point Programme for social education is as follows-

Literacy Classes. By 1953, 400,000 individuals were made literate through 40,000 classes. By 1955, 7,000 classes provided literacy to 89,000 individuals. In community development centres, 85,000 classes helped to make 600,000 individuals literate.

Community Centres. Community centres perform the functions of providing literacy, recreation and information.

Youth Clubs. Youth clubs have been organised in villages with the result that village protection groups, youth welfare centres and other such units work for social education have come into existence.

Women's Committees. In each development centre, women's welfare groups and women's councils should be set up so that women can be given information about and involved in hymn singing, social discussion groups, use of smokeless stoves, knitting, stitching, nutrition and balanced diet, domestic skills, general health care, domestic economics, home decoration, literacy, etc.

The following means or instruments are employed in social education- (a) the common audio-visual aids, (b) black-boards and chalks, (c) charts and flash cards, (d) flannel and other materials, (e) other audio-visual materials, (f) films, (g) radio, (h) television.

The Education Commission has expressed the views that every possible effort should be made to overcome these obstacles, even though 20 years may pass in the process. It has suggested that- (1) For the 6-11 year age group, universal education must be achieved in 5 years. (2) Arrangements must be made for part time education. (3) Arrangements must be made for vocational education.

Different Approaches

The Commission has suggested that the following two methods should be adopted for this purpose-

Selective Approach. In this context, those groups are included which can be controlled easily, it also includes vocational training, in which industrial and commercial enterprise, large industrial enterprises and the government itself can take up budgets against illiteracy. In this method the following fields can be comprehended-(a) Most workers in industrial establishments are illiterate, and hence such establishments can be required to make arrangements for the education of their own employees. (b) The state should make arrangements for the education of their own employees. (c) The state should make arrangements for the education of all illiterate classes concerned with social and economic growth, since the number of such individuals is very large. (d) Programmes for imparting literacy should be an invariable part of every scheme of social education.

Mass Approach. This is concerned with developing a general method of public or mass education in which advantage will be taken of all educated men and women for eradicating the illiteracy of their brothers and sisters. Voluntary organisations can take effective steps in this direction. Existing schools can be converted into community centres. Regarding this approach, the Kothari Commission has argued that a movement for collective or community literacy depends largely upon the voluntary services of all educated individuals, including governmental as well as non-governmental employees and other sections of society. It has suggested that students of the primary, secondary, under-graduate students and students of vocational schools should be engaged in the teaching of adults as a part of the National Service Scheme.

This Commission has made the following suggestions for accelerating the literacy movement:-

(a) Organising a curriculum for adult women through the central social welfare board, with 'rural sisters' teaching women in the rural areas with the help of the community.
(b) Generating social skills.
(c) Adopting education as a dynamic process.
(d) Running ad hoc courses.
(e) Training through units which should be for teachers and common people. In this, students should be given suitable opportunities, and use should also be made of radio and television.
(f) Generating a suitable atmosphere before initiating the programme.

(g) Preparing the adults psychologically to make them receptive.
(h) Making use of such means as radio, television, films, lectures, etc., so as to make teaching suitable.
(i) Making schemes for literacy in accord with local circumstances.
(j) Making the programmes attractive.
(k) Seeking the full cooperation of universities, industries, etc.
(l) Organising an effective administration.

Area of Operation

The field of social education presents vast opportunities for educating the public. Various kinds of efforts have been made for educating people all over the world, and for this purpose various experiments were conducted. The USA and USSR despite the fundamental differences in their political and economic structure, both accept and understand the importance of kind of education. There, the schools, colleges, clubs and institutes and other institutions which work for improving the standards of the fore mentioned have been provided with extensive cultural facilities. In India, too, various experiments have been conducted in the sphere of social education. These are -

Organisation of Tours and Camps. In such schemes, adults are sent to camps for completing a pre-determined course of study which aims at teaching them reading, writing and healthy citizenship. K.G. Saiyadain has laid special emphasis upon the utility of such organisations, because in camps, the atmosphere generated is suitable for the growth of brotherhood as well as leadership. However, it must also be kept in mind that the organisers of tours and camps should have adequate knowledge of mass psychology. These camps can prove to be the nerve-centres of social education, and so they should be managed with sympathy and understanding.

Janata (Public) Colleges. Like the 'folk schools' of Denmark, Janata or public colleges were established in India, too. After observing their work, one observer commented that the most important element was not the quantum of knowledge obtained by the students but the fact that their thoughts and sentiments were stimulated. It is conceivable that they would forget much of what they had learnt, after they left school, but after leaving school, they appear to be completely changed. By that time, they have learnt to listen, observe, think and make the best possible use of their abilities.

According to Pyare Lal Rawat, the foundation stone for a public and cooperative life will be laid in the social centres in rural society. Janata colleges have been set up to produce educated and trained workers for such social centres. Leadership will take birth in these colleges. They will not have the form and structure of the ordinary colleges because their purpose is to train young men and women to perform activities of social, cultural and educational value among the rural people so that they may be able to provide leadership to the rural areas. In other words, their purpose is to generate knowledge and education among the rural people, to teach the rural people better ways of living so that they may lead a better and more contented life. The objective of these colleges will be to make Indian rural people responsible citizens of a democratic society by arousing their civic, social and cultural awareness.

Community Centres. Community centres were set up in rural areas to provide education, sociability, recreation as well as education in good citizenship. These centres were set up in the village squares (chaupals), panchayat houses and schools, and provided with such materials as carpets, furniture, books, radios, newspapers, periodicals, sports goods, etc.

Intensive Libraries. Where community centres have not been established, intensive libraries have been set up. These libraries contain literature suitable for the adults, as well as books on agriculture, cottage industries, cooperative societies, health and other such subjects of utility.

Educational Caravans. Educational caravans were put into use in the rural areas around Delhi. These caravans are equipped with film projectors, health materials, libraries and other teaching materials. This caravan sets up camp at one place, and then its workers spread all round, making arrangements for adult education.

Adult Education Departments in Universities. The Rajasthan university has made adequate efforts towards adult education by setting up a department, which has also initiated a number of schemes for continuing education. Other universities should imitate Rajasthan in this respect. Universities can make their contribution to social education through postal courses, short-term education, extension services, post education contact programmes, etc.

Mass Education Movement. 20 years ago, the 'Parichaya' (acquaintance) trust was set up for the spread of mass education for the Gujarati speaking people. So far, this trust has published as many as three hundred books on various subjects. This movement was strengthened by the activities of Wadilal Dagli (Editor, *Commerce*) and Yashwant Doshi (Editor, 'Parichaya' trust publications). Dagli was inspired in this endeavour by the Chicago University pamphlets; which he saw at Berkeley (California). He thought of spreading mass education in his mother tongue. The work began with only Rs. 500. Each pamphlet was priced at 0.40 paise. In the first year, the organisation enrolled six hundred members. The publication was based on the principle of giving 10% royalty to authors and Commission to the middle men.

This movement brought about a social revolution, and also provided the illiterate people with a ray of hope. So far, the trust has published 300 pamphlets, thus providing the neo-literates with reading material on a variety of subjects. The trust now plans to publish similar literature for neo-literates in other languages also.

Informal Education. In the fifth plan, one important experiment in the sphere of social education was that of informal education. In this context, the Central Education Advisory Council has prepared a scheme for linking social education with national development. The scheme envisages providing further opportunities for education to those who were compelled to abandon their education too early, Correspondence courses, evening classes, etc.; are part of this scheme. It will provide free and informal opportunities of education for everyone.

Village Education Muhim. This experiment was carried out in Maharashtra. Some social workers conducted adult education classes. In. Vidharabha, some enthusiastic workers were given training and the number of adult education centres was thus increased. This movement was based on the declaration of the workers that they would maintain their own literacy, send their children regularly to school, maintain unity in the village and seek to fulfil the goal of integral development of the village.

Now, this programme is being conducted by District Councils. It has three objectives:-

(i) Putting an end to illiteracy among adults (14-50 age group)

(ii) Granting neo-literates opportunities to remain in constant contact with education.

(iii) Bringing about the comprehensive development of villages through social education centres.

Village Vidyapeeth. This experiment was initiated in Mysore. Through it, the spread of education in economics, agricultural education, etc., was achieved. The project received inspiration from the Danish folk high schools. In these institutions, a class has to remain at the school for 5 or 6 months for studies. This helps to develop a harmonious community life.

Punjab Literacy Project. Mrs. Helen Butt developed an intensive literacy method (Hindi) in the Neelokheri block of Karnal. After its initiation by Mrs. Butt, the project continued with the help of 20 teachers, 7 lady teachers (planning and panchayat department), and 4 supervisors. Its success is proved by the fact that 36 classes for men and 11 classes for women were started. 1000 adults attended these classes. Each full time teacher taught two classes on alternate days. Classes were held on three days a week basis over a period of six months. The learners were taught to read and write Hindi. In addition to literacy, a programme of continuing education was also conducted over 3 months. A short nine-day programme for training teachers was also conducted. Besides, literacy was spread through the Immediate Learning Method. When the project was introduced at the state level, the farmers showed exceptional enthusiasm for it, proved by the fact that attendance in the classes was as much as 19.4%. Mrs. Helen Butt has said after her experience of this project that the total expenditure on adult literacy scheme should be borne by the education department and the institutions (panchayats) which stand to benefit from them.

Adult Education Department Rajasthan University Jaipur. In 1965, the Rajasthan University at Jaipur set up a department of adult education in order to explore the possibilities of adult education by spreading continuing education. This department organises conferences and seminars at regular intervals. It also organises a variety of short-term courses for the neo-literates as well as-the semi-literates. This department has done the following kinds of work with the assistance of the government, the university and voluntary organisations- (i) studies in the philosophy and concept of adult education. (ii) education in literacy- social, economic development and literacy, adult literacy and the methods of teaching, teacher training, village education muhim, (iii) portable audio visual materials, library, conferences, discussions, (iv) liberal education, (v) public cooperation, (vi) training in leadership (Mysore Vidyapeeth), (vii) the sphere of continuing education industrial and vocational development, (viii) education of adult women, (ix) agencies and organisation. This department continues to think upon and discuss such issues as the university and social responsibility, the work done in foreign countries on adult education, the educational requirements of community, continuing education,-vocations, agriculture, training, liberal teaching, evening colleges, correspondence courses, adult education and related disciplines, etc.

Role of Commission

Adult education is one of those aspects of education on which the Kothari Commission has thought at length. The Education has expanded the scope of adult education, and for its success and spread, it has suggested the following six-point programme- (1) eradication of illiteracy, (2) continuing education, (3) correspondence courses, (4) libraries, (5) role of universities in adult education, (6) the organisation and administration of adult education. We will now consider the recommendations of the Commission in the light of its programme.

Movement for Education

The Education Commission has pointed out that as compared to the situation in 1951, there were 26 million more illiterate people in 1961. As compared to 1951, there were 20 million more illiterates, despite the fact that literacy had increased from 16.6% to 28.5%. It also accepted the fact that the nation was paying a heavy price for this illiteracy, because. illiterate persons are not really independent and complete citizens. Besides, illiteracy acts as an obstacle in economic, social and political development, control of population, creation of security, etc.

The Commission has suggested that any programme for the eradication of illiteracy should have the following bases - (i) As far as possible, adult education should be based on work, and it should aim at change of attitude, creation of interests and skill. The information given should bring about an increase in the learner's skill. (ii) Adult education should stimulate the learner's interests in national problems and also make a powerful and effective contribution to the nation's social and political life. (iii) It should make adults capable of reading, writing and calculation. If the learner's wish they can ensure their own improvement through informal knowledge.

It is evident from these three bases that the literacy drive will have three stages - (a) in the initial stage, the adult should be taught reading, writing and calculation, and also given information about citizenship and national problems. Besides, information about his vocation should also be imparted to the learner. (b) In the second stage, the knowledge obtained in the initial stage should be reinforced and the skills developed further. Adults should be enabled to understand and face their personal problems. (c) The third stage should help the adult to participate in continuing education.

A useful programme of adult education depends upon the acceptance of certain basic facts. We must see such programmes in the light of industralisation and modern agricultural progress, as making illiterates useful instrument in the country's general as well as economic development, as turning them into an effective work force. For this, the following facts should be considered:

Targets. The success of adult education depends upon successful planning. There should be a proper time schedule for programmes for the people, preparation of resources, training of workers and provision of other needs. The Commission has recommended that the programme should not be prepared for the whole nation, instead, state-wise planning should be adopted. The progress of adult education depends upon the educational facilities, public co-operation and existing organisation in each region. The Education Commission has expressed the hope that, on the basis of proper planning and implementation, 60% illiteracy can be eradicated by 1971 and 80% by 1976. Consequently, the Commission has recommended that every effort should be made to eradicate illiteracy. It has hoped that within 20 years, no part of the country should remain backward.

Programmes for Eradication of Illiteracy. The Commission has suggested the following programmes-(i) Providing for compulsory education of at least five years for the 6-11 years age-group. (ii) Providing for part-time education of the children in the 11-14 age-group who had to give up their education for some reasons. (iii) Making arrangements for the part-time general as 'well as vocational education for individuals in the 15-30 age group. This group will include individuals who have received education partially.

Strategy of Approach. The Commission has rightly argued that every effort must be made to overcome obstacles to adult education. We must consider the population in our country and determine our strategy accordingly. According to the Census of 1961, there were 1 million illiterates in the 15 + age-group. Literacy in urban areas was 47%, while in rural areas, it was 17%. The distribution of literacy also depends upon the region. While in Delhi it was 52.7%, in NEFA it was as low as 1.8%. Besides, there was considerable differences between the literacy among men and women. Social groupings, caste and class and the nature of the community have always hindered adult education. Besides, the differences in the nature of a region lead to different levels of motivation towards adult learning. The Commission has felt the need for the acceptance and observation of certain general principles, and so it has suggested two approaches for success in this endeavour- (i) Selective approach, and (ii) Mass approach. Programmes based on both approaches should run simultaneously.

Typical Approach

According to the Commission, the selective approach is suitable for the group which can be identified easily and also kept under control with relative ease. Such a group can be effectively motivated to obtain education. Such a group can be made useful and the literacy programme can achieve success. Even vocational training can be given to such groups. Under this approach, the following programmes can be formulated :

1. Almost 4% illiterate people are employed in industrial and professional organisation. Hence, the Commission has recommended that large firms, trading and industrial organisations and institutions may be legally made responsible for the adult education of their employees. They should be made literate within three years. The owners of such organisations must bear the entire responsibility of making their employees literate. The government should bear all expenses related to education, such as supply of teachers, teaching materials, books and other tools. The Commission is convinced that the owners themselves will, in the long run, benefit from the education of their employees.
2. The Commission has suggested that large organisations managed by the administration must give primacy to the important programme of adult literacy.
3. The humanitarian attitude is necessarily linked with all programmes for social and economic progress. They include a large number of people who have never even seen a school. Hence, it appears logical to argue that provisions must be made for the education and training of all workers in the schemes for industrial, agricultural, and trading development or improvement in health and education.
4. The Indian government has implemented numerous schemes for social welfare and economic development.

These include such schemes as the creation of the Khadi and Village Industries Commission, community development schemes, child welfare schemes, etc. The Commission's view is that adult education should be made an integral part of all such programmes.

In order to put an end to illiteracy, it is necessary to mobilize all literate people in society. This approach is unorthodox, and it has not yet been adopted in practice in India. Russia has achieved spectacular successes in adult education through this approach. In India, Maharashtra has achieved notable success through its Village Education Muhim. In this approach, the workers seek the cooperation of the community and make schemes for mass education. The only difficulty in this approach is the laxity in follow-up, but this can be taken care of. Such a programme possesses the following characteristics:

1. This approach depends more upon political and social institutions rather than administrative educational institutions.
2. Adult education, by its very nature, is voluntary, and the drive behind it is the individual's own motivation. Hence, national unity and security, health and social welfare should be implicit in adult education, a fact which must never be lost sight of by educational planners, administrators or workers.
3. This approach depends upon the voluntary services contributed by such educated individuals in society as doctors, lawyers, teachers, students, engineers and other individuals, though, of course, the brunt of the responsibility falls upon the teachers and students. It is for this reason that the Commission has recommended that adult education should be propagated, through compulsory national service at every level of education.
4. In connection with adult education, a new responsibility should fall upon the schools. This will also help to modify the attitude of the school. This approach comprehends not only the student in the school, but the entire community. It provides an important sphere for extension service.

A programme of adult education cannot be run successfully as long as a proper plan is not formulated. For the success of such a programme, the following points must be considered:-

1. Before the implementation of the programme, the government, and all social and political leaders should arouse the interest of the community and bring about mobilisation.
2. The individual adults taken into the scheme should be psychologically motivated in a suitable manner. They should become aware of the importance of literacy.
3. All means of mass communication, such as radio, television, films, slides, drama and literary organisations should be made use of in such programmes.
4. Whenever the programme is to be implemented, the necessary teaching aids such as books, charts, graphs, guide-books, etc., must be prepared before-hand.
5. In planning for literacy local, needs and conditions should be kept in mind.
6. The literacy programme should also have provision for the continuing education of neo-literates. Follow-up programmes should also be organised.
7. The adult education programme cannot be left entirely and exclusively to the teachers. They must be offered the cooperation and assistance of the following- (i) extension services, agricultural and industrial departments, (ii) the use of mass media instruments, such as the All India Radio.
8. Libraries should also extend their cooperation to this programme.
9. Training in leadership should also be part of this programme.
10. Students, teachers and others interested in the spread of adult literacy should be given suitable training.
11. A powerful administrative and supervisory mechanism must be evolved.
12. In this progamme, schemes should be devised for bringing people into contact with each other through study groups, committees, clubs, recreation groups etc.

13. The public, too, should recognise and appreciate such programmes.
14. The percentage of illiteracy among women is greater than among men. In the urban areas, 34.5% women are literate while in the rural areas this percentage is 8.9, a situation similar to that found existing in the whole world. Hence, as many lady teachers as possible should be appointed to speed up the education of women.
15. The success of any activity depends upon the follow-up action given to it. Hence, for adult literacy also, properly planned programmes of follow-up action should be devised.

At the Doorstep

Adult education occupies the most important place in our country's educational set-up. In the rapidly changing circumstances of today, life as a whole should be conceived of as a continuing process of learning. It is now being generally accepted that the modern method of education does not provide extensive education for one's entire life. Hence, to complement it, full-time, part-time or in-service educational programmes are devised for those who have left school and reached adulthood: Generally, the system of continuing education is devised for two classes:-

(i) Those people who participate in part-time education along with other individuals. Individuals of this class increase their qualifications by receiving part-time education in schools and colleges.

(ii) Those persons who can study only at home, but who need some assistance in getting official recognition for their study.

Continuing education is meant for persons who want to complete the education left incomplete by their leaving school. Individuals working in institutions also need opportunities for improving their qualifications and abilities. There are also some individuals who wish to study literature, language or some special subject merely for the pleasure of it. Adult education seeks to bring education within the grasp of every kind of person by catering to his special needs.

Hence, the Education Commission has suggested the following steps for developing continuing education- (1) For part-time education, a parallel system must be developed within the educational structure. Just as degrees, diplomas and certificates are granted to full time students, similar recognition should be available for part-time curricula and courses also. (2) Education institutions should provide the necessary leadership in this process they should understand the individual's problems, solve them and help them in obtaining knowledge as well as the necessary help. (3) Through special part-time courses and mixed programmes, efforts should be made to improve the mental horizon of workers and employees ; their knowledge and skills should be improved and a sense of responsibility engendered in them. (4) Specialised institutions should be established, for example, the Central Women's Welfare Council, Vidyapiths, etc.

For millions of those people who have to stand upon their own feet very early in life and struggle for livelihood and survival, correspondence courses provide a means by which they can satisfy their ambition for education, which would otherwise remain unfulfilled. Such courses are very much in use in foreign countries, such as the USA, Sweden, Japan, the USSR, Australia, etc. In India, too, experiments have been conducted in this form of education by the Delhi, Meerut and Himachal Universities. Although this method does not provide any immediate and direct contact between the students and the teachers, the relations between the two can become quite intimate through exchange of correspondence. Besides, it is also to be noted that there has generally been a dearth of teachers who can inspire students through direct contact.

Correspondence courses should be designed to encourage an exchange of views, and they should not restrict themselves merely to the exchange of written information. Individuals who wish to study science through the correspondence courses should be allowed to make use of laboratories during vacations. Even in education as a subject, there should be arrangements for correspondence curricula through Programmed Learning, a method which has been productive of good results.

The correspondence system of education should also get the assistance of radio and television, which can be used for the expression of fundamental and emotional ideas. Courses of this kind should be designed not only to enable students to obtain degrees, but also to give information and knowledge to individuals engaged in agriculture, industry and other productive activities. These courses should be organised through the extension departments.

The following are the recommendations of the Education Commission for the development of correspondence courses:

1. Those individuals who can take part in courses or curricula should receive education through correspondence courses. For this, extensive correspondence courses should be organised.
2. Students studying through the correspondence system should be given opportunities to meet the teachers at regular intervals. As far as possible, they should also be allowed to avail of library facilities existing in schools and colleges.
3. Correspondence courses should be assisted by the radio and television network.
4. Correspondence courses should also be organised for those individuals who wish to develop their literacy or aesthetic values.
5. Correspondence courses should not limit themselves to helping students merely to obtain university degrees. Instead, they should also contain courses which may lead to increased production in agriculture and industry.
6. Through correspondence courses, school teachers should come into contact with fresh knowledge, new methods of teaching, etc.
7. The education ministry, with the assistance of other ministries, should set up a National Council of Home Studies. Its functions would be to evaluate the correspondence courses, the agencies involved in such education, and the identification of spheres in which correspondence courses can be introduced.

8. Those individuals who wish to appear at examinations conducted by Boards or universities, on the basis of self-study, should be allowed to do so.

Libraries have always played a leading role in the growth of knowledge. In their absence, the possibilities of developing the habit of reading are very few, especially in rural areas. The Commission has suggested that, for the spread of mass education, school libraries should be utilised as public libraries. It has suggested that:

1. The suggestions of the advisory committee on libraries should be accepted, and on its basis, a network of libraries should be spread over the entire country.
2. School libraries should be organised and structured as public libraries.
3. Libraries should be dynamic; they should attract adults towards themselves.

The importance of libraries is reflected in the following statement from UNESCO. It says that in the whole world, and especially in developing countries, there is great need for the expansion of free libraries as a part of the educational programme. Libraries satisfy the needs of the prevailing educational system and help the teachers in their work. In the absence of public libraries, many adults and young men gradually sink towards illiteracy on leaving the school.

Commenting upon the importance of universities, the Education Commission has declared that the image of a university is that of an intellectual, 'closed' community which gives rise to knowledge, spreads and preserves it, but this is the traditional image. The walls which divide 'town and town' no longer exist. There has come about a revolution in the life of the university, with the revolutionary idea that the community can be linked to the university for the mutual benefit of both.

The Delhi University introduced the correspondence courses and soon found that the demand for them was growing rapidly. In the same manner, the Rajasthan University set up a department of adult education, which was widely applauded. The idea was widely appreciated in Meerut University also.

The function of the university is to bring about a growth and improvement in the social, economic, educational and cultural spheres, and through special agencies it can have a profound impact upon these spheres. Universities should organise effective and powerful programmes for various vocations. It is their duty to ensure that their teachers are constantly in touch with the latest editions to knowledge. In the context of adult education, the Education Commission has made the following recommendations regarding the role of universities:-

1. Indian universities should shoulder a heavier burden in educating the adults in the country. This can be done in the following ways- (a) departments similar to the Rajasthan University's department of adult education should be set up in other universities. (b) Universities must contribute to social and economic growth. (c) They must nourish community life and cultural values.
2. A Board of Adult Education should be constituted by taking representatives from the various departments involved in making the adult literacy programme a success.
3. Universities should be given financial aid for the proper implementation of the adult education programme.

Managing Institutions

The Commission has clearly felt that the basic weakness in the efforts being made by governmental, non-governmental and voluntary agencies towards the spread of adult education lies in the absence of proper planning and cooperation. Hence, it has suggested the establishment of a National Board of Adult Education to overcome this shortcoming. The council should have representatives from all related ministries. It should have the folllowing functions:-

1. Advising the central and state governments on informal adult education, offering for consideration blueprints for teaching and training.
2. Wherever necessary, setting up institutions, helping in the preparation of literature, teaching materials and necessary teaching programmes.

3. Creating harmony between the efforts of various departments and governmental as well as non-governmental agencies.
4. Evaluating the achievements from time to time and making suggestions for future improvements.
5. Encouraging research, evaluation and survey activities.

Similar organisations should be established at the state level also. At the district level committees should be set up to function as integral parts of the district councils. They should be assisted by village and block committees. They should also be in intimate contact with extension programmes in the spheres of agriculture, cooperatives, health, community development, etc.,

On the question of administration, the Commission's view is that a separate department within the ministry of education should organise this work. The government must accept full responsibility, and every department of the government should be cognizant of the importance of adult education. In addition, every department should help in implementing this programme. Undoubtedly, adult education is the concern of the department of education, but it is also true that, in order to achieve success, it will be necessary to depend upon some particular mode of action.

As far as the question of voluntary agencies is concerned, they should be given financial and technical assistance. Adult education is a sphere in which such agencies can work freely. Besides, the nature of the work is such that its progress and mobility provides a necessary background for the success of all our planning for national development.

Bibliography

Aali, K.R. : *Problems of Schools in India*, Lancer Publications, Bombay, 1995.

Addaval, S.B. : *The Third India Year Book of Education : Educational Research*, NCERT, New Delhi, 1968.

Aftab, R.M. : *School Education in India*, Pearl Publications, Chennai, 2003.

Aggarwal, J.C. : *Development and Planning of School Education*, Vikas Publishing House, New Delhi, 1993.

Alva Myrdal : *The Power of Education*, Lancer Books, New York, 1965.

Anderson, C.A. : *Education and School Development*, Frank Cass, London, 1981.

Andrew, W., Halping : *School Theory in Education*, MacMillan Company, New York, 1997.

Aparna Basu : *Growth of Schools and Development*, Oxford University Press, Delhi, 1971.

Bhatia, S.C. : *Education and School*, Xerxes Publications, Delhi, 2002.

Biswas, Dutt : *The New Educational Pattern in Schools*, Vikas Publishing House, Delhi, 2001.

Chourasia, G. : *Challenges in School Education,* Sterling Publishers, New Delhi, 1977.

Crites, J.C. : *Vocational Schools,* McGraw Hill, New York, 1999.

Denis, Lawton : *Education and Schools,* Sage Publications, London, 2001.

Desai, A.R. : *Social Change and Educational Policy,* NCERT, New Delhi, 2003.

Dharni, P. Sinha : *Descriptive-cum-Critical Study of Education System,* Administrative Staff College of India, Hyderabad, 1976.

Ehsanul, Haq : *Education and School Culture in India,* Sterling Publishers, New Delhi, 1991.

Gandhi, Kishore : *Issues and Choices in School Education,* B.R. Publishing Corporation, Delhi, 1997.

Gandhi, M.K. : *My Views on Education,* Bharatiya Vidya Bhavan, Bombay, 1970.

Ganguly, S.N. : *Tradition, Modernity and Education,* MacMillan Company of India, Delhi, 1997.

Ghosh, S.C. : *Schools in Developing Countries,* Sterling Publishers, New Delhi, 1976.

Goel, S.C. : *Education and Economic Growth in India,* The MacMillan Company of India Ltd., Delhi, 1975.

Gopinathan Nair, P.R.: *Primary Education,* Allied Publishers, New Delhi, 1981.

Inamdar, N.R. : *Educational Administration in Schools,* Popular Prakashan, Bombay, 1985.

Iqbal Narain : *Educational Administration,* Aalakli Publishers, Jaipur, 1976.

James, A.R. : *Vocation, Education and Guidance,* Charles E. Marril Publishing Co., Columbus, Ohio, 1970.

John Vaizey : *Schools for Tomorrow,* Penguin, London, 1996.

John W., Hanson and Cole S. Brem Beck: *Education and the Development of Nations,* Holt, Rinehart and Winston, New York, 1966.

Joshi, R.N. : *Education—Elsewhere and Here,* Bharatiya Vidya Bhavan, Bombay, 1979.

Julian, E., Butter Worth and Howard A. Dawson : *The Modern Rural School,* McGraw Hill, New York, 1952.

Kidd, J.R. : *Education for Perspective,* Indian Education Association, New Delhi, 1969.

Kishore, Gandhi : *Issue and Choices in School*, B.R. Publishing Corporation, Delhi, 1997.

Kochhar, S.K. : *Pivotal Issues in School Education*, Sterling, New Delhi, 1991.

Lakshmana, Swamy Mudaliar : *School Education in India*, Asia Publishing House, Bombay, 1975.

Louis Malassis : *Education and Development,* Croom Helm, London, 1976.

Mukherjee, R.K. : *The Social Structure of Schools,* S. Chand & Company, New Delhi, 1994.

Mukherji, S.N. : *Administration of Schools in India*, Acharya Book Depot, Baroda, 1973.

Naik, J.P. : *Policy and Performance in Indian Education,* Dr. K.G. Saiyidain Memorial Trust, New Delhi, 1955.

Naim, M. Kazim : *Educational Institutions in India,* Allied Publishers, Bombay, 1995.

Niblett, W.R. : *Essential Education,* University of London, London,1955.

Nural Hasan, S. : *Challenges in Education, Culture and Social Welfare,* Allied Publishers, Bombay, 1977.

Oldhan, J.N. : *Village Education in India*, Oxford University Press, London, 1922.

Panchamukhi, P.R.: *Financing of Primary Education in India*, NCERT, 1970.

Pandey, S.N. : *Education and Social Changes*, Motilal Banerasidas, Delhi, 1976.

Paulo Freire : *Education : The Practice of Freedom*, Writers and Readers Publishing Co-operative, London, 1976.

Prem Kripal : *A Decade of Education in India*, Indian Book Company, Delhi, 1968.

Premi, M.K. : *Educational Planning in India : Implications of Population Trends*, Sterling Publishers, New Delhi, 1972.

Raghunath Safaya : *Innovations and Latest Trends in Education*, The Associated Publishers, Ambala Cantt., 1976.

Rajagopal, M.V. : *Kothari Commission on School Education*, Telugu Vidyardhi Prachuranalu, Machilipatnam, 1967.

Rao, M.S. : *Education Social Stratification and Mobility*, NCERT, New Delhi, 1997.

Ratna, G. Revankar : *The Indian Constitution*, Associate University Press, Canbury, New Jersey, 1941.

Rudolph & Rudolph : *Education and Schools in India*, Harvard University Press, Cambridge, 1982.

Russell, Bertrand : *Education and the Social Order*, Unwin, London, 1977.

—*On Education*, Unwin Books, London, 1971.

Saini, S.K. : *Development of Schools in India*, Cosmo Publications, New Delhi, 1991.

Shipman, M.D. : *Education and Schooling*, Faber and Faber, London, 1981.

Shri Prakash : *School System of India : An Econometric Study*, Concept Publishing Company, Delhi, 1981.

Shrimali, K.L. : *A Search for Values in Indian Education*, Vikas Publishers, Delhi, 1974.

Shukla, P.D. : *Towards the New Pattern of Education in India*, Sterling Publishers, New Delhi, 1976.

Siqueira, T.N. : *The Education in India : History and Problems*, Oxford University Press, London, 1952.

Stephen, J., Knezevich : *Administration of Public Education*, Harper and Brothers, New York, 1962.

Sundaram, P.S. : *Education or Catastrophe?*, Vikas Publishing House, New Delhi, 1976.